Touching
the Heart

Touching the Heart

Why Sport Matters

David Miller

Foreword by
Marcus Rashford

First published by Pitch Publishing, 2021

Pitch Publishing
A2 Yeoman Gate
Yeoman Way
Worthing
Sussex
BN13 3QZ
www.pitchpublishing.co.uk
info@pitchpublishing.co.uk

A CIP catalogue record is available for this book
from the British Library.

ISBN 978 1 80150 012 8

Typesetting and origination by Pitch Publishing
Printed and bound in India by Replika Press Pvt. Ltd.

Contents

FOREWORD

MARCUS RASHFORD MBE

I'm incredibly proud to call myself a footballer, to call football my profession. That round ball is one of the most consistent realities I've ever enjoyed in my life. That one opportunity I've found which offered me purpose, structure, discipline: all vital for a child who grew up in what might be referred to as an 'under-privileged' community. That ball provided an avenue out of difficulty, not just for me, but my family too.

For many, football is the most common language we all can speak. It has the ability to bring people from all walks of life together as one. I have been privileged enough to experience the broadest available geography lesson through my professional football career: visiting places I couldn't have ever imagined. I've met people from different cultures, races and religions, learnt something different from every one of them. The game has this rare ability to bring people together without the need to say a word. Thereby, football offers a sense of belonging.

I've stood on a seat at the Stretford End of Old Trafford as a child, trying my best to see the fullest of the action. Absorbing every moment, that feeling of unity and freedom which is so difficult to recreate elsewhere. In that stadium, alongside

74,000 other emotional fans, I felt part of something special. Today I still feel that, but it has become a sense of pride, able to play an active role in that collective passion, that mutual investment of commitment and community.

Sport, and football in particular, is something spontaneous. Success is built from mistakes, it's adventurous: more importantly, it's *togetherness*. Sport teaches us how to handle success, to handle failure. Sport can fill a void in us that might be blind to the masses. It's our escape, our common language, belonging.

Sport has also offered me a voice, a platform where that voice can be heard, which speaks for many who are speaking but not being heard. Sport has the power to influence positive change, truly a force to be reckoned with in society at large, especially for deprived children. Sport is my everything. My identity. My forever story. The remorse will remain from that missed penalty for England against Italy, letting everyone down. I long to compensate by helping win the World Cup once more in 2022.

With his seven decades' experience in sport, from 12-year-old inter-county schools XI, internationally respected David Miller illustrates just why sport does indeed matter to all of us.

PREFACE

'Success? Enduring repeated
failure, maintaining enthusiasm'.
Winston Churchill

As political frictions rupture global equilibrium in China, Hong Kong, North Korea, Myanmar, Yemen, Iran, Syria, Ethiopia, Belarus, Brazil, Mexico, the USA and elsewhere, and COVID-19 has ravaged every nation, sport – not only professional events but the many millions who enjoy, and need, leisure expression – has been repressed.

Yet the truth is that one of the prime iniquities of the 20th century, South Africa's apartheid regime, was driven towards resolution partially on account of the influence of the Olympic Games. As a journalist for *The Times*, I closely followed the negotiations, from 1989–91, by the IOC's special Apartheid Commission, appointed by then-president Juan Antonio Samaranch, to achieve South Africa's return to the Olympic arena in 1992 after an exclusion of 28 years – a springboard towards a free democracy. At the heart of this political jigsaw were clandestine meetings with Nelson Mandela, released from Robben Island prison after 27 years, dehumanising for an African National Congress rebel. I was there on the occasion of strategic deliberations in Ulundi,

Kwazulu, as the tide of social revolution utilised the catalyst of sport.

It was a privileged private moment when, on an afternoon in Johannesburg in 1995, as South Africa were about to meet New Zealand in the Rugby World Cup Final, I was introduced to President Mandela by Joe Pamensky, president of South Africa's by now multi-racial cricket union. In the briefest informal conversation, the transformative national leader elected the previous year confided, 'I am hopeful that today will be remembered as a landmark in our new liberated nation.' Later, presentation of the trophy to Francois Pienaar – once an emblematic white, now converted democrat – was confirmation. My rollercoaster journey through countless stadia, embassies and conferences has involved me in many stories, many exchanges with notable leaders reflecting on the relevance of sport.

Nelson Mandela, president of South Africa 1994–99, Nobel Peace Prize winner 1993, in celebration of South Africa's hosting of the Rugby Union World Cup 1995 and prospective FIFA's World Cup 2010:
'Sport has the power to change the world … the power to inspire. It has the momentum to unite people in a way that little else does. It speaks to youth in a language they understand. Sport can create hope where once there was only despair. It is more influential than governments in breaking down racial barriers.'

Thomas Bach, ninth president of the International Olympic Committee, maintaining the IOC's global cache, upholding Tokyo's postponed Olympic Games:
'Athletes personify how sport touches our hearts. Lofty pinnacles, application, emotion, their joy, their tears – as in

the Olympic Games. The beauty of sport is its universality: humanity shares its emotions, sport transcending all boundaries. Current extraordinary times have revealed that the role of sport has never been more important. As we grapple with a health crisis, and divisions within and among nations widen, sport offers hope, individually and collectively. Sport is a low-cost, high-impact opportunity assisting all countries, rich or poor, in reaching long-term objectives, and sustaining health. The Olympic Games are the only event that embraces the world in peaceful competition. When all 206 NOCs and the IOC Refugee Olympic Team gather, this ignites a message of shared diversity. Athletes reveal the values of excellence, friendship, respect and solidarity: through competitors, simultaneously coexisting under one roof, free of discrimination, bound by the same rules regardless of social background, gender, religion or political belief. All are equal. Sport reminds us that co-ordinated humanity can be more coherent than all the forces which emerge dividing us.'

Mangosuthu Buthelezi, Zulu Freedom Party chief, whose recognition of the impetus generated by sport was emphatic:

'Sport will hasten the process, and the progress, of rationalisation. Sport is a tool for change, an example to other cultures, for sport is as much a way of life for South African blacks as for South African whites. Sport coaches people for higher office, and does so in such a way that the checks and balances which are there in democracy are made to work because people want them to work. There is so much aggression in South Africa, as a consequence of many decades of racist rule, that anything that will help turn political competition into political co-operation is vitally needed. The lesson sport has for us is that competition is only permissible when it is played within the rules. There are rules of the game to be played in South Africa, and it is vital that South Africa's political leaders should borrow from the sports world the spirit with which competition becomes exhilarating.'

Sir Geoff Hurst, West Ham and England centre-forward, scorer of a hat-trick in the 1966 World Cup Final:

'Everyone can try to do their best in whatever leisure is suitable for them. Sport provides the platform for that: a chance to achieve, in fairness, generosity, discipline, team spirit, amusement. At the competitive level, it promotes values like resilience and strength. Even now in my 80s, I go to my local gym regularly, though the pandemic has interrupted that routine. When the gym was shut, I'd exercise in the park, six days a week. The fitter you are, the better you meet challenges. Mental attitude is important too. Not everyone can win an Olympic medal, heavyweight boxing title or play for their country at football, cricket or rugby. When talking about my career, I stress that sport matters beyond winning, matters to society, as does culture: literature, music and theatre. England team-mates of that day in 1966, winning the World Cup, celebrate that it carved a unique niche for them, still receiving requests for signed photographs and World Cup memorabilia from all over the world. We were privileged to play elite sport, success that encourages youngsters to aspire to their own sporting achievements.'

Juan Antonio Samaranch, Current IOC Executive Board:

'The 1992 Olympic Games in Barcelona are remembered for great athletic achievements, the quality of the organisation and some exceptional moments, but the Games were much more than that. Barcelona received an invaluable legacy from being host city, not only in infrastructure that expanded the city, but also, and more important, a transformation and development for its citizens in becoming a vibrant, self-confident and modern community – for instance, running the original railway underground and opening an expanse of beach to the population. There was a before and an after for Barcelona: 29 years later, take a walk in the city and experience the most important legacy from the Games … a welcoming community of friendly and Olympic people.'

Sir Matt Busby, manager of Manchester United, 1947–69:

'It is pleasant to succeed, but winning at all cost is not the test of true achievement: nothing wrong with trying to win, so long as you don't set the prize above the game. There is no dishonour in defeat, so long as you play your best. What matters is that the game should be played in the right spirit, with skill and courage, fair play and no favour, playing as a member of a team, the result accepted without bitterness or conceit. I love the game's drama, its great occasions: feeling a sense of romance, wonder and mystery, a sense of poetry. On such occasions, the game is larger than life.'

David Hemery CBE, Olympic 400m hurdles world record in Mexico 1968; author, teacher, charity co-ordinator:

'Playing sport requires us to take personal responsibility, rather than to depend on others, learn the rules and skills, aspects such as self-development and self-discipline, dealing with injury, maintaining our own integrity in mind and spirit. Some are against competition, but that's life: for university places, jobs, working relationships. Equally important is visualisation, planning in your mind's eye your successful actions, the impetus given by personal bests to your self-confidence. Inner motivation is a key. Yet a vital element is enjoyment, research indicating that enjoyment is ten times more important than any other reason for involvement in sport. If this is team-orientated, there is the benefit of camaraderie, sometimes of valuable coach relationships and the mutual respect generated by these.'

Richard Pound QC, Canada; Olympic swimming finalist in Rome 1960; IOC Executive Board/vice-president 1983–99; inaugural chairman World Anti-Doping Agency:
'I had fun and some success in high-performance sport, including the Olympic and Commonwealth Games, learning much about myself and the world. The benefits derived did not end when I ceased competing; they enriched my post-competition life, the ability to plan, set goals, manage my time, work collaboratively with others, understand the wider community, deal with success and failure, adjust to changing circumstances and be myself measured. All this derived from involvement in sport. So too did respect for others, understanding the principles of society conduct. Self-discipline, a particular legacy, crosses seamlessly into post-sport life. Any athlete knows that the only place where success comes before work is in the dictionary. Former athletes are ready to work, understanding this is an investment in their future.'

Dr Henry Kissinger, US Secretary of State, campaign chairman for US host election for 1986 World Cup following Colombia's withdrawal (Mexico elected):
'I've been interested ever since I was a boy, honorary chairman of the North American Soccer League, so bringing the

World Cup here would elevate the sport in the States. I've gathered American executives and political leaders to back the enterprise, show this is not a commercial venture, but broad-based support from business and political communities. Either FIFA should give us the World Cup on the basis of our written presentation, or delay their decision until they send a team to look us over. We think we deserve a visit. The quality of our stadia, our advertising facilities, and the importance of showing the international game here in a way it has not been previously seen, must be advantageous to FIFA. It would make soccer a major sport in the US and become focused in a country as sports-minded as the US. It could be, and should be. We'd have serious crowds for the semi-final and final, substantial for the second round, the first round being problematic, as it has been since it was expanded to 24 teams. By giving us the World Cup, FIFA would be investing in the future, and it would be a point of honour for all of us to ensure that it was a success.'

Andrew Young, aide to Martin Luther King; US Ambassador to the United Nations; 55th Mayor of Atlanta, campaigning for South Africa's reinstatement, 1989:
'Nothing can make any more powerful impact on the attitude of all South Africans than the emotional involvement of sports teams, which reflect the kind of pride and spirit that country desperately needs, the first South African to win an Olympic gold medal will become a national hero. Most nations have realised the importance of sport for multi-national unity and pride. We have seen it clearly with high school athletics in small towns here in Georgia. Recognition of the new NOC in South Africa was no reward for those still trying to hold

back progress, but a new force for freedom and dignity. Soon the youth of South Africa may be able to live out the drama and conflict of life on the athletic fields rather than on the battle fields (of townships). That day cannot come too soon.'

Gerhard Heiberg, president, Lillehammer Winter Olympic Games 1994; IOC Executive Board/ Marketing Commission 1994–2017:

'I have spent much of my life not only practising sports but in management of many sports activities. I believe in the principle of the Olympic Charter, "To contribute to building a better world through sports." This should take place without discrimination; the rules for sports are the same worldwide: fair play, tolerance and friendship. As president of the Winter Olympic Games of Lillehammer in 1994, I witnessed joy, enthusiasm, togetherness, equality … it was all there! Athletes, spectators, all agreed, what an experience, the world coming together and all were smiling. Wherever I go, people are interested in sport: politicians, royals, regulars; it's a common language, and not just physical activity but the promotion of health and an educational tool which fosters cognitive development, enhances social behaviour and supports integration within communities.'

Andrew Young, campaigning for Atlanta's host city election for the Centenary Olympic Games of 1996:

'As a theology student in 1951, I forsook an Olympic dream – being a collegiate sprinter – to compete in the wider event of the cause for racial harmony. There was a choice: the Olympic challenge or that of social and political change. Atlanta was destroyed by the Civil War and racked by racist division, yet we have been able to heal those divisions, moving from total segregation to living in peace and prosperity. We now have 37 nationalities in the city, all learning English as a second language. In my eight years as mayor, we have attracted $70bn in investment from across the world and created 700,000 jobs in a metropolitan population that has grown in 30 years from half a million to 2.7 million. I cannot think of a better way than the Olympic Games to lead this region into the 21st century. We are asking the Olympic family to entrust the youth of Atlanta with extending the Olympic ideal.'

Sir Craig Reedie, originator of badminton's inclusion on the Olympic programme; retired chairman of the IOC's World Anti-Doping Agency:

'As the Italian newspaper, *Gazzetta dello Sport*, once proclaimed, "Of all the things which are unimportant, sport is the most important!" How true. For young people sport is fun, and when well organised, either at school or by club membership, an essential part of our education, entrusting a lifetime's values. In adulthood it offers social benefits ranging from personal enjoyment, maybe a level of excellence, even to professional employment. For the older, it offers companionship as well as good health, protection in declining years. We need to hope that governments will promote sport as being critical in the processes of recovery that can enable us to return to what we once called normal.'

Kevan Gosper, Melbourne Olympics 1956 silver medallist; IOC Executive Board/vice-president:

'For me as an Australian Olympian, in 1956 at Melbourne, and a home Games administrator, I believe Sydney 2000 demonstrated many benefits, bringing our nation together cheerfully and proudly. Sport provides global guidance in human behaviour across all languages and conditions. An equal playing field, always inspirational, can be configured anywhere. Rules are universal, the umpire's word final, all this reflecting the fundamental rules of life.'

Dr Rania Elwani, Egyptian gynaecologist; Olympic All-Africa record-breaking swimmer, Sydney 2000:

'The Olympic Games are not merely about competition. The most memorable experience is participation, a rare occasion where athletes from worldwide feel a sense of belonging, a group that shares passion, dreams, hopes and sometimes disappointments: although coming from many backgrounds establishes communication on another subliminal level, creating its own language. You discover friendship, exchange laughs, pins, uniforms, even though maybe not understanding each other's language. Athletes have this special bond, not created but simply *there*. My most memorable moment in 2000 was being under the huge flag covering all the athletes at the closing ceremony; an amazing experience, pride and excitement all in one, wishing the values and spirit of those 15 days could have lasted all year long.'

Dr Francois Carrard, Swiss lawyer; IOC director-general 1989–2003 during constitutional reviews; FIFA Reform Committee chairman:

'We have a body, a brain, and perhaps a soul. Developing harmoniously, men and women alike, requires a balanced education, partly through family and partly through educational institutions. Sport is basic and essential in development for all. While traditionally Anglo-Saxon states have incorporated sport in education, providing an established curriculum, there are too many governments that have not understood sport's importance – beyond improving health – now more than ever evident during the pandemic: teaching us the self-respect fundamental in society and the essence of the Roman motto *"mens sana in corpore sano".*

John Boulter, British Olympian 1964–68; executive director, Adidas:

'Leaving a banquet in Toronto in 1992 on the eve of the General Assembly of the International Yacht Racing Union, I fall in with a group of middle-aged men. Can you tell me how to get to the InterContinental Hotel, I'm asked. Yes, we're staying there, come with us, where are you from, I ask one of them. "From Norway." And what do you do when you're not busy with sailing? "I'm a king," he replies. In 2005, I find myself sitting next to David Beckham, and seek his autograph for my nine-year-old granddaughter. She wants to know if we had made contact. Our shoulders had touched, I say. She goes into a trance, strokes my shoulder, chanting repeatedly, "David has touched this shoulder!" From the highest in the land to a star-struck nine-year-old, sport is an important part of a full life for millions, from every corner of the planet.'

Ser Miang Ng, IOC member; chairman for Singapore's Inaugural Olympic Youth Summer Games, 2010:

'Sport is an integral part of nation-building for Singapore. Ask anyone what they were doing on 13 August 2016, and the odds are they were watching swimmer Joseph Schooling win the nation's first Olympic gold medal. For a young nation who struggled as a poor developing colony in the 1950s, to a prosperous modern independent country today, sports have never played a more important role. From accessible outdoor spaces and facilities everywhere, to robust national programmes encouraging young and old to be active, the benefits of staying healthy through sport have gained momentum. Coming from obscurity never diminished Singaporeans' aspirations to excel on the world stage.'

Sir Hugh Robertson, Conservative MP 2001–15; Minister of Sport 2010–13; British Olympic Association chairman; Camelot Lottery Fund chairman:

'Sport touches both the head and the heart, the head explaining why it matters. Sports events benefit the economy and tourism, having a major impact on GDP. Redevelopment opportunities engendered can transform a neighbourhood, witnessed with Manchester's Commonwealth Games, or Stratford after London 2012; more locally with various redevelopment of football stadia. Volunteers assembled to serve events often remain as community volunteers, while disabled athletes value the effect that showcasing their talents reflects on how society views them. Yet sport also matters on a more emotional level, being the bedrock for many ordinary lives, an element of their emotional happiness and an educational tool for children. Sport can expose a nation, as with London 2012, and define the way we are regarded internationally.'

Dame Katherine Grainger, Olympic rowing champion; four silver medals; six-times world champion; UK Sport CEO – supervision of elite funding:

'Sport has been a huge part of my life since primary school, has taken me on an incredible journey of highs and lows, laughter and tears, has taught me more about myself than anything imaginable, has given memories and friendships that will remain forever, irreplaceable. Sport can provide a home for people, create a common language, form an extended family, discover somewhere to belong. Love of sport, of a team, can be a short cut to human connection, providing collective experience: showcasing drama and tragedy, complex cliff-hangers, sweet revenge, the gift of redemption. It teaches, motivates and inspires, yet provides that crucial human element of hope.'

President Vladimir Putin, email interview in the wake of Russia's doping scandal, 2010–14:

'Besides Russia's cultural, social and political relations, retaining international sport and Olympic frontline prominence remains important. Russia always has been, and I hope always will be, one of the leading international sports countries. Our athletes still produce great results in international competition, set new records and win gold medals. Like any country, we might have experienced certain ups and downs with regard to results, but in no way does this cast any doubt on Russia's status as one of the leading sports countries. I have always had a problem when someone tries to place sport in a social or political context. Sport is a separate and unique kind of human activity, which functions under its own rules and principles. It has nothing to do with the political agenda, and neither should it. When politics interferes with sport, injustice happens.'

Tony Estanguet, triple Olympic champion; president of Paris Olympic Games in 2024:

'I was lucky to belong as a youngster to the Canoe-Kayak Club in Pau, south-west France. Access to sport from early childhood, coupled with other activities, enabled every child to find the sport that suited them best: that's really essential. It allows us to imbue in each child the values that only sport brings: resilience, teamwork, pushing your limits, respect for rules and competitors, discipline, but also inclusion and the acceptance of differences that disappear out on the field of play. It's a mindset that translates into everyday life and lays the foundations for a more inclusive and caring society. Our Olympic Games in 2024 – the third in Paris – will personify this global ethic.'

Tim Higglesworth, CEO of Sport England:
'Right now, sport matters more than ever. London 2012 showed sport in all its glory, but the solution to raising activity levels lies increasingly by ensuring it can accommodate everyone's regular lives, while highlighting its benefit to physical and mental health. Focusing on inequalities, we've seen sustained games in the nation's activity in subsequent years. Coronavirus has restricted this, yet emphasised its importance. Sport helps address society's serious challenges. Where Sport England chooses to focus, energy and money will be governed by three principles: investing in those who need it most; achieving a blend of national and local support; providing guidance and support that is simple to give and receive.'

Jade Jones, taekwondo double gold medal champion:
'Not being top ranked at London 2012, I wasn't fancied as the winner, and it wasn't until reaching the final I realised I could actually do it. Towards the end of the match, I kept on incurring penalty points ... then I heard the home crowd starting a countdown, heard the number one being called … and knew it had happened. I still can't put into words the sensation of achieving that first gold. It was surreal. Becoming the target as number one, pressure mounted at Rio in 2016. Primarily, I just wanted to become remembered for all time, not just as someone who had won the Olympics once. With a minute to go, I kicked my opponent straight in the head and determined not to stop,

keep getting at her, and that's what I did. Finally I'd made it. I'll be attempting the triple in Tokyo, I hope.'

Sebastian, Lord Coe: President World Athletics, sole successful defender of Olympic 1,500 metres title, 1980–84:

'Unquestionably, sport can be defined as one of the most potent ingredients in the social equation. Many politicians do not realise or understand the effectiveness of sport as one of the forces of diplomatic power. They forget the ping-pong diplomacy of 1968 which brought Maoist China to the international table, enabled President Nixon to engage, via Henry Kissinger, with Chinese hegemony. To go anywhere, sport can shine the spotlight: even for politicians seeking trade deals.

Sport can inevitably be a personal passport. Its impact on me was systemic, fashioned my future, anything I went on to do, providing a clear indication of the human condition more than could any other environment arena. In the struggling local community of Sheffield, or the inner city confinement of London's Haringey athletic club, sport could provide the only anchor of the week within a troubled society: creating friendships otherwise unavailable for teenagers.

The momentum from London's Olympic Games, where a new city was built inside an old city, inspirationally generated more medals at Rio '16, the impact inestimable.'

The national pride fostered in 2012 regrettably was not to be replicated when hosting the final stage of the postponed European football championships in 2021. After 55 years of frustration, including World Cup semi-finals in 1990 and 2018, and European semis in 1996, the astute management of Gareth Southgate – unluckily responsible for a losing missed penalty in '96 – had guided England, founders of the game, to a second summit. Now there was none of the scepticism that had surrounded taciturn Alf Ramsey – his tactical perception beyond public recognition – during a fundamental tactical revolution across the game: the arrival of Total Football and Ramsey's reputed 'wingless wonders', a mere decade after our two most illustrious players were wingers Matthews and Finney.

National pride in the Sixties was still cautiously restrained during post-Suez loss of Empire and Cold War anxieties. Remember that my generation's schoolboys were as equally in awe and admiration of the RAF Spitfire as any footballer: in those days unethically expected socially to know their place on £10 a week, travelling to home matches by bus with the fans.

While I readily had fantacised about sport and its tempting horizons, an enduring emotion had been kindled by Noel Coward's haunting verse honouring Bomber Command's lost 50,000, 'there's one debt you'll forever owe':

> *Lie in the dark and listen.*
> *It's clear tonight so they're flying high,*
> *Hundreds of them, thousands perhaps,*
> *Riding the icy, moonlit sky.*
> *Men, machinery, bombs and maps,*
> *Altimeters and guns and charts,*
> *Coffee, sandwiches, fleece-lined boots,*
> *Bones and muscles and minds and hearts,*
> *English saplings with English roots*
> *Deep in the earth they left below.*
> *Lie in the dark and let them go;*
> *Lie in the dark and listen.*

Has my career championing sport, that social cement and emotional release, been worthy of life's deeper responsibilities?

CHAPTER ONE

DISCOVERING A SPORTING LIFE

The Greeks got it right. They knew a thing or two in 2700 BC – the inseparable link between humanity's intellectual and physical instincts. The urge to chase a ball, throw a spear or win a race as distinctive then as in 2020. The psychology dates back to hunter-gatherer millennia, to our survival, and the basic urge is no different for the COVID-19 generation. We need, enjoy and thrive on challenge, essential to both mental and physical equilibrium. The assault of COVID-19 has been a demonstrable threat to our collective sanity by its imposition on exercise, fundamental to a healthy population. Sport provides dual benefit: fitness for the individual, while reducing national medical costs, alongside the entertainment which is provided by many professional sports. Football engages hundreds of thousands, whether amateur players or the professional game's audience. The Coe–Ovett contest in Moscow's Olympics embraced 23 million UK viewers. The Queen was riveted by Torvill and Dean four years later. The world has held its breath at three contemporary Olympic Games, spellbound by Usain Bolt's sprinting treble-treble;

elsewhere by Jonny Wilkinson's dropped goals and by Roger Federer's cross-court backhand.

Sport is different from most cultural activities in that almost everyone can be engaged, playing or watching. It is non-lingual: a Mexican can compete with a Russian, whether it's swimming or snooker, fencing or football, as long as they know the rules, and it is discipline which conditions sport – a mobile, unpredictable drama, a flexible art form, occasionally physically beautiful, and not to be scorned by intellectual snobs. Yet pause for a moment. Sport is also potentially a vehicle, in parallel with regular life, for helping us better to comprehend intellectual civic strategy within critical relationships, domestic or international: how humanity behaves collectively in crisis. There is a plausible correlation, with hindsight, of, say, the outcome of the blindside battle of Waterloo, Marchal Blucher's crucial Prussian flank attack – or the insane Peterloo massacre, or the contemporary Clapham Common demonstration police conflict – with the sporting sophistication of Hungary's football in the 1950s when England's centre-half captain Billy Wright was effectively left as a bystander in a 6-3 defeat, or Holland's jigsaw of the '70s, the epic technical *volte face* of Arthur Ashe's defeat of overwhelming favourite Jimmy Connors. Parliament might occasionally act more wisely if more male MPs played mixed doubles at tennis. Even sport itself is only latterly adapting to gender-awareness integration. In a mere two words, sport is *sensible* and *civilised*: a microcosm of life.

My mission here is to capture the personal dramas of elite performers: emotional, circumstantial, racial, rather than statistical, all of whom bar three in the early 20th century I have met or reported on. It will begin with three contemporary icons – Lionel Messi, Jessica Ennis-Hill and Lewis Hamilton

– plus the sorrow of Lillian Board's abrupt death 50 years ago; then from segregated black rebel Jack Johnson through the 1930s of Jesse Owens, early post-war Fanny Blankers-Koen and Emil Zátopek, and on to current times with Usain Bolt and social campaigning footballer Marcus Rashford. I hope to portray how, across a century, sport has evolved towards becoming more classless, more integrated, more accessible for everyone: for both the elite and the average. It is the anonymous games teachers, gym instructors and public volunteers who breed the base of the sporting pyramid which ultimately generates champions. They propagate the eventual headlines but seldom receive the credit. My theme precludes debate on triumphant teams as opposed to individuals, teams being part of sport's massive canvas. The elite 50 I have selected as illustration and inspiration of why sport matters, serve to encourage the rest of us to respond to nature's subliminal instincts.

George Orwell derided sport, following Moscow Dynamo's visit to Britain in 1945, as being war without the bullets, 'unfailing cause of ill will'. He was so wrong: sport is about so much more. There are five universal languages in life – money, politics, art, sex and sport. The latter mostly embraces the first four, additionally and disconcertingly nowadays a sixth in racialism.

The global COVID-19 pandemic has witnessed parallel acceleration of the social and climate agitprop campaigns, movements spearheaded by Black Lives Matter and Extinction Rebellion, platforms which inevitably attract extreme political interventionists. This tide has aroused demands for staged protests on the Olympic medal podium to be acceptable, removing the International Olympic Committee's prohibition under Charter Rule 50. The fundamental virtue of that regulation is, in an echo of Greek philosophy, that the Olympic Games be free of political grandstanding. What sport should propagate is consensus, not division.

Competitive sport forms an emotional medium for identity, whether for an individual, a city, a race, a nation. It can be as emblematic as a play, a poem, a monument, which is not to deny that in excess the emotion can be adverse and even damaging. Yet reflect on what is the most ecstatic experience of the Pacific island of Fiji – winning the rugby sevens at the Rio Olympics in 2016. When cynics argue that the Olympics ruin a city, it is more often the reverse: that a city or an individual corrupts the Olympics. Whether competitive or recreational, sport is a vehicle of self-expression. Even when confined to the humblest mode of exercise, many discover self-improvement merely by a look in the mirror. Sport helps tell us who we are, whether as individuals or nations, but should do so gregariously, not aggressively, even when under the banner of Black Lives Matter.

A suggestion last year by Dominic Raab, Britain's foreign secretary, that the nation should boycott Beijing's Winter Olympics of 2022 on account of genocidal attitudes towards China's Muslim people of Uighur, was imprudent political opportunism. History proves Olympic boycotts carry no momentum: failed attempts to oppose Berlin's Nazi-orchestrated Games of 1936 are wholly remembered for the glory of Jesse Owens, Afro-American, and his spontaneous friendship with rival German long-jumper Lutz Long; the consecutive boycotts of 1976, '80 and '84 harmed only those who stayed away. A boycott in 2020 by Britain, a minor winter sports nation, would have zero impact on domestic Chinese policy. Not only does the British government have no jurisdiction over a constitutionally independent

British Olympic Association, but effective reprisal would have to be diplomatic or economic. Disapprove of a nation? Do not elect them as hosts in the first place, rather than harangue them later. The Olympic Games must never be a political tool.

The objective of my amalgam of memories of elite performers across a century, having met and recorded their deeds, is to emphasise how significant is sport in society. Irrespective of millions of spectators – those paying handsomely to watch professional dramas, humble families attending village contests, those exploiting modest leisure gymnasia – the sports industry in Britain employs over 300,000 people. Irrevocably, sport matters. I hope my recollections, tracing individual landmarks of history, may provide a sense of what sport generates in the passage of life as a fundamental culture: a sensation of emotion, no less profound than that experienced in the heroic Greek battle episodes of Marathon, where soldier Pheidippides ran 40 kilometres to relate victory over Persia in 490 BC, or that at Thermopylae in 480 BC when Leonidas and a thousand outnumbered compatriots fought to the death to hold a pass against invading Persia. The peacetime deeds of Indian-American Jim Thorpe, Afro-Americans Owens and Arthur Ashe, Aborigine Cathy Freeman, Anglo-Saxon Steve Redgrave or Caribbean Usain Bolt, have symbolised for us all the human spirit: sometimes sorrowfully or disappointing, as with track stars Lillian Board or Dave Bedford. This is my story.

Greece kindled the flame. Spiritually believing their gods and goddesses lived on Mount Olympus, they founded the ancient Olympics, bound by a truce demanding cessation of any war for the duration, an olive wreath decorating the winners. That historic initiation was echoed in 1850 by Dr William Penny Brookes, establishing in Shropshire the Wenlock Olympic Games, for 'moral, physical and intellectual promotion'; events included athletics, football, cricket and quoits. Significantly, it was a visit by Baron Pierre De Coubertin in 1890 which spurred the French aristocrat for his launch in 1894, at the Sorbonne in Paris, of the IOC. And here we are today, countless modern champions financially sponsored by that ancient goddess of victory – Nike. We owe so much to the wooded Mediterranean grove of Olympia.

Sport, as suggested, is a microcosm of our existence: of success and failure, effort and frustration, celebration and dismay, or sometimes, below the anxiety of serious competition, simply the fun and laughter. And never forget – this being an historic ingredient of the Olympic Games – it should essentially be founded on friendship, whether international or domestic, 'getting to know the other side'. In one sense, Orwell is correct: that sport is an alternative to war, to some of the emotions, jealousies and injustices that provoke war, so that sport can be a kind of safety valve, a testosterone escape mechanism that induces pride rather than rage, beauty instead of horror. It is no coincidence that a pillar of sporting achievement should be the marathon race. The courage that sport often requires is so often a mirror of the battle. The psychology of sport can indeed be profound.

On the other hand, we should not be obsessive about sport; it is not the ultimate but part of life's cultural fabric. For the last two centuries, the romanticists have been attempting to find the alternative to the industrial revolution, and sport offers part of that enterprise, providing social relativity and individual or collective gratification. Viv Richards, the celebrated West Indian cricketer, striking a lofted six at Lord's Cricket Ground in London, or Pelé's rasping 1,000th goal at Rio's Maracanã cathedral, can briefly lift a nation's morale. Yet while Jean Giraudoux, French author and playwright, reflects that 'the ball is that thing which most easily escapes the laws of life', those without the eye-to-hand (or foot) synthesis of bouncing-ball dexterity should not be scorned. They may well excel at static competition such as chess or bridge, or the professions of science, engineering, law, medicine or industry. Yet they, in turn, should not be dismissive of physical games, as many respected, avowed intellects such as the late, esteemed Bernard Levin have been. Briefly editor of *The Times*, Simon Jenkins, subsequently chairman of the National Trust among public cultural appointments and publications, adopted a patronisingly condescending but ignorant attitude towards sport: once archly writing prior to an Olympics 'wake me up for the mile', unaware this was an event never contested.

Jenkins indulged in a veritable minor hobby, denigration of sport and its management, bypassing the IOC's basic ethic of global friendship and communication and instead condemning the inadequacies of certain members, or constantly suggesting alterations to sports' governance: such as widening football's goalposts or the size of the hole in golf, abolition of the second serve in tennis to eliminate ace dominance, unaware that grass courts have become a minority surface and that the second serve is the salvation of grassroots players in a sport conspicuous for the level of errors.

Even articulate critics of sport tend to underestimate either the economics or the emotions. For Olympic cities there are two budgets: the cost of more than 30 sports venues, and then the ancillary budget of a city seeking to expand its social, industrial or tourist reputation. Nor can the likes of Levin or Jenkins comprehend what brings thousands to line the streets for the funeral of, say, Stanley Matthews or George Best, almost on a par with the acclaim for Admiral Nelson at St Paul's Cathedral, truly touching the heart.

What would-be intellectuals also tend not to comprehend, especially concerning elite and therefore nowadays predominantly professional sport, is that it requires total mental and physical commitment. There is no hiding place when intently observed by either a live audience of thousands or, additionally, by millions on television. The merest hesitation, whether emotional, or moral in the context of regulations, will be instantly apparent. Architects, lawyers, physicians and the like have their character flaws but are protected by professional qualifications. The sports performer is wholly exposed – though I am excluding for the moment the wretched escalation of cheating, drugs-wise or other. Yes, there has always been an element of bending the rules – foul tackles in football, no-balls in cricket, below-the-belt blows in boxing, all either accidental or occasionally intended but governed by correction laws.

Character is part of the public appeal. Above and beyond appreciation of commitment, of loyalty to club, country, by and to supporters in team games, is sportsmanship. And I do not mean old-fashioned amateurism of supposed English gentry of the 19th century, but simple honesty. It is so often character which defines sport, whether immaculate West Indies all-rounder Gary Sobers or Roger Federer from Switzerland. There is no stronger currency with the public, even if a minority will occasionally extol a braggart or a bully. Idealistically, spectators give their soul to perfection in sport. To Muhammad Ali or Usain Bolt or Lionel Messi: occasionally, as with Ali or ethnic minority social reformers such as Aborigine fountain-head Cathy Freeman, there being social addenda.

One of my earliest journalistic memories is from the renowned Kop grandstand at Liverpool Football Club's emotional Anfield stadium. A gifted but somewhat timid winger was summarily clobbered by the opposing full-back. As a moment's silence awaited Liverpool's free kick, a lone voice drifted from the Kop, "It 'im with yer 'andbag, Brian.' I'm granting anonymity to 'Brian'. How often might we wish to shout at a lawyer, politician, town planner, police chief – or journalist – to 'give us their best'? Symptomatic of what I mean is the tribute on the title page of that tennis bible by America's journalistic doyen of the game, Bud Collins. From an avalanche of historically memorable players from around the world, for sportsmanship without equal, Collins thanked Arthur Ashe: black campaigner for humanity on and off the court. Contrary to Orwell's concept of inherent ill will – which understandably can exist, with evidence of football violence from London to Moscow to Latin America, or boxing-ring malevolence in the Olympic Games – sport not only promotes generosity in the arena, but extensive financial charity from wealthy professionals such as Federer and Messi, or Marcus Rashford, Manchester United's disciple for adequate school meals for the impoverished; increasingly in the late 20th and early 21st century, sport has expanded, pre-COVID, the reach of social, racial and gender mobility.

Part of the magic of sport is dependent upon spectators, themselves skilled or unskilled, but optimistically waiting to be captivated by a theatrical act, the outcome of which is unknown. How did I stumble into such good fortune of employment as a writer? Frankly, by child accident of severe scalding and subsequent skin-grafting which rendered me ineligible for National Service, plus the cancellation of an appointment in education, wartime loneliness, and an emerging, rewarding degree of my own moderate sporting aptitude. Scalded by near boiling water across my back from my shoulders to my knees aged three, I should have died and didn't. A devoted hospital nurse soothingly stroked my forehead for the first 48 hours, my limbs tied to the bed corners to prevent movement, all memory hitherto obliterated. Survival was immense luck.

My father, an aspiring stage actor, joining the RAF on the outbreak of war, my mother losing two infant daughters, our house blitzed, I was evacuated to a great aunt and then to a boarding prep school aged seven. Weeping nightly inconsolably, I planned my imaginary escape by the number 18 bus from Epsom to anywhere I could safely hide in Surrey's woods, being a boy scout adroit with campfires. My ally and solace was nature, the blossom of spring, then and always. Yet suddenly football and cricket came to my rescue.

Inadvertently, though small I discovered I could drop-kick a football higher than anyone else. Esoteric. Refuge. Instant semi-celebrity. The pelting with acorns or conkers by senior bullies, long tolerated, now ceased. My incentives with the leather mounted when a visiting professional coach from Charlton Athletic – his name now sadly evaporated – demonstrated he could kick a ball from Surrey almost into Kent. Here could be my echo of father's theatrical stage.

Alongside was cricket. An early voracious reader, I had been religiously absorbing the red-ball gospel from the age of six. My dear wartime nanny, uninformed, was duly alarmed when discovering me immersed in a *Sunday Express* exclusive, 'Don Bradman's Secret Sorrow', supposing I was prematurely into illicit romance documentation.

To relieve interminable leisure boredom – wartime re-engaged retired schoolmasters fell asleep at weekends – I engaged in protracted two-man Test matches with another loner, Joe Hyams: he England, I Australia, every ball bowled, struck, fielded and the possible runs mutually debated, with our saga lasting for days. An unplanned journalistic discipline was being fashioned. Addiction to the game was furthered immediately post-war, aged ten, fielding at long-on for the straight drives, when the touring Australian Test side, led by the incomparable Lindsay Hassett, indulged in net practice at the Saffrons Ground at Eastbourne where I could clamber over the brick wall. Rewardingly, at close, they would bowl a couple of overs at me.

From there on – with maths, Latin, and chemistry taking their chance with this unacclaimed but academically comfortable student – sport accelerated with increasing rhythm: Surrey Prep Schools XI, Public Schools v FA Youth XI (including future England captain Johnny Haynes); spellbound by the sorcery of the Matthews FA Cup Final of 1953; junior 100 metres at the August Bank Holiday Games at White City; 220 yards hurdles for Cambridge University; javelin performer (undistinguished) for Achilles Club; orchestrating the goal against Oxford which the *Daily Mail*'s chief correspondent described as 'one of the best ever seen at Wembley'; coached by such experts as Arthur Rowe and Bill Nicholson of Spurs, Joe Mercer of Everton, Arsenal and England and manager of Manchester City, and by former Corinthian winger Norman Creek with England Amateurs; missing an open goal for England Amateurs at Loftus Road against QPR and being the only player not selected against Scotland the following Saturday (remembered daily for the next 60 years!).

Coached at cricket by the physically towering but gently cheerful George Geary, of Leicestershire and England, considered in the late 1920s the most accurate medium-pace bowler in the world (5-35 in Sydney), who could pitch a ball on a proverbial handkerchief in the nets to force you to play a particular stroke; coached at squash by inimitable Nazrullah Khan; at rugby – merely conversationally – by England full-back Nigel Gibbs; at athletics by Cambridge hurdler Brian Young, he as headmaster turning up at the track somewhat inappropriately in pinstripe trousers; and morally in the classroom by inaugural Everest summit pathfinder Wilfred Noyce, a man of serene disposition.

The Bank Holiday Games had been specifically memorable. An ardent reader of Olympic lore and the likes of such legends as Jim Thorpe and Jesse Owens, a distant hero at London in 1948 had been Mal Whitfield, 800 metres champion with such melodic stride, no visible rise and fall of the shoulders even when accelerating, that he seemed to float. He had retained his title at Helsinki in 1952. Now here I was at the old White City, home of London 1908, warming up for my semi-final (eliminated in fourth place) alongside Whitfield himself, there being no external warm-up area beneath the grandstand. I felt elevated by our shared preparation. As we each independently took a breather a few yards apart, the legend's quiet friendly word was profound. 'What we're doing here is as important as what we do on the track.'

At school, in the lingering 'amateurism' of the 1950s, even wearing a tracksuit and warming up was unflatteringly regarded as professionalism. Prior to arriving at Cambridge on a county scholarship – my father's fluctuating stage career, including the inaugural performance of Shaw's *Saint Joan*, scuttled by RAF service as a radar operator in the Battle of Britain and thereafter, and embarking post-war as an impecunious prototype Basil Fawlty – I languidly read zoology, with a view to entering medicine, and at Cambridge the philosophy of science, lectured by renowned young American philosopher Russell Hanson (a Harvard shot putter) who sadly died young in pursuit of his flying hobby. Philosophy seemed more absorbing than dissecting a frog.

The social vault from school adolescence to university trainee-manhood was for me something of a nightmare. Britain in the 1950s was undergoing – having elected a Labour government in 1945, with evolutionary disposal of their totemic and inspirational war leader – a dress rehearsal of class reorientation, which would pervade the established domestic, cultural and employment structure in the 1960s. I was in no-man's land: where did I belong? My mother descended from landed gentry, who had founded one of the earliest newspapers, the *Mercury* of Manchester in 1752, but the family had squandered inherited wealth. Regarded as a valueless daughter, my mother had rebelled, scandalously left home aged 17 – her parents never searched for her – to join an immigrant White Russian (Belarus) orchestra, and precariously married a penniless actor who now post-war was socially and economically adrift among the professional classes while running a downmarket 19th-century coaching inn, short on trade in a bankrupt nation.

My father Wilfred was an emotional conundrum, simultaneously affectionate yet insecure and self-protectively ill-tempered. A late child of a frail, bed-ridden mother, and his gifted but irascible church-organist and actor-manager father, of 19th-century old-school theatre's dramatic exaggeration, who would pursue his unwelcome children down Shaftesbury

Avenue with a carving knife when not otherwise occupied composing the libretto for Stephen Philpot's *Dante and Beatrice*: a turn-of-the-century opera widely performed in Britain and America. My father left school at 15, tumbled into teenage drama school with Bernard Lee (James Bond's spymaster M) and thence into the esteemed West End company of Sybil Thorndyke launching Shaw's inaugural *St Joan*. Yet he was so lacking in confidence that he hid behind his father's name, 'William Miller Junior': until I was ten or so I was puzzled why all his friends referred to him as Bill, and by then I had identified that if we were coherently to relate the initiative had to come from me.

My only professional 'contact' was mother's (family-preferred) brother, a GP in distant Galloway, digging through snowdrifts to reach his patients in an era when bedside courtesy was still a medical flagship. Having attended an independent school, Charterhouse, courtesy of a benevolent great aunt sympathetic to mother's loss of two infant girls, the only cultural structure I knew, beyond academia, was sport: a ladder towards respectability and status, possible economic administrative foothold; as Gary Lineker, vastly talented son of a Leicester market trader, and many others, were to discover.

Cambridge, unintentionally, opened the gate. Suddenly there was the objective of playing at Wembley against Oxford: a privilege extended by the FA, through to the 1990s, to promote the game at schools in rivalry to rugby. That Wembley glamour at the time was magnified by the emergence of Pegasus, a combined Oxford and Cambridge team founded in 1948 and twice winning football's FA Amateur Cup, this abolished with the termination of the amateur distinction in 1973. Crowds of 100,000 witnessed Pegasus at Wembley: the club dissolved after 20 years. Yet this team of part-time amateurs, assembled from their professional jobs in all corners of England for a Saturday afternoon, were an echo of former Corinthians for adventure and romance – 19 gaining international honours – the victorious side against Bishop Auckland in 1951 being considered by some professional commentators as superior to FA Cup winners Newcastle United.

Whatever my football career might have been, never mind my father's repetitive assurance that 'football will never earn you a living', my path, by abstract association, was determined. Attention to chemistry and zoology became flagrantly irrelevant. I was so fortunate: sport was to provide, unexpectedly, an iridescent career – though not as performer. I think my convoluted background combined to guide me towards supporting as journalist, almost alone in Fleet Street for the *Daily Telegraph* at the time, the freedom from English football's maximum wage in 1960/61; then celebrating Wimbledon abolishing the institutional sham amateurism of tennis, and simultaneously, US silver millionaire Lamar Hunt's creation of a professional tour; most significantly, subsequently for *The Times* campaigning for the abolition of South Africa's apartheid regime; later Olympic acceptance of professionalism in 1987 to prosper egalitarian training, in acknowledgement of 50 years' reality of 'shamateurism'.

With my laboratory disillusionment at Cambridge and the withering disintegration of my parents' union, my prospect of Olympic football selection evaporating at grassless Loftus Road, and my residing loneliness detonated by falling in love under the willows caressing the idyllic Cam, I abandoned, to a headmaster's ire, an appointment to teach chemistry. So what now?

I had university subsistence bills to pay, I needed a summer vacation job and through the benign influence of Geoffrey Green, eminent but in those days anonymous football and tennis correspondent of *The Times*, was offered the post of 'relief' sports sub-editor – which enabled staff to relax on holiday. Green himself had been an iconic centre-half for the famous Corinthians, said by ace professional Charlie Buchan to have been the best in the land, amateur or pro. My task as sub-editor was to handle, daily, up to 14 simultaneous County Championship scorecards in full, including bowling analysis, and not to provoke a dozen retired clergymen's letters by omitting 'extras'. In late summer, a fellow sub was promoted to rugby correspondent, whereby I was able to fill the desk vacancy – on 18 guineas a week, some 30 per cent better than a lowly chemistry master. Sixty-five years later, gratuitously I am still there, so to speak.

Relating the exhilarations of legendary figures is to capture, I hope, something of the fascination that envelops all of us, of whatever race or origin, in some shared joy. The laudable perfection of, say, Lew Hoad, Olga Korbut or Seve Ballesteros at their peak cannot be precisely defined: any more than a Constable or a Gauguin. One moment an unexpected epic, the next gone forever, bar a two-dimensional TV reminder.

Imperative within the contemporary social equation is an elevation, in both performance and media promotion of both women's sport and ethnic integration, within the ugly racist controversy which so damaged the European final between England and Italy. Women's right to receive proportional exposure and appreciation as half the human race, being equally as capable as men of creating drama, say, on the ocean waves as at an indoor hall. Women, and women in sport, also matter: equally essential is ethnic identity and tolerant integration, whether for Jews, blacks, Muslims or whichever immigrant races seek to establish a contribution to Britain's historic multi-tribal and complex society. Sport is anyone's vehicle.

CHAPTER TWO
MODERN MAESTROS

LIONEL MESSI
Nourished Daydreams

'Jewels rather than bullets'

The gift to society by supreme sports performers is not simply the professional drama of unpredictable entertainment, the conclusion of a delayed secret, but the imagined *idea*, the fantasy for many of us somehow privately emulating these exotic deeds. A million young boys around the globe, and nowadays girls too, inspired by the vision of Lionel Messi's unending magic, harbour an ambition that perhaps, even just *once*, they could conjure on the playing field or in the street a moment as fulfilling as those which Messi has contrived for Barcelona – less often for Argentina – almost every time he touches the ball. The phenomenon of Messi, so ordinarily Mr Average in civvies without his boots, is that his magic – and I do not use the term casually – has been so consistent over 20 years that it has become 'normal'. Spanish and Argentinian media publicly acknowledge that, professionally, they have exhausted appropriate superlatives. As Marcus Rashford observes, 'The way Messi finds spaces, he's unbelievable. In a sense, he doesn't move, yet he's everywhere, because he lets everybody else move.'

The cultural impact of Messi on society is difficult not to exaggerate. He is the perfect manipulator with that instrument, a ball, which the majority find perplexingly unmanageable, yet because he does so with such ease, millions are captivated by it: many go out to the playing fields, between the age of six and 46, *pretending* to be Messi, and thrilled by their illusion. It is entertainment therapy: now perhaps to be continued by Kylian Mbappé of Paris Saint-Germain, at 22 already a World Cup winner with France in 2018 and a dribbler/goalscorer in the Messi style.

I've had close friends in that hero make-believe mould: John Moynihan, a benign colleague on the *Telegraph*, 6ft 2in and minimum balance, who from boyhood to middle age, on Sunday mornings from Hyde Park to Hackney Marshes, believed he *was* Tommy Lawton – centre-forward for Everton, Chelsea and Notts County from 1938–48, with 21 goals in 23 England appearances. John's shooting and the net were seldom closely acquainted. Such pleasurable illusion was shared by Brian Glanville, the novelist, eminent international commentator, football historian and would-be left-back, under whose tutelage the ball was often as immune to flight as a bale of hay, yet whose conviction was such that at times he would engage conversationally with England's then impeccable left-back, World Cup winner Ray Wilson of Everton, to offer advice. For several decades, Glanville aided national health by orchestrating Chelsea Casuals, an itinerant Sunday leisure team of eccentric characteristics. It is genuinely so that the likes of Stanley Matthews, Bobby Charlton and Messi have nourished the daydreams of ordinary folk and even our recreational realities. Whether Mbappé can sustain for 20 years the team ethic of Messi remains to be seen. The genius of Messi has been not just his individualism, but the extent to which he has co-ordinated cohesion with colleagues.

Yet how to define, today, the status of Messi, now 33, repetitively asserted by some to be the ultimate technician of all time: the rivals being, by common consent, Alfredo Di Stéfano, Pelé, Johan Cruyff, Diego Maradona and Messi's contemporary, Cristiano Ronaldo of Portugal. My immediate comment would be that while Messi, like Di Stéfano and Pelé, has been primarily a one-club man, an itinerant Ronaldo has given evidence at times of playing largely for himself. For all his extraordinary escapology, Messi is transparently a team player, devoid of conceit: off the field, shy to the point of being uncommunicative. His childhood offers some explanation.

Born in June 1987 in Rosario, the third of four children, taken to football aged four by his maternal grandmother and joining traditional Newell's Old Boys aged six, and scoring nearly 500 goals in the next six years, Messi discovered aged ten that he had a growth hormone deficiency: so small and fragile that his playing prospects seemed bleak. Yet such was his evident talent on the ball – entertaining first-team crowds with half-time juggling – that at 13 he relocated to Barcelona's youth academy for subsidised hormone therapy. In almost any other sport, 5ft 6in Leo, the future assassin of defenders, would have been a wimp.

Mercifully, he was headed for stardom, as endlessly recorded: first-team debut at 17, in October 2004; 33 trophies in the next 16 years, including ten league titles, four Champions Leagues, six Spanish Cups; the La Liga goals record of 456 at the time of writing; record La Liga goals in a season 50;

record 36 La Liga hat-tricks, and eight in the Champions League; over 750 career goals for club and country (heading towards Pelé's 1,000-plus); Olympic champion at Beijing in 2008; record six Ballon d'Or awards; in 2006, the youngest Argentinian to play in a World Cup finals; as Argentinian captain from 2011, leading them in three consecutive finals – World Cup 2014, Copa America 2015 and '16, then qualifying for 2018 World Cup and bronze medal Copa America 2019.

Such have been the pinnacles of Messi's career that it is rare for him to excel beyond anything he has already done before: except in the first of his Champions League hat-tricks, in the second leg against Arsenal in December 2010 when he scored four goals. Even sceptical media from Madrid were obliged to bow. As *El Pais* headlined, 'Messi Ate Arsenal'. The embarrassment for Castile was that the maestro might have scored six, twice grazing the bar and post amid his fourth hat-trick of the season: at only 22, having already notched 119 goals for the club, a routine bordering on ridiculous. The stunning impact for Arsène Wenger's men was that in the 2-2 first leg, Messi had been comparatively subdued, though having twice as many shots as any Arsenal player. For his fourth goal in the second leg he dribbled past three defenders before shooting, Maradona-style. His second Champions League treble was the 4-0 away leg against Plzen the following year, and was innocently easy.

His third hat-trick came two years later in a 7-1 home thrashing of Bayer Leverkusen: this time, Messi became the first man to score five, for a 10-2 aggregate. Part of his unique speciality is an ability to chip over an alert goalkeeper from close range, a matter of only a few yards: this he did against Leverkusen, once with each foot. His fourth hat-trick was a four-goal rout of Ajax at home in September 2013, the third goal a feint to shoot to the right, then calmly placing the ball to the left. Number five was an unusual triple of easy close-range nudges away to Apoel in November 2014. Number six was the humiliation at the Camp Nou of Celtic by seven goals, a South American monopoly as Neymar of Brazil set up Messi's first two and Suárez his third.

The seventh in Messi's unrelenting haul, in October 2016, was cruel: former Camp Nou guru Pep Guardiola, having returned 18 months earlier to suffer defeat with Bayern Munich, now was back with Manchester City, his ex-protégé striking three in Barcelona's 4-0 stroll. And the eighth in September 2018: five years to the day after shredding one Dutch team, Messi now dismembered another, PSV Eindhoven. The first goal was one of Messi's sublime, geometric free kicks. These sometimes have to be seen to be believed.

Immediately prior to the infamous Heysel disaster in Brussels at the 1985 Liverpool v Juventus European Cup Final, I had witnessed a lone training session by Michel Platini, Juve's captain, taking 20 free kicks from the edge of the penalty area, bending the ball over a wooden fake wall. Only once had the adroit Frenchman failed to curve his shot a fraction under the bar. What Messi contrives to do – slim, undersized and with none of the muscularity of Platini or Ronaldo – is to send the ball on a climbing, swerving and then dipping parabola which leaves any goalkeeper confused. If you don't believe me, watch the clip on the internet of his free kick in December 2018 during the four-goal victory over local rivals Espanyol. Diego Lopez, Espanyol's keeper, is tall and agile. Messi has been fouled just outside the penalty area, slightly to the right of a line on to Lopez's left post. With an exceptional right-lean, Messi strikes the ball with the inside of his left foot: it is climbing initially towards Lopez, but then curves to his left (Messi's right) and, still climbing as if on a conveyor-belt like a COVID vaccine phial, eventually dips into the smallest gap between crossbar and Lopez's left post. Physically almost incomprehensible. At Espanyol's stadium, there is incredulity. 'A Magnum Opus' claims *El Mundo*. Public astonishment fuelled parallel news: that Messi now ranked only *fifth* in the current Ballon d'Or standings. Had he now himself normalised the abnormal?

Wherever you turn in the record books, Messi defies normality. He and Ronaldo are the two players to have surpassed one hundred goals in the Champions League. Early in 2018, Messi did so in a comprehensive defeat of Chelsea. Ronaldo was already there ahead of him, with 117, but Messi reached the milestone in 14 fewer appearances and over 250 fewer shots (as addictive statisticians record).

Returning to the theme of 'greatest ever', what distinguishes Messi from the other five maestros I mentioned earlier is the gentleness of so much of his guile. Pelé, Maradona and Ronaldo have all been conspicuous for muscular bravura: Di Stéfano and Cruyff less so, though infinitely agile. Messi effortlessly whirls like a gyroscope, the ball his servant, his instant acceleration from zero seemingly supercharged yet gone almost silently like a puff of exhaust, comparable to Matthews 80 years ago. There was an instant in 2015, during Bayern Munich's destruction, when Messi left three defenders prostrate on the ground as he skated goalward: more Rudolf Nureyev than Mike Tyson, his two goals jewels rather than bullets.

Debate swells among Argentinians on the respective merits of Messi and Maradona, the latter achieving World Cup triumph and Messi falling short. Comparisons are inevitably subjective: my reflection would simply be that, of all candidates for heavenly supremacy, Messi's claim is serenely effortless. Arsène Wenger was unequivocal, 'Messi is the best player in the world ... by a distance.' Alex Ferguson was more specific, 'The best striker, the best dribbler, the best midfielder.'

The truest measure is the awe in which Messi is regarded by other contemporary players. Nélson Semedo, a Portuguese international defender for Benfica, Barcelona for two seasons and then Wolves, once observed, 'I never ever saw him take a free kick in training. We all used to practise shooting from a distance, yet Messi never with a free kick. For him it was just natural – no practice but still perfect. I've seen him dribble past five players, wondering "how can this guy do this?" He makes good players look bad.'

Just like Stanley Matthews, of whom more later.

JESSICA ENNIS-HILL
Motherhood Mastery

'More than just a British heroine'

A smile goes a long way. Maybe I am prejudiced, but my experience, as child and adult, is that smiling comes more readily to women than men. An opening for women, exploratory communication is simpler than words, which men use for sparring. Two of the most conspicuous smiles in my lifetime – apart from my mother's, which punctuated her various misfortunes – have come, unaffectedly, from two women in identical occupations: Mary Peters and, 30 years on, Jessica Ennis (or Ennis-Hill once married). Each a beacon of the multiple athletic event, in Peters' time the pentathlon's five events, for Ennis the even stiffer seven-leg heptathlon; their respective lives, while professionally necessarily self-contained, were at the same time socially welcoming. Mary Peters, of whom I write about elsewhere, all her life has enjoyed more friends than she has had breakfasts: Jess Ennis has, involuntarily, also had a whole city, Sheffield, and much of Britain opening their hearts in her support.

The momentum of this spontaneous public emotion swelling behind a sports performer became accentuated – as it had 67 years earlier for Fanny Blankers-Koen – when Ennis-

Hill won her third world championship, in Beijing, the year following the birth of her son Reggie: still with that sunshine aura, in the immediate aftermath, of someone enjoying a summer holiday. Regular women could not *do* that after seven soul-shredding events. There has always been something uniquely appealing about this daughter of Jamaican Vinnie Ennis and Derbyshire's Alison Powell. It might be said that in the nine-year period of Ennis's senior performing peaks, British sport has lacked a profusion of rival women's sports figures, but nonetheless the pride of Sheffield has been the recipient of more civic honours than a bride's confetti shower: not to mention, as with Peters, a damehood. Moreover, she has weathered the acclaim, by a profusion of public institutions, with the quiet modesty of a church warden who has won the lottery.

Many experts, both in sport, medical anatomy and physiology, and even her career-long coach, Toni Minichiello, doubted whether motherhood could withstand the demand of seven running, jumping and throwing disciplines which would assail Ennis-Hill in Beijing, three years after her epic gold medal at London 2012. Admittedly, her points score in Beijing, 6,669, was over 200 short of the London performance, and without any single-event peak, but the consistency was there. The speculation now would be whether the following year she could retain her Olympic title in Rio.

Born in January 1986, Ennis ran her first race aged nine, at the Don Valley Stadium, joining City of Sheffield & Dearne Athletic Club the following year. A high jump prize came at the National Schools Championship aged 14, her development already schooled by Minichiello, with aside guidance in javelin from world bronze winner Mike Hill. At 17 she was eighth in the World Junior Heptathlon Championships in Italy; a year later came the European junior title in Lithuania; then, aged 19, senior level bronze in the University Games in Turkey with a personal best of 5,910 points. Another 'high-grade' bronze was gained in Melbourne's Commonwealth Games of 2006 with a further PB of 6,269, this marginally rising to 6,282 in eighth place at Gothenburg's European Championships, including individual event bests in 200m, shot and javelin. The real feel of 2007 came with fourth place at the World Championships in Japan, with a PB of 12.97 in the 100m hurdles, but expectation for Beijing's Olympic Games the following year was scuppered by injury and a 12-month interlude.

No lasting harm: at Berlin's World Championships in 2009, Ennis took her first major title with the highest score of the year, 6,731, including a first-day score that was the third-best ever posted, behind world record-holder Jackie Joyner-Kersee, with 4,124. Her ceiling was steadily rising: a new British, Commonwealth and world record came at Doha's World Indoor Championships, defeating all three medal winners from Beijing's Olympics; followed by the European outdoor title with 6,823 points, a mere eight points short of Denise Lewis's Commonwealth record. At the 2011 World Championships in Daegu, South Korea, Ennis was second behind Russia's Tatyana Chernova, notwithstanding that Ennis won five of the seven events and recorded PBs in the shot and 800m. Retrospective testing would disqualify Chernova, upgrading Ennis to gold in 2016 – her second Olympic year. For now in 2011, she would have to make do with her bust in Madame Tussaud's.

The waxwork was not her only replica. Walls, advertising hoardings and pub windows were alight with expectant pictures of Britain's Olympic poster girl heading for London's

Games, the nation taking a preparatory deep breath alongside her. Could this gentle girl with the inner streak of steel ride the tide of patriotic pressure? She could, and did. Her first day included two PBs: 12.54s in the 100m hurdles and 22.83s for the 200m, the hurdles having been the fastest ever in heptathlon, equivalent to the winning solo race time in Beijing's Olympics. Another PB in the javelin, 47.49m, meant she was assured of gold prior to the concluding 800m. To the thrill of the Olympic Stadium's audience, Ennis raced away from the field, defeating runner-up Lilli Schwarzkopf of Germany by over 300 points, disgraced Chernova taking bronze. In a cape of stadium affection, Ennis gathered all her opponents for a communal lap of celebration: more than just a British heroine. Ennis would be welcomed back in Sheffield by a crowd of 20,000 prior to a mayoral reception in the town hall: a parade of further civic awards ensued at home and from abroad.

Problems arrived in 2013 and '14: Minichiello's contract with UK Athletics expired and he declined to join a high-performance unit at Loughborough University; Sheffield closed the Don Valley Stadium; Ennis suffered an ankle injury mid-summer, its continuation excluding her from Moscow's World Championships. Pregnancy closed the 2014 season yet, indomitably, she was back in training by the following May, finishing fourth in Gotzis, Austria, to qualify for Rio's Olympics of 2016. Her fitness confirmed at London's Anniversary Games, she was ready for that remarkable third world title in Beijing.

Awards continued to accumulate faster than baby laundry duty. Defending her Olympic crown in Rio, she was runner-up to Nafissatou Thiam of Belgium, who hit three PBs. Only two women Olympic champions have ever retained their title in Games intervened by motherhood: Shirley Strickland of Australia in hurdles, 1952 and '56, and Francoise Etone, French Cameroonian, in triple jump, 2004 and '08. Ennis-Hill hung up her champion's spikes on return from Rio: a woman who had illuminated a path of opportunity for any able and ambitious girl in Britain, the ordinary having become extraordinary.

LEWIS HAMILTON
Lone Black Supremacist

'Never makes mistakes in wheel-to-wheel combat'

There are four elements surrounding the acclaim engulfing newly knighted Lewis Hamilton, a national figure iconic for his physical achievements and wealth, and the fame accompanying their combination. One paramount quality is that he is black, a common enough fact of life, yet being the one and only in the history of Formula One motor racing. Second is the honour bestowed in the wake of his record seventh Formula One championship; third is the inestimable debate on whether he is the greatest of all time in his field and, lastly, whether a sport essentially powered by multi-million-pound engine technology can rationally be rated internationally alongside muscle-powered cyclists, cricketers and rowers. These debates serve only to emphasise the arresting characteristics of Hamilton's engaging personality.

Perhaps I should declare my personal racial perception regarding Formula One being, seemingly subjectively, exclusively white (at the wheel). Since boyhood, my sporting heroes have been multi-racial from across the world, including Indian-American Olympian Jim Thorpe through Maharajah

Ranjitsinhji, the silken Indian cricketer, and Afro-American Jesse Owens, to Afro-Caribbean Usain Bolt. As mentioned in Chapter One, as a schoolboy competing in London's Bank Holiday Games, I was exhilarated to be warming up side-by-side with double Olympic 800m champion Mal Whitfield. A close friend at Cambridge, and during my brief association with the England Amateur XI, was right-back Jerry Alexander, the genial West Indies veterinary student with whom I shared a room on tour in Sweden, who was later West Indies cricket captain. Emanuel McDonald Bailey, flexibly Trinidad-British in hangover Empire years, was my guest at an annual Sports Writers' Awards function. I was the first, I think, to advocate Viv Anderson of Nottingham Forest to be England's first black inclusion. In 1978, following the Commonwealth Games in Edmonton, I was so convinced Daley Thompson could win the decathlon in Moscow that I offered to contribute ten per cent to any subsidy the *Daily Express* would donate towards his training, there then being no sponsors. Victor Matthews, *Daily Express* owner, declined: he was interested only in golf, and Thompson was never informed of the rebuff. My allegiance to any British champion, aside from character assessment, is colour neutral – just as was McLaren chief Ron Dennis's when signing on Hamilton as a teenage super-prospect.

Hamilton's existence at school, and as a go-kart upstart aged ten unfailingly supported and financed by his father, was gruesomely antithetical, as he once explained, 'I experienced a lot of racism growing up, bullied at school, but as with battle wounds, it just makes you tougher. My dad said "do your talking on the track, results speak louder than words". You don't *have* to address racists. We'd arrive at racetracks, the kart crammed in the boot, just amateurs, with everyone looking at us as though we didn't belong, the only blacks, every weekend.' Later, in Formula One, Hamilton was advised not to discuss racial issues, not to offend sponsors and the existing social framework. 'Yet I saw what went on, had my own feelings, knew I was justified, that my reasons were right, seeking integration, though it was hard to see a social balance. There came a point when I really cared, but with age you find you don't need other people's validation. I knew how hard I worked, my values, who I am as a person … and that I enjoyed my life.'

So, as Hamilton's Formula One prestige ascended during 14 years from 2007 to 2020, beyond previous records, and gold medal winners had been receiving royal honours almost before they had time for a shower, debate arose on Hamilton's exclusion. Colour-coded? Non-residence tax evasion? Tobacco sponsorship, unethical international federation? Dame Margaret Hodge, Labour MP and former Public Accounts Committee chair, protested against Hamilton's nomination. It was noted that the only previous Formula One knighthoods had been those of Jackie Stewart, in 2001, with his dementia charity credential – notwithstanding Swiss tax haven residence – and Stirling Moss, who had to wait for 50 years. It allegedly required a bureaucratic nudge from Boris Johnson to ensure Hamilton's 'approval' within the 'overseas list': a pool that regularly has more financial donor candidates than an occupation of an aquarium. It is significantly relevant that since Hamilton's frontline emergence in 2007, in reflection of his popularity input, Formula One's annual global revenue has risen over 50 per cent to nearly $2bn; much of his influence is evident within UK engineering projects.

An irony of the debate on Hamilton's eligibility in the honours list was that simultaneously he topped the *Powerlist 2021* for influential British black persons, ahead of Professor

Kevin Fenton, Public Health England's regional director in London, and historian David Olusoga. Simultaneously, Hamilton was winner of the BBC's Sports Personality of the Year award: an equivocal honour because the voting figures are never revealed, and seldom except in lean years includes motor racing among the frontrunners. Prior to the knighthood, Hamilton had been respectfully restrained about speculation, 'When I consider the possibility of that honour, I think more about my granddad who served in the war, about unsung heroes. I've not saved anybody. All I can say is that standing on the podium [in victory] and hearing the national anthem, I am very, very proud, a special moment representing the nation, an incredible honour. Yet there's more work to do in this sport [in integration]. I think we've had an awakening; people are starting to hold themselves accountable.'

Hamilton was born in January 1985 in Stevenage, Hertfordshire. His white mother, Carmen, and black Grenada-born father, Anthony, separated when he was two. His father bought him a radio-controlled car when he was five, a go-kart for Christmas when he was six, though he was still living with his mother, his father having multiple jobs to sustain his son's evident driving instincts. Father would remain his son's racing manager until he was 25. Hamilton had learned karate to counteract bullying; played football as a fan of Arsenal; attended John Henry Newman School at Stevenage; at 16 joined Cambridge Arts and Science College, an independent sixth form at Cambridge, having already signed at 13 with McLaren's young driver programme, and been UK junior kart champion aged ten. In climbing the rungs of minor racing, at 15 he had won the European Formula Super A title, the following year finished fifth in Britain's Formula Renault winter series, and third on the international circuit in 2001. By 2004, aged 19, having flirted with the Williams Formula One stable, Hamilton was launched in the Formula Three series by McLaren, finishing fifth in the championship.

Hamilton's McLaren Formula One debut came in 2007, aged 22: a black innovation which largely remained an undiscussed sensation, joining a partnership with defending champion Fernando Alonso. Hamilton distinguished himself by finishing runner-up to Kimi Raikonen by one point, alongside records for the most consecutive podium finishes for a debut year, nine; most wins, four; and most points, 109. There was conflict between the rival partners; a season's end departure by Alonso, with Hamilton signing a multi-million-pound contract until 2012. In 2008, overtaking Alonso on the last corner of the last lap of the last race, Hamilton became the youngest Formula One champion by one point, ahead of Ferrari's race winner Felipe Massa, and the first British champion since Damon Hill in 1996. In the next four seasons, comparatively inferior form and inadequate engines produced placings no higher than fourth – and a transfer to Mercedes for 2013.

What was perceived as something of a gamble, Mercedes having a slender reputation at the time, brought Hamilton a single victory in Hungary, but a renewed partnership with teenage kart colleague Nico Rosberg. Hamilton finished his first season in fourth place, for the third time in five years. However, turbo-hybrid regulation adjustments raised Mercedes' pedigree with 16 wins in 19 races by the pair, 11 of them by Hamilton, regaining him the title. In the 2015 season, winning ten races with a further seven podium places, Hamilton matched Ayrton Senna's three titles, and extended his Mercedes contract by three years for beyond a reputed £100m.

Questioning 'the greatest of all time', someone my age will immediately ask how about Juan Manuel Fangio of Argentina? A Spanish immigrant engineer-cum-taxi driver, the Second World War delayed Fangio's racing impact: he was 41 by the time of his first Formula One title in 1951, with a further four from 1954–57. I interviewed Stirling Moss, Fangio's most stubborn rival, a couple of times, and he was adamant that Fangio was the best ever, if latterly perhaps equalled by Ayrton Senna, who was Hamilton's idol. What can I think be said is that, compared with the technological advance over the past 70 years of engine/gear box/brake/aerodynamic design synchronisation, in the Fangio/Moss era the skill of the driver was paramount. Yet this consideration does not exclude calculation of Hamilton's all-time ranking. Many contemporary rivals and/or mechanic directors or team leaders rate Hamilton supreme: notably, say, on account of the fact that in 14 consecutive seasons he has won at least one race in each, when achieving a victor's performance from less than a perfectly pitched machine, especially while with McLaren from 2007 to 2013.

McLaren leader Ron Dennis intuitively detected genius in the teenage Hamilton: Toto Wolff, Mercedes' CEO, has described him as 'maybe the best driver who ever existed', on account of a brand of telepathy between mind and machine, comparable to that which was attributed to Senna. Sky Sports commentator and former driver Martin Brundle reflects, 'He just never makes mistakes in wheel-to-wheel combat ... he doesn't fade, mentally or physically.' In the turbo-hybrid engine era, Hamilton is unbeaten in any race affected by bad weather since 2014 (the same as Senna, notably in Australia '95). Gerhard Berger, former partner of Senna, is unequivocal, 'The great champions were Piquet, Lauda, Prost and Schumacher. There was always one above them, Ayrton. Now I see Hamilton in the same way. Losing life the way Ayrton did magnifies the legend. Now Lewis is advancing from one stage to the next.' Hamilton acknowledges that his attitude and style has been moulded from youthful study of Senna, 'I thought this is how I want to drive.'

In 2016, Hamilton surrendered the title to colleague Rosberg, with some friction rising between them; Hamilton allegedly opening gaps to allow other rivals potentially to rob Rosberg of the title in his own favour. After his victory, Rosberg retired and was replaced at Mercedes by Valtteri Bottas from Williams. A 2017 duel with Ferrari's Sebastian Vettel ensued; Hamilton establishing 11 pole positions, finishing every race with points and nine victories, to gain his fourth world title. The 2018 contest was a parallel battle between Hamilton and Vettel for a fifth championship each, in a story of two halves: the first Vettel's domination, the second, decisively, Hamilton's, with six wins in seven races, plus a renewed two-year contract at $80m. He retained the title with two races to spare: a total of 11 victories plus another six podiums, five poles and a record points total of 408. The defence of 2019 resisted challenges from team colleague Valtteri Bottas, from Max Verstappen with Red Bull, and Ferrari's Charles Leclerc, Hamilton's 11 wins plus six podiums sufficient with an increased points record of 408.

A 2020 season shortened by COVID-19 witnessed Hamilton's summit: equalling Michael Schumacher's seven titles and surpassing the German's 91 victories, with 11 wins, three more podiums and ten poles. The record was clinched in the Algarve, Portugal, in October, with a 92nd win in 262 races in circumstances which defined Hamilton's mastery at 35: recovering from a start in which he lost his place on cold tyres, somehow subsequently preserving the grip of worn tyres while maintaining by then a slender lead, and finally winning by 25 seconds.

The supposedly impassable Schumacher was in the shade, father Anthony in tears as his son bestrode the podium, erasing their rift a decade earlier. Maybe son was now primed for a new eclectic fashion release in New York with Tommy Hilfiger. Whatever, Hamilton has expanded the social dynamics of Britain.

LILLIAN BOARD
Limitless Expectation

'Creating rare attention'

In January 1970, the BBC staged its first episode of television quiz show *A Question of Sport*. The opposing captains were Henry Cooper and world rugby doyen Cliff Morgan, the participants joining them George Best, Ray Illingworth and Tom Finney. The lone woman was Lillian Board, just awarded the MBE in the New Year's Honours. Unknowingly, as she took her seat alongside five of the most illustrious names in British sport, she had less than a year to live: a talent with almost limitless expectation, for herself and also the British women's track relay teams, at Munich in two years' time. Her sudden death from cancer 11 months later was a truly bleak moment in 20th-century British sport, Board being the epitome of the schoolgirl-next-door soaring to international acclaim. Her departure, like that of centenarian Tom Moore 70 years later, touched the heart of the nation. Other than a handful of tennis stars and equestrians, Olympic 800 metre champion Ann Packer from 1964 and cricketer Rachael Heyhoe-Flint, we did not have many female icons in those days.

Board was born in December 1948, with twin sister Irene, in Durban, South Africa, of Manchester emigrants Frances and George. The family shortly returned to Manchester, then in 1956 moved to Ealing, west London. Sue Gibson, Middlesex discus champion and PE teacher, detecting Board's potential, introduced her aged 12 to women's athletic club London Olympiades, where she became a sprinter and long jumper. By the age of 14 she was English Schools long jump champion at 17ft 3in (5.26m), then Women's Amateur Athletic Association junior champion with 17ft 5.75in (5.33m).

Motivated by prominent Olympiades pentathlete colleague Mary Rand, Board switched attention to sprints; from there, guided by father George, she moved up the range to 440 and 880 yards. Dividends were immediate. In 1965, with Board aged 16, Olympiades gained the 4 x 100m Women's AAA junior title; versatility remained, improving both her short sprint times to 10.9s (100 yards) and 24.7s (220 yards). The following year, with fourth place in the Southern Counties Championship at 440 yards, Board precociously gained the same position in the women's AAA senior final with 54.6s, a European junior record. By now she was on a secretarial course at Chiswick Polytechnic.

Board's one-lap form was sufficient for inclusion in the England team for the 1966 Commonwealth Games at Kingston, Jamaica; just short of her best time, she finished fifth. Surprisingly omitted from Britain's selection for the European Championships in Budapest, Board compensated with fourth place in 55.9s on her international debut against France in Lille. She was on track for more serious demands. Still a junior in 1967, her stunning finishing kick brought 400m victory for a Commonwealth team against the USA at Los Angeles in July, her 52.8s aged 18 the second fastest ever by a European woman, a live television broadcast at home creating rare attention.

Board had now risen from national expectation to the level where she was the target to be beaten. Winning five consecutive international races, hers was Britain's only victory, at 400m, in the European Cup in Kiev in September, while simultaneously improving personal bests for 200m and 880 yards. Mexico's Olympics in 1968 lay ahead: she was ready.

In a preparatory 400m in Moscow, Board leapt to the front of the world rankings with 53.5s, then confounded expectation by taking silver for 800m in the Women's AAA with 2:02, the second fastest ever by a British woman, behind defending Yugoslav champion Vera Nikolic, who established a new world record with 2:00.5. Board was all set for Mexico in October, having just anchored a world record by Britain for 4 x 110 yards. She was the 400m favourite in Mexico, won her semi-final with a personal best of 52.56s, and led into the home straight of the final only to be pipped at the line by nine hundredths by Collette Besson of France, never mind Board's UK record of 52.12s.

Revenge against Besson would come in 1969, defeating her in a Britain–France meet at Middlesbrough, following an earlier GB relay world record of 3:37.6 for 4 x 400m. A back injury had punctured the season, more evident in short sprints, so Board's target for the European Championships in Athens was the two-lap middle distance. Winning her heat, she stormed through the final, triumphant by eight metres in a new championship record, the first British woman to take the title. To compound this prestige, Board again outpaced Besson on the anchor leg of the 4 x 400m, edging a photo-finish decision for a 3:30.8 world record. Few young British sportswomen had ever been held in higher regard.

Ambition continued into 1970, enhanced by her MBE honour. The first Brit to embrace both sprints and middle distances, Board made her mark for the mile with 4:55 and was selected for an international against Italy in Rome; finishing second behind former world record holder Paola Pigni. Yet doom hovered.

Returning from Rome, Board was stricken with stomach pain, yet nonetheless contributed to a 4 x 800m world record at Edinburgh, bravely continuing from there to the women's AAA championship at Crystal Palace and a faltering 800m third place. To confront death through illness when in the prime of life is simultaneously heroic and humiliating; doubly so when you are the nation's darling. Board's plummeting demise was a bolt of lightning.

Withdrawing from Edinburgh's Commonwealth Games in July, it was thought she had inflammation of the bladder: by autumn, bowel cancer was diagnosed. Vainly she departed in November for a specialist exploratory clinic in Bavaria, and then to a hospital in Munich, all the while accompanied by her sports journalist fiancé David Emery. The ravage rampant, treasured, smiling Lillian Board surrendered on Boxing Day.

Queen Elizabeth sent condolence. Cremation was at Putney in January, with a memorial at St Paul's Cathedral. Not every prime minister is accorded similar acclaim. Such was the esteem for a nation's effervescent icon: the silent pride that can swell alongside someone as ordinary yet appealing as a runner. Was it not thus at Marathon 25 centuries earlier? Lillian Board set 11 UK track records, four world records: at Munich's Olympic Stadium, where gold medal dreams for 1972 lay unfulfilled, a footway posthumously bears her name, 'Lillian Board-Weg'. She is not forgotten: a girl who lifted women's sport on to the front page.

CHAPTER THREE

SETTING THE TONE

JACK JOHNSON
Brazen Black Rebel

*'No one ever taught me
whites were superior'*

There was never the chance for me to have met, let alone observed, one of the most culturally controversial, proud, extravagant, racially abused yet magnificent sportsmen of all time. Jack Johnson, first African-American world heavyweight champion, recklessly yet predictably died at the wheel in a car crash aged 68, infuriated by rejection from a restaurant, when I was 11. More than a century before today's equivocal Black Lives Matter movement, Papa Jack's life epitomised the shameless segregation horror which has throttled American society for four centuries. Bizarrely, he relished, exploited, and challenged the conflict. Subsequent Afro-American heavyweight champions Joe Louis and Muhammad Ali would experience an echo of Johnson's social torment, Louis with dignity and aversion to Johnson's irreverence, Ali with a jesting, calculated provocation.

Few in the world noticed when, in May 2018, 105 years after Johnson's contrived conviction under the Mann Act – immoral interstate transport of women – a posthumous pardon was invested by President Trump, fulfilling a petition successively sought by President George W. Bush, Senator John McCain, champion Mike Tyson and President Obama. Such had been Johnson's deliberate discourtesies throughout life – consorting with a succession of often wayward white women, marrying three of them – that slave-descendant Black America, characteristically demure and law-abiding, had widely disowned him. Noted 20th-century black scholar Booker T. Washington observed, 'It is unfortunate that a man with money should use it in a way to injure his own people, in the eyes of those seeking to uplift his race and improve its condition.'

When Muslim-converted and temporarily suspended Olympic champion and Vietnam refusenik Cassius Clay defeated white Jerry Quarry, Ali's cornerman Bundini Brown chanted that here was the return of Johnson. Bookstores and television thrived again on Johnson mementos. A 1960s current Broadway hit portraying Johnson earned multiple awards. Yet while Ali was unequivocally a black promoter, Johnson's contempt, and white-friendly affiliations, had often roused scorn.

Boxing's dichotomous lure engaged me early on at junior boarding school. Older, unobserved bullies enjoyed dragging 'newhops' through nettles on the playground fringe: a reputation in the ring could dissuade them. Our glove game was governed by a long retired, parchment-skinned First World War staff sergeant: a benign grandfatherly figure (prior to the sport's abolition in schools) who understood the inherent self-defence and camaraderie that boxing generates. Through him,

I first gained knowledge of Louis, and a growing library of past champions' biographies: James Corbett, Henry Armstrong, Georges Carpentier, later Mills, Cooper, Ali, Bruno, famed historians Leibling and Fleischer, and Johnson biographer Randy Roberts. I enjoyed my senior school boxing team until I exceeded eight stone (60kg), at which level serious pugilists at rival schools became disconcertingly too damaging.

Johnson was born in Galveston, Texas, in 1878, the third of nine children of former slaves Henry, a Union Civil War infantryman, and Tina. Jack was an early segregation rebel, joining white gangs, sharing hobbies, and never feeling victimised. 'No one ever taught me that whites were superior.' Quitting school and moving to New York as a stable boy, with a West Indies welterweight he learned to box. Returning to Galveston, his first, illegal prize fight earned him $1.50, aged 16. At 21 he suffered a fifth-round knockout against Chicago's John 'Klondike' Haines, professed 'black heavyweight champion'. Johnson kept afloat financially with four-dollar sparring rounds at small clubs, by 1901 winning a string of minor bouts across the south and the Pacific coast. A third-round knockout in 1901 by experienced Joe Chonaski, an illegal bout in Galveston, brought 23 days in jail for both: the two happily sparring for inmates' entertainment, subsequently released and good friends.

By 1903, Johnson had won some 50 bouts against both black and white opposition, and now came his first formal title, world black heavyweight champion, defeating Denver's Ed Martin on points over 20 rounds: a title he would defend 17 times over five years, with no reigning white heavyweight prepared, in trenchant racist prejudice, to face a precocious black. The hate level across America, deepened by his brazen exploitation of white women, closed the door for even megabuck bouts repeatedly on offer, including several for the return of retired, undefeated white champion James Jeffries.

Nor would the new white world champion, Tommy Burns of Canada, countenance a bout, Johnson ostentatiously taunting his target around the world, repeated financial rewards being rejected while Johnson's prestige climbed: a knockout of former white world champion Bob Fitzsimmons in two rounds. Burns – born Noah Brusso in 1881 – was finally run to ground in Sydney, agreeing to defend for a guaranteed $30,000, a landmark fee in prize fighting, especially for a man only 5ft 7in and regarded as lightweight in the top division, though his career record was an impressive 42 victories, eight draws and only three defeats.

Just as Johnson pursued Burns, so avid racism pursued Johnson: as in post-colonial USA, so in semi-colonial Australia, where Tasmania's ethnic race had been obliterated and antipathy to Johnson was rampant in a nation where the *Australia Bulletin* banner proclaimed, 'Australia for White Men'. To encourage Burns, the *New York Times* preview suggested, 'If the black man wins, thousands of his ignorant brothers will misinterpret victory as justifying claims to much more than physical equality with white neighbours.'

For all the local momentum in Sydney behind Burns, he appeared anything but confident entering the ring, while Johnson merely smiled at the insults being hurled at him. It soon became apparent that Burns was outclassed, suffering a first-round knockdown, recovering but finding that Johnson's masterful defensive weaving, feinting, blocking, left Burns clutching at air: his beckoning taunts of 'c'mon and fight, n****r' tamely hollow. Johnson merely chatted to the ringsiders. Burns had nothing left but pluck as his whipping continued, police attempting to halt the rout in the 13th round. Burns refused to concede but was then floored in the 14th. A black man now occupied the throne: the media howled in disdain about a primordial ape. Johnson fuelled the anger, unsportingly declaring Burns had been useless. Intensifying the mood of social fury was his accompanying Hattie McClay, a prominent blonde courtesan.

Johnson might have just climbed the Himalayas. The problem was, with national desperation to find a white challenger to 'correct' the disaster, that racist lock-jaw dissuaded potential bidders, 'a great white hope' not readily apparent until the following October. Up stepped hugely respected middleweight champion Stanley Ketchel. Historian Nat Fleischer suggests, in his authoritative *The Heavyweight Championship*, that there was a private tacit deal on a formidable money-making contract: neither would look for a knockout in an essential 'exhibition' bout, thereby encouraging other white hopes not to be fearful of Johnson's power.

For 11 rounds the two toyed with each other, Johnson sheathing his renowned lethal uppercut, Ketchel then unceremoniously flooring him in the 12th. Response? The right uppercut left Ketchel on the deck, his front teeth embedded in Johnson's glove.

A year on, public pressure obliged the undefeated Jeffries to suspend retirement: white honour demanded action, Jeffries asserting his sole purpose was 'proving a white man is better than a negro'. The temptation offered by his backers was said to have been a purse of today's equivalent of $3m, split 60-40 for Jeffries. The bout was to be in Reno, Nevada. All America was intent, 20,000 fans flooding into town; inspections were mounted to exclude firearms from the stadium, along with alcohol. Pre-fight prejudice ran amok; historian Roberts relates that a psychologist forecast in London's *Lancet* that

Jeffries' brain would be the deciding factor, while a local brass band serenaded the fighters' imminent appearance in the stadium with 'All Coons Look Alike To Me'. The outcome? Another slow waltz for Johnson, his calm evasion, ambling counter-punching all but making a fool of ageing Jeffries, whose cornerman's incessant insults screamed at Johnson merely incentivised the ruling champion: Jeffries twice felled, for the first time in his career, throwing in the towel in the 15th round, and admitting, 'At my best I could never have beaten him.'

The devastating consequence, from Atlantic to Pacific, was the conflagration of jubilant black celebration, rioting; at least 20 were murdered and hundreds injured as whites and blacks abused each other. During WW1, a heavy-duty Howitzer was labelled a 'Johnson'. In Georgia shots were fired. The defending champion, however, was supremely alive – for another undefeated five years. In 1912, there was a successful defence against Jim Flynn in Las Vegas, but then followed conviction under the Mann Act, causing Johnson to flee to Europe, safe from extradition in Paris and twice more disposing of challengers. With his lustre declining aged 37, and still a refugee, he accepted a challenge from a towering Kansas cowboy, Jess Willard, scheduled for Havana in July 1915.

A younger Johnson would have experienced no bother. Even now, for ten rounds, he inflicted a technical lesson on Willard, but the Texan's immense strength evaded any knockdown. Johnson's stamina in the Caribbean sunshine began to fade in, unbelievably, a scheduled 45-round bout. In the 25th he indicated to his wife to leave the stadium: in the next, Willard's looping right hand put Johnson down. There he remained, one arm shielding his eyes from the sun. The game was over: white America breathed again.

The fact that Johnson had seemed conscious, with an arm lifted, prompted accusations of fix: that he granted Willard the title allegedly prior to arranging his return to the US to serve his time in jail. However, a year later he sold a story to Fleischer, implying there was indeed an agreement. Yet in Fleischer's seemingly conclusive subsequent history, the author countered, 'I am in a position to state flatly that Johnson was not being truthful [in his confession]. I saw the fight and can vouch for its honesty.' Fleischer adds that Johnson's Canadian trainer, Tom Flanagan, confirmed, 'The battle was on the level. Willard was the better man. Johnson was not at his best … in the 14th, he tried to land a knockout … when he felt Jess was fighting back harder, he just lost heart … in the 26th he went down with sheer exhaustion.'

Following the Havana defeat, Johnson and his wife Lucille Cameron – cited in the Mann Act conviction – remained in exile in Mexico for another five years. Surrendering to federal authorities at the Mexican border in July 1920, Johnson walked serenely from his car, without handcuffs, into Leavenworth US Penitentiary to serve his time; then emerging to continue a life of luxury, of non-segregated controversy, financed by exhibition bouts even into his 60s and a succession of nightclubs, including what subsequently became New York's celebrated Cotton Club. Lucille had sued for divorce in 1924 for infidelity.

His was the life of unending confrontation: racial, sporting, social, sexual, political. He simultaneously championed and exploited both blacks and whites with unabated charm and cynicism. His love life was more hazardous than his appearances inside the ropes ever were. His autobiography in 1927 related an early marriage to black Mary Austin of Galveston, undated and undocumented. Affairs with black

Clara Kerr and Alma Toy, a white Australian in Sydney, came and went. A tempestuous marriage to Etta Sureya in 1911 ended with her suicide a year later. The same year he married Minneapolis prostitute Lucille, divorcing 12 years later. In 1924, he met Irene Pineau at an Illinois racetrack, married the following year, and was with her until his death in 1946. Asked at his funeral what she loved about him, Irene answered, 'His courage. He faced the world unafraid.'

On Johnson's boxing credentials, Fleischer is in no doubt. His assessment concludes, 'After years of studying heavyweights, I have no hesitation in naming Jack Johnson as the greatest. He possessed every asset – big, strong, with perfect co-ordination, a good hitter, powerful counter-puncher, a master of feinting. All round, the tops.' Historian Roberts is intellectually distanced, 'Taken as a whole, his life inspires respect. He faced a sea of white hate without fear. He refused to regard himself a second-class citizen, and wrote the rules for his own life. But the self-centredness that allowed him to do these things left most observers cold. It is only from a safe distance, intellectual as well as physical, that Jack Johnson could honestly be admired as a man.'

The irony of Johnson's accidental death was that it characterised not his exemplary discipline in the ring but his hazardous attitude almost everywhere else. I hesitate to imagine what independent gesture he might have adopted, in the realm of today's Black Lives Matter, on the Olympic podium in an era still ruptured by inequality: he a statue for freedom that would still be in question a century later. Author Denzil Batchelor concludes in *Jack Johnson and His Times*, 'All his offences came during his champion days: he was a well-behaved citizen after he left prison.'

JIM THORPE
Unsurpassed Native Indian

'Simply an Indian schoolboy,
I didn't understand'

The impact of sport upon our lives can influence society's history, viewed retrospectively. The deeds of Jim Thorpe over a century ago, so much more than a revelation at Stockholm's Olympic Games in 1912, still carry momentum in the Indian-American Pine Reservation of South Dakota, with its Lady Thorpe's School and Pine Ridge School under the direction of the US Department of Education, for the advantage of descendants of the Wounded Knee genocide of 1890 and elsewhere. There is the thriving Thorpe Apparel Stores. A still-renowned national figure remains an icon of forgotten culture.. In an agricultural state heavily supportive of Donald Trump, the indigenous population was united behind president-elect Joe Biden, though Trump won by a wide margin. The Jim Thorpe Association runs the Oklahoma Sports Hall of Fame and directs fitness and arts programmes, with a Jim Thorpe Scholarship for indigenous students.

When Thorpe was stripped of his Olympic medals a month later, improperly for a paltry professional irregularity, his ethnicity was an underlying motive. When selection for Stockholm was imminent, the *New York Times* ran the headline, 'Redskin from Carlisle [Oklahoma] will strive for place on American team'. As a commentator on international sport for many years, including 24 Olympics, I beg to proclaim Thorpe as, unequivocally, the foremost sportsman of all time: he was unsurpassed not only in Stockholm, his only Olympics – gold in both multi-events, pentathlon and decathlon – but in baseball and American football, and a fourth discipline, basketball, only revealed accidentally in 2005. A couple of browsers in an antique bookstore casually purchased a Wild West history, and out fell a basketball entrance ticket for 1927 'Jim Thorpe and his famous Indians'. Research at Warren, PA., Public Library reveals an extensive tour, including at Warren YMCA gymnasium, by Thorpe's all-star team, hitherto ignored by 'white' America. Dave Thomas, curator of Anthropology at the American Museum of National History, relates, 'To understand Thorpe, you have to understand Indian country at the time – vanishing Americans who didn't vanish. What Thorpe was trying to change was to give Indians jobs. The tour would have done this.'

Bob Reising, biographer of Thorpe, recognises the icon's lifelong generosity, 'He was accepting of everything and everyone. You could call it simplistic. His daughter, Grace [one of eight children from three marriages], calls it fatalistic. He just loved to compete. His tribal people were giving, with a naivety within the real world … Thorpe was an ideal person to be exploited.' Substantiation of my opinion of Thorpe's all-time sporting supremacy is prominent: official polling as 'Greatest American Footballer', institutionalised in the various halls of fame: of college football, professional football, US Olympic and US track and field. A 2000 poll by ABC Sport (TV) ranked him 'Greatest Athlete of the 20th Century' ahead of Muhammad Ali, Babe Ruth, Jesse Owens, Wayne Gretzky, Jack Nicklaus and Michael Jordan.

Consider first Thorpe's most public pinnacle, the Stockholm Games. An only recently relative novice athlete, he had come to notice when, almost as a passer-by in his working overalls, he had cleared five foot nine in the high jump without a run-up. Both pentathlon and decathlon were comparatively new events on the track syllabus: Thorpe would proceed to win eight of the 15 disciplines in the two events, additionally finishing fourth and seventh respectively in the separately competed individual high jump and long jump. In the initial pentathlon, he won four of the first five events – long jump, 200m, discus, 1,500m – coming third in javelin behind Hugo Wieslander of Sweden. He had won the event before running the 1,500m.

The following day, he took part in the two individual jumping events, and the next day the decathlon for the first and only time. He won the shot-put, discus, high hurdles and 1,500m, for a ten-event world record of 8,413 points, 688 ahead of Wieslander, which would have earned him a silver medal 36 years later at the London Games of 1948. Besides the gold medal, he received a chalice from Tsar Nicholas of Russia and a bronze bust for the pentathlon victory from King Gustav of Sweden, who, handing him the trophy, stated, 'Sir, you are the greatest athlete in the world.' This triumph, having had his track shoes stolen just beforehand, had come in a mismatched pair retrieved from a bin. There was nothing second rate, however, about a ticker tape welcome back home in New York. For now, Thorpe – and America – were truly great.

Weeks later, in Queens, NY – where he had qualified for Stockholm – and the home of the Irish American Athletic Club, Thorpe captured the American Athletic Union all-round championship, winning seven of the ten events and finishing second in the other three, breaking the existing record of 1909 with 7,385 points. Martin Sheridan, former champion and holder of eight Olympic gold medals in 1904 and '08, was present to see his record broken, generously congratulating Thorpe. 'My boy, you're a great man. I never expect to look on a finer athlete,' he said, and later told the press, 'Thorpe is the greatest athlete to have ever lived … in my prime I could not do what he did today.'

Early in 1913, the *Worcester Telegram* reported that Thorpe had received $2 a match playing baseball for Rocky Mount, North Carolina, in the East Carolina League 1909/10. The AAU, led by secretary and Olympic addict James Sullivan, highlighted accusation of professionalism. Thorpe innocently but ineffectually apologised, 'Simply an Indian schoolboy, didn't understand, doing what others did.' Yes, but others used an alias. The IOC, disregarding their own regulations, which required notice of irregularity within 30 days, not six months, stripped Thorpe of titles and medals, immediately opening him to professional offers.

There followed almost two decades of illustrious achievements in both baseball and American football, never mind his Indian heritage. Thorpe was born in a single-room pauper's cabin, five-eighths Native American: father Hiram, half-Irish, with a Sac and Fox mother, his mother Charlotte with a French father and Potawatomi mother, a descendant of Chief Black Hawk, son James's native name Wa Tho Huk, or Bright Path. Jim shuttled between various schools prior to Carlisle, Pennsylvania, in 1904, a trades education for the indigenous with a view to 'integration'. It was here that Thorpe fortuitously came under the eye of noted coach Glen 'Pop' Warner, pathfinder to the Olympic stage. With Carlisle, Thorpe prospered with two All-America awards for football. In 1912 he had been the powerhouse behind Carlisle's exceptional wins against Harvard, Syracuse and Pennsylvania. In a 27-6 victory against the Army, Thorpe scored 22 of the points, intermittently scalping one Dwight D. Eisenhower, who recalled in a speech in 1961, 'There are some people supremely endowed. I remember in particular Jim Thorpe. He never practised in his life, and he could do anything better than any other footballer I ever saw.'

Following Stockholm, Thorpe signed for New York Giants, with six seasons in Major League Baseball from 1913 to '19, while simultaneously joining the Canton Bulldogs American football team in 1915, helping them win three professional championships. Thorpe would reflect, 'I was never content unless I was trying my skill against my fellow play-mates, testing my endurance and wits.' In 1920, he became the first 'president', and commercial selling point, of the American Football League, subsequently National Football League, in the wake of his 91-run baseball career over 289 games. The money, while it lasted, was good: $250 a game with match attendances soaring. He played for six different teams from 1920 to '28. On a world tour with Chicago White Sox, he had played before a 20,000 crowd in London, including King George V. Retirement came at 41 in 1928: finance for an educationally unqualified Indian would begin to slump. By 1932, living in a caravan park, he was too poor to attend the Olympic Games at Los Angeles. US vice-president Charles Curtis invited him to attend the opening ceremony. The *Boston Post* had written way back on Carlisle's crushing of Harvard, 'An unequal conflict between the white man's brawn and the red man's cunning.'

Kate Burford, author of *Native American Son: The Life and Sporting Legend of Jim Thorpe*, observed how Thorpe had found employment at Hollywood, 'Because he was so famous, he not only sought out as spokesman for Indian causes, but formed his own casting company to pressurise studios to hire real Indians in stereotypical Westerns, in which they would hire Italians, Greeks and Mexicans to play Indians.' Rates of indigenous suicide and a diagnosis of PTSD are at the same level today as that of war veterans.

During the Great Depression, in 1931 Thorpe sold the rights of his life story to MGM for $1,500 ($25,000 today), and subsequently for a $15,000 fee to Warner Brothers in 1951 for *Jim Thorpe – All-American*, starring Burt Lancaster. Yet circumstances frayed: an operation for lip cancer in 1951, his third wife Patricia pleading he was broke – having donated to many relatives – and death arriving with heart failure in 1953, aged 65, his funeral following at St Benedict's Catholic Church, Shawnee, Oklahoma. Unknown to the rest of his family, Patricia made a financial deal with the twin Pennsylvania towns, where he had never been, Mauch Chunk and East Mauch Chunk, to have his body transferred, the two towns merging under a new name: Jim Thorpe. His son Jack filed lawsuits seeking to remove his father's remains to the family environment in his Oklahoma birthplace, but the Native American Graves Protection Act was overruled, and this upheld by the Supreme Court. Thorpe's monument and grave rest on soil from his native Oklahoma and from the stadium where he won his Olympic gold medals.

The IOC's confiscation of those, soullessly instructed by Avery Brundage, AAU and subsequently IOC president – an insignificant contender against Thorpe in 1912 – was transmuted, after prolonged negotiations, by IOC president Juan Antonio Samaranch in 1982; the originals were lost but replicas were presented to two older children, Grace and Bill, in what, behind the scenes, became an uncomfortable dispute regarding their final resting place. IOC records, however, which had been assigned in 1912 to 'victories' by Ferdinand Bie of Norway and Hugo Wieslander of Sweden, now bear the name Jim Thorpe, as my *Official IOC History 1894–2018* records. Thorpe's Olympic glory is an epitaph to a phase of humanity shamefully erased.

MILDRED (BABE) DIDRIKSON
Sporting Astronaut

'I never wore stockings'

If sport matters, if black lives matter, then it ought not to be forgotten that women matter and, as much to the point in this story, that women's sport matters. It is not that long ago, less than a century, that the concept of women indulging in physical competition was anathema. Down the ages, there have been forthright, heroic women, such as Joan of Arc, Florence Nightingale, or politician Nancy Astor, but no one sweating *for fun.* By the late 19th century there were some female archers, a handful of tennis players, but athletic aggression was socially a non-starter. Women were not permitted to *run* in the Olympic Games until 1928.

So just imagine, only four years later, appearing in the land of the free, the most remarkable woman as yet in human history leaps on to the stage at the Olympic Games in Los Angeles. Mildred 'Babe' Didrikson breaks not only three world records, aged 21, but is the only athlete, man or woman, ever to win three individual running, jumping and throwing events in a single Games. She would surpass most contemporaries in a dozen other sports, becoming a champion golfer at the first attempt, and arrogant enough to enter male tournaments: simultaneously acclaimed and detested for corruption of conventional femininity. Even Olympic heptathlon champions of the 21st century pale in comparison with Didrikson's sporting ubiquity – an affront to myopic global male sexist prejudice.

Did this phenomenal woman carry an excess of testosterone, say, similar to the sadly jeopardised South African Caster Semenya nearly a century later? Certainly not from physical appearance. Born Mildred Ella in 1911, the sixth of seven children of Norwegian immigrants, she was a mere 5ft 5in, allegedly nicknamed 'Babe' upon hitting five home runs in a childhood baseball game, in reflection of famed Babe Ruth. Her ferocity lay in masculine temperamental extravagance rather than outward physical abnormality, while possessing rare timing co-ordination. Across her career she allegedly excelled – and I am assured by historic accounts – at athletics, basketball, baseball, billiards, bowling, boxing, cycling, diving, handball, golf, skating, swimming, tennis and volleyball. The only activity absent from a schoolgirl's curriculum had been dolls; yet she was adept as a seamstress, fashioning many of her own clothes, including golf tunics, winning a Dallas sewing championship aged 20 and when idle, if ever, recording a few quick songs for the Mercury Records label plus an occasional tune on her harmonica.

Comparatively average academically, while playing basketball for the local Beaumont High School, Didrikson was offered employment in Dallas so as to be able to represent the works team, though paid as 'secretary' to preserve amateur status. Simultaneously discovering track and field, she soon won four events in an American Athletic Union meeting then, in 1932, as the single-handed competitor for her employers, winning the national championships solo; in three hours competing in ten events, winning five of them and setting records in javelin, 80m hurdles, high jump and baseball throw.

Didrikson qualified for the Olympic Games, these being confined for women by the International Olympic Committee's regulation to three events. Her autobiography, *This Life I've Led*, reveals her headstrong independence which characterised every objective: prodigious Olympian historically setting four world records. As she related, 'The javelin took place on the first day, late in the afternoon when there were shadows coming up over the stadium and it was turning cool. Warming up, I was watching the German girls because they were reputed to be the best. They'd been taught to loosen up by throwing the javelin into the ground ahead of them. I'd been told this was the way to practise, but could never agree. It seemed to me this gave you the wrong motion – I always thought you should warm up with the same swing you used in competition. There was a flag stuck in the ground to show how far the new Olympic record was. It was a German flag because one of the German girls had just set the inaugural record … which was some distance short of my own best. When my turn came, what with the cool air and my lack of warm-up, I wasn't properly relaxed. Yet the javelin kept flying to set a new Olympic record of 143ft 4in [43.68m]. In practice, I'd been close to 150ft, but I tore a muscle in my shoulder making that first throw, and in my last two attempts some people maybe thought I wasn't trying.'

These being inaugural events for women – in a previously hallowed male arena where founder De Coubertin had considered women were eligible only for applause – Didrikson was unabashed at the prospect of hurdles, 'The new best was 12.2 seconds, while my record set a couple of weeks before was 11.9. I beat that in my heat with 11.8. In the finals the next day, I was so anxious again to set a record that I jumped the gun. A second time, and I would have been disqualified, so I held back, and it wasn't until the fifth hurdle that I caught up and just beat Evelyne Hall of Chicago. In horse racing, you'd say I won by a nose. Even with the late start, it was another world record of 11.7.'

With her stated, unabashed ambition as a teenager to be 'the best athlete the world has seen', Didrikson confidently faced the high jump alongside compatriot Jean Shiley: 'I wanted to win to make it a clean sweep. Jean and I were better than we'd ever been, the bar climbing to 5ft 5in [1.65m], nearly two inches higher than we'd jumped in the trials. We both cleared and had now beaten the world record, but there was still first place to be settled. The bar rose another three quarters of an inch – we both missed, so they dropped the bar back down to five foot five. We both cleared. The judges weren't used to seeing my Western Roll and under the rules of the day your feet had to cross the bar before your head, otherwise it was a "dive" and didn't count. They suddenly ruled that I had dived, which cost me a first place tie. Pictures proved my feet cleared first. I'd been jumping the same way all afternoon, all year for that matter. I told the judges so, but they merely said, "If you were diving before, we didn't see it!"'

It was during Didrikson's residence in the Olympic Village that she encountered the diversion of golf, thanks to a spare-time invitation by sports journalist Grantland Rice to join him and two colleagues at Brentwood Golf Club, Didrikson never having previously played a complete round. Never mind – she proceeded to win at the 18th, prompting Rice to declare that he 'may have been looking at the greatest future women's golfer of all time'. Close to the mark. Within another three years Didrikson had won the Texas Women's Amateur, shortly after which the US Golf Association ruled her now ineligible having competed professionally in other sports. She would be reinstated as an amateur in 1943. When asked how she could drive 250 yards, the reply was 'loosen your girdle and let it rip'. Ever versatile, in 1934 Didrikson had been occupied in Major League Baseball, playing consecutive exhibition games for Philadelphia Athletes against Brooklyn Dodgers, for St Louis Cardinals against Boston Red Sox, finally for New Orleans Pelicans against Cleveland Indians.

Reinstated as an amateur, Didrikson was nominated as Female Athlete of the Year three times in succession from 1945 to '47, having won 13 consecutive golf tournaments in '46, and become the first American to win the British Women's Amateur, one of 55 tournament victories. Turning professional again, she won 17 of 18 tournaments including her first US Women's Open in 1948. During these past ten years, Didrikson's career had been managed by George Zaharias, a wrestler with whom she had been paired in the Los Angeles Open: the first woman, aged 27, to encroach male exclusivity. She had not made the 36-hole cut but had found a husband. In 1948 she made a vain attempt to enter the men's National Open at LA's Riviera Club, but was rejected by the USGA. No room yet for women astronauts.

By 1950, Didrikson had won a gross 82 tournaments, amateur and professional, the *New York Times* later observing that 'no golfer other than Arnold Palmer has ever been more beloved by the gallery'. Yet the admiration had not always been uniform, on account of her often boastful nature, her breach of accepted female courtesies. There had been a hint of this social ambivalence at the opening ceremony of the Olympic Games, of which she had recalled, 'It was a thrill to march into the stadium, but to tell you the truth, I couldn't enjoy it once we got out there. We all had to wear special dresses and stockings, and white shoes. That was the first time I'd ever worn stockings in my life, and the shoes really hurt.'

Didrikson's masculinity and self-acclaim would regularly be frowned upon, notwithstanding that Byron Nelson, a prominent American golfer, considered that only a handful of men could out-drive her. Grantland Rice held a detached assessment, 'She is beyond belief, until you see her performance … the flawless muscle harmony of complete mental and physical co-ordination.' The Didrikson brand was such a contrast to the then European perceived feminine ideal of elegant Joyce Wethered, with half the power. Some sexist commentators disregarded her fame, one New York columnist reflecting, 'It would be better if she and her ilk stayed at home, got themselves prettied up and waited for the phone to ring.'

It is not the business of history to debate the sexuality of distinguished sporting personalities. In the 21st century, gay individuals declare themselves in rugby or football, women in boxing or tennis. Didrikson's sexuality was ambiguous, notwithstanding her marriage which ultimately faltered, and she was living with fellow golfer Betty Dodd, having met on the course in 1950 and toured together. That is by the way when reminiscing about a woman of astonishing, multiple sporting capabilities which captivated public attention. In 1995, Associated Press voted her 'Women's Athlete of the Twentieth Century'. Iconic *Sports Illustrated* named her second behind Olympic heptathlete Jackie Joyner-Kersee. In my humble opinion, though too young by 20 years to have had a chance to be a witness, I would say *S.I.* got it wrong. Didrikson was to women's sport what steam was to railways.

JESSE OWENS
Friends Gather No Dust

'Dreams need dedication and self-discipline for reality'

Eighty-odd years before the Black Lives Matter campaign, Jesse Owens, grandson of slaves who was himself a cotton-picker aged seven, was pursuing the integration of southern oppressed Afro-Americans. Owens is venerated for his sensational, anti-Nazi supremacy at Berlin's Olympic Games of 1936: it is less recorded that, little educated, he was articulate beyond the command of many politicians. Moreover, for this young English schoolboy innocent of global demography imbalance, the charm of Owens, an instant hero, was that he always seemed to be smiling, that engaging nature evident when meeting him in the media centre at Montreal's Olympics in 1976. Professionally familiar by then with most racial groups, I never thought about his being black, simply someone with a cherished history. At every stage of his life, he was profoundly observant: reflecting on his athletic career, 'People come to see you perform and you've got to give the best you have – the lives of most are patchwork quilts, or at best one tidy outfit with a laundry bag full of inconsequential accumulation. I had a lifetime of training to meet just ten seconds. Friendships born on the athletic field are the real gold. Awards become corroded – friends gather no dust.'

Returning from Berlin in 1936, though fundamentally non-political, Owens aligned himself with Republicans for the upcoming election. Appearing at Baltimore, in front of a 9,000 multi-racial crowd at the Fifth Regimental Armory, he declared, 'I can't tell you how to vote, you are mostly old enough to be my parents, but I believe the term "negro race" should be abolished, replaced by "American people" ... In the field of athletics, racial prejudice is broken down, so I think every youth should take part. I was so proud in Berlin when the US flag was raised, but was embarrassed that I couldn't remember all the words. We should all know them. I have to say that sometimes coloured people are their own worst enemies, a hard pill to swallow ... I am supporting Governor Alf Landon as Republican nominee.'

Owens continued his backing for Landon elsewhere, including New York City on 4 September, as reported by the *McDowell Times*, both Owens and world heavyweight champion Joe Louis proclaiming their backing for Landon. Owens stated, 'I'd like to use my leadership gained by Olympic victories ... I don't consider Alf Landon a man to make false starts!'

Memory tends to focus on Berlin: the revelation of Owens's supremacy in fact occurred a year earlier. He had attended Ohio State University, coached by Larry Snyder and winning eight national championships in 1935/36. As an Afro-American he was obliged to live off campus and when travelling with the team to eat at blacks-only restaurants and stay at segregated hotels. On 25 May 1935, during the Big Ten meet at Ann Arbor, Michigan, in under one hour he set four world records and tied a fourth: 100 yards in 9.4s; 26ft 8.25in

(8.13m) for the long jump, which would last for 25 years; 220 yards in 20.3s; 220 yards low hurdles in 22.6s. Arguably, he simultaneously bettered the world records for respectively both 200m events. In his junior year at Ohio State, he won all of 42 contests. He reflected, 'I always loved running – it was something you could do by yourself, under your own power, fast or slow, as you felt like, fighting the wind if you wished, seeking new horizons on the strength of your feet and the courage of your lungs.'

Two weeks later, he married Minnie Ruth Solomon, two years his junior at 20. Childhood sweethearts since 13, they already had a daughter, Gloria, and were to have two more. Of his lifelong partner, he would affectionately write, 'Minnie was unusual, because even though I knew her family was as poor as ours, nothing she said or did seemed touched by that, or by prejudice. Or by anything the world said or did. It was as if she had something inside her that somehow made all that not count. I fell in love with her some, the first time we ever talked, and a little bit more every time after that, until I thought I couldn't love her more than I did. And when I felt that way, I asked her to marry me … and she said she would.'

Owens was born on 12 September 1913, the youngest of ten of Henry, a sharecropper, and Mary Emma, in Oakville, Alabama. The family had moved, as part of the Great Migration of 1.5 million Afro-Americans from segregated south to industrial north, to Carolina, where 'James Cleveland' joined Fairmont Junior High School: giving his name as 'JC', which his teacher misheard as 'Jesse'. It stuck: Owens doing odd jobs to help pay subsistence. He once recalled, 'We used to have a lot of fun, never any problems. We always ate. We didn't have steak? Who had steak?' More important was his association with a shrewd coach, Charles Riley. 'Every morning, just like

Alabama, I got up with the sun, had breakfast even before mother, sisters and brothers, went to school, winter, spring and fall to run and jump and bend my body this way and that for Mr Riley.' That sense of purpose was echoed at Ohio University under coach Snyder: 'He was constantly on at me about the job I was to do, the responsibility I had – how I must be able to carry myself, because people were watching me.'

In December 1935, Walter White, a national athletics administrator, was one of many seeking a US boycott of the Berlin Games because of Nazi anti-Semitism, but the campaign – fronted by US IOC member Ernest Jancke, who was expelled in consequence – failed due to the wilful opposition by American Athletic Union and subsequent IOC president Avery Brundage, who labelled White and the rest as 'un-American agitators'; never mind Nazi propaganda denigrating the US team's inclusion of Owens and others as 'black auxiliaries' and 'non-humans'. Contrary to Nazi adverse publicity, crowds awaited the arrival of an already celebrated Owens, and Adidas founder Adi Dassler was on hand to provide running spikes to the first sponsored Afro-American runner.

On 2 August 1936, Owens won his first two 100m heats, successively equalling then beating the Olympic and world record, the second time being discarded for being wind-assisted. Late that day, team-mate Cornelius Johnson won the high jump with a new Olympic record of 2.03m. In attendance, Hitler had earlier congratulated German medal winners but had ignored Afro-American Johnson. Controversial accusations suggested he subsequently ignored Owens's triumphs, though the truth was that IOC president Henri de Baillet-Latour had advised Adolf that protocol required him to meet all winners or none. Hitler thereafter remained discreet.

The following day, Owens gained his first gold, the 100m in 10.3s, defeating compatriot Ralph Metcalf by a tenth with Holland's Timus Osendarp in bronze. Owens later recalled that on his way subsequently to a broadcast, 'Hitler waved at me and I waved back.' He was more forthright about the nature of fulfilment. 'To a sprinter, the 100 dash is over in three seconds, not nine or ten. The first "second" is when you come out of the blocks. The next is when you look up and take your first few strides to attain a leading position. By that time the race is actually about half over. The final "second" – the longest slice of time in the world for a sprinter – is that last half of the race, when you really bear down and see what you're made of. It seems to take an eternity, yet is all over before you can think what's happening.'

On 4 August, Owens predictably won the long jump – after a qualifying-round scare. A normal testing run-through, getting the feel of the track, had pompously been ruled a 'no jump', and with a succeeding 'no jump' there was only one more attempt to qualify. At that moment his main rival, Lutz Long, blond idealist-looking Aryan German yet good-natured rival, offered Owens advice on an adjusted run-up. Owens's response was to qualify, then take the title with 26ft 5in, slightly short of his world record (he would be there at Rome in 1960 to witness Ralph Boston break his record, admitting that in Berlin 'panic had crept in, taken me over'. Long would be killed in the Second World War, but Owens continued to correspond with his family.

The parallel with Afro-American subjugation is centuries-old Jewish discrimination, to which Owens inadvertently probably owed his fourth Olympic gold. On 9 August, Owens and Afro colleague Metcalf found themselves suddenly promoted into the 4 x 100m relay team in place of

Jewish sprinters Marty Glickman and Sam Stoller; the new combination with Frank Wycoff and Foy Draper setting a world record of 39.8s. Owens had unavailingly protested about the switch and had been rebuked by management. The record would last for 20 years, and Owens's four golds would not be emulated until Carl Lewis did so in 1984. It was widely believed at the time that an insensitive Brundage, a fulsome backer of Berlin's swastika parade, had heeded Nazi subterranean requests for the removal of Glickman and Stoller. Nonetheless, Owens could but reflect on his remarkable accomplishment, 'We all have dreams. To make them reality, it needs an awful lot of dedication and self-discipline. If you don't try to win, you might as well stage the Olympics in somebody's back yard. You need to win to prove yourself.' Doing so back home was not so easy.

Greeted in New York City by a ticker tape parade and Mayor Fiorello LaGuardia, at the Waldorf Astoria, he was obliged to take the freight elevator to enter the reception staged for him. 'It became increasingly apparent that, never mind my four Olympic medals, with the slaps on the back and the shaking of hands, no one was going to offer me a job … I couldn't ride in the front of the bus, only the back, I couldn't live where I wanted. No, I wasn't personally greeted by Hitler, nor was I invited to the White House, not even a telegram. I wanted no part of the function of politics, but I did want to try to make things better [for integration].' As stated, he endorsed Alf Landon, Roosevelt's Republican opponent.

A harsh domestic rejection now confronted him. To exploit potential endorsements back home, Owens had declined joining the Olympic team's invitation to then compete in Sweden: the US Olympic Committee promptly withdrew his amateur status on presumption of professional breaches, yet opportunities were scarce: gas station attendant, playground janitor and, demeaningly, sprinting against racehorses, as at half-time in a soccer match against thoroughbred Julio McCaw – 'Bad enough to be toppled Olympian, but now to make a living competing against animals!'

In 1937, he briefly toured with a jazz band affiliated to Consolidated Artists. 'I couldn't play an instrument, I'd just stand up front and announce the numbers. They had me sing a little, a horrible mistake, I can't carry a tune in a bucket. We played black theatres and nightclubs all over hell, one night in Harlem, another in Philadelphia. It was big time for blacks.' Finally, a friend from the University of Michigan organised a position as assistant pensions director at Ford Motors in Detroit, which he held from 1942 to '46, then he joined the West Coast Negro Baseball League, becoming vice-president and owner of the Portland Rosebuds franchise in Oregon, though that shortly disbanded. 'There was no TV, no big advertising, no endorsements, not for a black man anyway.' Bankrupt and prosecuted for tax evasion in 1966, he was rescued by a government appointment as 'goodwill ambassador', travelling the world as a US promoter; including, ironically, the once-hostile US Olympic Committee.

Financial insecurity having shackled much of his post-Berlin life, Owens was initially unsupportive towards the podium racial protests by sprinters Tommie Smith and John Carlos at Mexico in 1968, telling them, 'The black-gloved fist [raised on the podium] is a meaningless symbol. When you open it, you have nothing but fingers. The only time it has significance is when there's money inside. That's where power lies.' This cynicism at the end of a fraught career would be revised in a late biography, *I Have Changed*, stating, 'I now realise militancy, in the best sense, is the only answer for the black man, that anyone who isn't a militant in 1970 is either blind or a coward.'

A guest at Munich in 1972 and at Montreal four years later, Owens tried to persuade President Jimmy Carter to withdraw the proposed boycott of Moscow '80: that the Olympic ideal was suspension of war, he being still the idealist to his dying day in March 1980 from lung cancer. Carter's posthumous epitaph spoke for all the oppressed, 'No athlete better symbolised the human struggle against tyranny, poverty and racial bigotry.' Owens, in effect, had some time before sentimentally written his own, on the inevitable loss of Olympic and world records. 'It's like having a pet dog for a long time. You get attached to it, and when it dies, you miss it.' Honour awards exceeded his medals: Presidential Medal of Freedom by President Gerald Ford in 1976; Living Legend Award by President Jimmy Carter in 1979; Jesse Owens Award (annually to the top athlete) by USA Track and Field in 1981; Jesse Owens Allee, the adjacent road to Berlin's Olympic Stadium in 1984; Congressional Gold Medal by President George W. Bush in 1990. Yet no award can mitigate America's enduring segregation.

WINIFRED BROWN
Britain's Greatest All-Rounder

'The headmistress can go to hell'

The topic of this memoir is the achievements of exceptional sports performers, predominantly full-time professionals, or those who, under older regulations, had been classified as amateur, especially in the Olympic Games. In the realm of former gender discrimination, I am including a woman who defies definition: someone who fundamentally personified female emancipation, ambition and fortitude in the first half of the 20th century, a woman fearless, forthright, romantic, adventurous. Additionally, the most extraordinary woman for her son Tony to have had as a mother and effectively doubling as his father. Alongside illustrious Olympians or global football luminaries, Winifred Brown unquestionably qualifies for inclusion by her astonishing originality: aeronautic champion, Arctic sailor/navigator, Amazon explorer and an accomplished ball-games performer. Truly Britain's greatest ever all-rounder.

Let me begin between the wars. Win, aged 31, is by now owner of her own plane, an Avro Avian bought by her wealthy father, owner of a string of butchers in Manchester. Women across Europe had been 'airborne' since early century; Raymonde de Laroche of France becoming the first to gain a pilot's licence; in 1912, Harriet Quimby being the first English woman to fly across the Channel; Marie Marving of France the first to fly combat in 1915; English woman Mary Bailey, the first to fly to South Africa in 1928; Amy Johnson, the first all the way to Australia in 1930. In the same year, Win was entering the redoubtable round-Britain King's Cup. Her competitive motivation had arisen when driving a racing car in the early 1920s with a friend who observed, 'The way you drive, why don't you try a plane!'

Established in 1922 by King George V to encourage aero engineering, and in rivalry to the Schneider Trophy, the inaugural competition from Croydon Aerodrome – still open in the Second World War – had been won by Frank Barnard, and never as yet by a woman. Now starting the six-leg contest from Hanworth in the Midlands, Win was refused accommodation by the Royal Aero Club, obliged to put up at a pub. Helping her navigate was Ron Adams, a regular sailing companion with whom she had played mixed doubles for Lancashire. The weather played into her hands.

'On the Manchester–Newcastle leg, the weather closed in,' she recalled, 'with low cloud over the Pennines. Fortunately I knew the area well, and was able to cut through the valleys.' The rest of the entry, more than 50 male pilots, were forced to climb above the cloud: descending into Yorkshire, many were confused, navigational aids then underdeveloped. By now experienced, and knowing at low altitude which railway lines to follow, Win landed safely back at Hanworth. As ground crew chocked the wheels, she asked who had won. 'You have!' she was told.

Here was instant celebrity. Royal Aero Club were profuse with immediate apologies: of course there was accommodation available. Demonstrative Win, who had been rolling her own cigarettes from about the age of five, politely declined and returned to the surprised hosts at the pub. Fame galloped. She, plus plane, was welcomed on stage at Blackpool's Palace Theatre on the same bill as comedian George Formby and subsequently at London's Coliseum. It would be 51 years before the next female victory, Josephine O'Donnell inviting the octogenarian to join the celebrations. Win had ceased to fly soon after her triumph, the sport becoming too commercial, too expensive and take-off freedom limited by ever-increasing air traffic control.

Sawley Brown, Win's father, had sported a 32ft cutter and was at one time the record-holder from Fleetwood to the Isle of Man. Win inherited the competitive gene and from the age of ten she had sailed with the all-male crew berthed in the for'ard locker. Attending Broughton High School, she courted expulsion at 14 for graffiti in the loo – 'the headmistress can go to hell' – and would have been sent to a convent in France but for the outbreak of the First World War. Instead she became a nurse in Manchester where she met the subsequent *Testament of Youth* author Vera Brittain.

It was a year after the war that Win first 'took off': a tourist spin for a fiver from Blackpool's promenade, and within four years her affluent father had provided an aircraft, enabling her locally to fly solo. She had studied navigation with the experienced O.M. Watts, well known for a long-running chandlers in London, and was aided by a devoted Ron, whom later she would marry. Theirs was a practical as well as romantic relationship; together learning the vagaries of the ocean, the skies and the tennis court where, Tony affirms, she could serve on to an exact square foot. Between times, Win was becoming a four-handicap golfer with equal spontaneity. Crucially, although she had been seriously overweight while still at school, by her athletic involvement she shed 30lb. Such was her eye-to-moving-ball co-ordination that she travelled with the England hockey team to Australia in 1927. Although she could not skate, she kept goal for England at ice hockey; being six feet tall, when kneeling with pads her entire frame filled the goal, requiring only assistance to stand for the national anthem.

In 1931, wanderlust had steered her Dr Livingstone-style to Brazil and a passage up the Amazon, by steamer and canoe, courtesy of four paddlers and an interpreter, sponsored by the *Daily Express* to which she dispatched details of the adventure. Now she married Ron, and it was immediately prior to the unexpected outbreak of the Second World War in 1939 that they had embarked on a hazardous voyage to Spitzbergen in the Arctic Circle, only 600 miles from the North Pole. In Win's never-less-than-complex life, despite her husband's presence, she knew, and Ron knew that she knew, a Norwegian lover Einar. Ron, who according to Tony adored his mother, nonetheless accepted the liaison. Tony, an actor and long-time stalwart of the television serial *Crossroads*, recalls that his mother's emotional breadth consumed all those around her, him included. He reflects, 'Although Ron persuaded Mother, whom he cherished, that they should be married, her individuality was anaesthetising. I never really had a father. Mother was both. I guess what you don't have, you don't know. For my mother, looking after me was more important than any career. Frankly, Ron's tolerance was amazing.'

With Norway having been invaded by Germany and the North Sea effectively 'closed', Win and Ron had been instructed that they could no longer sail home. Unperturbed, resolute Win merely said 'we'll fly the Norwegian flag', and off they went, hoisting the Union Jack when over the horizon, and criss-crossing U-boats en route to the Shetlands. Again 'quarantined' with Admiralty instruction to remain stranded at Lerwick, intrepid Win slipped moorings after midnight and stole back to the Menai Strait.

Wartime was a fresh adventure. Win's responsibility now was as mooring supervisor for the trans-Atlantic delivery of Catalina flying boats from assembly in Bermuda. On one occasion near midnight in 1942, Canadian pilot Hughie Green – later a UK television presenter – touched down and motored into Anglesey's harbour. Waiting for the towing launch, a crew man opened the bottom hatch. 'What's up with the launch man?' yelled an exhausted Green. 'Nothing, sir, but she's wearing an evening dress and a fox fur!' Not for Hitler was Win cancelling her social life.

Post-war was not easy for her and Tony. Ron, inevitably, had moved on, mother and son were living in a mean lower-ground-floor flat, dependent at night upon an adjacent street lamp to economise on their own electric meter: her grandfather, squandering his fortune on a mistress, had left Win without an inheritance. For a while she was sympathetically subsidised by a close friend from the Imperial Soap family.

When I first met Win, she was living aboard a gleaming old varnished motor yacht in Yarmouth, Isle of Wight, together with Tony and about to set sail for Jersey, where he was appearing for a summer season: she still rolling her cigarettes, cursing colourfully at irritants, ever ready to raise anchor if becoming bored. 'There were times as a boy,' Tony recalls, 'when I'd go to sleep in my bunk, and wake up and find we were at sea.' Mother had merely fancied a new location: a pioneer in women's sporting adventure still being explored to this day.

JOE LOUIS
White America's Black Hero

'The whole country was depending on me'

The first 'grown-up' sports book I had, with a birthday book token from an uncle, was *Ringside Seat* by Peter Wilson, the chief sportswriter of the *Daily Mirror*, a downmarket top-selling newspaper which energetically promoted 'the man they can't gag'. Wilson was one of a kind: hugely self-promoting, the nature of the job pre-TV, for a popular daily, he believing that if he wrote it, it must be true, which mostly it was. Wilson was well informed in three sports – boxing, athletics and tennis – but did not cover Britain's three main seasonal sports, football, rugby and cricket. He had a vivid style, more cliches and contrived metaphors to a chapter than most fighters threw punches in a 15-round bout: certainly not Shakespeare nor influential on my prose composition, but what he did was instil, in a 12-year-old flyweight in the school team, the beauty, bravery and the often-attendant baloney of the fight game.

There is an unerring truth about boxing, the so-called art of self-defence. Because it is dangerous, sometimes brutal at the professional level, it predominantly engenders a moral honesty in fighters: the manipulators, exploiters and cheats are those mostly found outside the ropes. Fighters, and the best trainers, see life for *real*: reading Wilson's hall-of-mirrors account, including tales of the greatest, such as Joe Louis, I prematurely began to understand, as a boy, the adult world of ferociously soaring or plummeting fortunes. It helped me handle the everyday hazards of disappointment or loneliness. Before any of the other elite performers I unexpectedly came to know professionally, Wilson presented me with an idealised celebrity: from a humble, racially deprived background, Joe became my internationally acclaimed hero. Aged 12, I had yet to learn the depths of racial prejudice: brought up on Kipling's *Jungle Book*, Mowgli or Joe Louis were simply 'people'.

Having been metaphorically brought to a halt when learning the measure of Louis's achievements, let me repeat them. Having gained the world heavyweight championship in 1937 – the first black champion since Jack Johnson – he defended the title 25 times, the most ever, over the next 12 years, the longest ever period. In a total of 69 professional bouts, he won 52 by knockout and lost only three, the last of which came when making a comeback after two years in retirement, against new champion Ezzard Charles: driven by financial necessity when harassed by tax demands on fight earnings in fact donated to Second World War military armament funds.

Louis was not just a magnificent pugilist but one of the first Afro-American heroes of America's white population, testified by his son Joe Junior, 'What my father did was enable white Americans to think of him as an American, not as a black.' To such an extent that his famous defeat, following a previous loss, of Germany's Max Schmeling, during mounting anti-Nazi momentum in 1938, was viewed as a national political as much as sporting triumph by the great grandson of a slave and great-great grandson of a slave owner: father Munroe of mixed race, mother Lillie half-Cherokee. With 'social' advice from his management team – never have a photo taken with a white woman, never gloat over a defeated white opponent – Joe Louis publicly charmed where 25 years earlier Jack Johnson had so controversially erred. He was invited to the White House in the wake of Schmeling's annihilation, where President Roosevelt told Louis that 'men like you' would be needed to overthrow the Nazis.

Louis was born in May 1914. His father was committed to a mental home when Joe was two: ten years later, during the Depression's migration northwards, the family moved from Alabama to Detroit, mother attempting to have Joe play the violin while he covertly joined a boxing gymnasium, making his amateur debut aged 17 in 1932. Soon he came under the wing of a black Detroit bookmaker, John Roxborough, winning a string of amateur bouts. Roxborough in turn knew a Chicago promoter, Julian Black, who hired as trainer Jack Blackburn, key to Louis's professional advance: his first fee in 1934, a knockout of Jack Kracken, being $59 ($1,150 today).

The following year, Louis had 13 bouts, prominently a six-round KO against former world heavyweight champion Primo Carnera of Italy. It was helpful publicity in associating Louis with anti-Nazi propaganda, Carnera being affiliated with Benito Mussolini and initiating Louis's media label, 'The Brown Bomber'. Increasingly was Louis marketable – admirable in a heavyweight division in decline since the retirement of Jack Dempsey more than a decade earlier, and even better for Louis's 'handlers', who had negotiated a contract giving them 50 per cent of their protégé's earnings.

White fans' lingering expectation for a fresh white challenger to the present heavyweight holder Jim Braddock rested on former champion Max Baer, who had been floored only once in his career. Louis proved far too smart for Baer, disposing of him with a fourth-round KO in a continuing run of victories in his first 27 fights, 23 by KO. A title challenge by him was imminent until Max Schmeling interrupted the sequence in their first meeting in June 1936. Schmeling, now 30, was a former champion only on the strength of a disqualification of Jack Sharkey: now he spotted a rare flaw in Louis's defence, his low left hand following a jab. A 12th-round KO, Schmeling catching him with a swift right hand, gave Louis pause for thought.

His defeat now potentially opened the door for Schmeling to challenge Braddock for the title, Braddock having a contract with New York's Madison Square Garden for any title defence. However, Louis's 'money men', led by Jacobs, worked behind the scenes, exploiting anti-Nazi sentiment and persuading Braddock's manager Joe Gould to accept a Braddock–Louis match. Swings and roundabouts: Louis would get the title shot, Gould and Jacobs a huge slice of the revenue – in Chicago. Louis's arrival as champion in June 1937, honourable black heir to divisive Jack Johnson, was detonated by an eighth-round right-hand KO that smashed Braddock's teeth and released uniform celebration across society, embracing noted commentators such as Malcolm X, and Anglo-American radio analyst Alistair Cooke, who observed, 'For one night, in all the dark towns, the black man was king.'

As new champion, Louis's compulsive urge was for revenge on Schmeling for that earlier defeat. Schmeling's camp was evasive, seeking an 'alternative' European rival title fight against hugely popular Welshman Tommy Farr, widely billed as the 'Tonypandy Terror'. The Louis camp out-manoeuvred them – in that gambler's world related by Peter Wilson – by offering Farr a $60,000 guarantee. He and Louis met at Yankee Stadium, Louis a fraction too casual against the nimble Welshman and taken the full 15 rounds before being given a narrow points decision. That defence was two months after gaining the title: the re-match with Schmeling came a year later, one of the most brutal encounters ever, again in New York.

While Louis was more emotionally committed for this than any bout in his 12-year reign, so was Schmeling, carrying the weight of Germany's assumed Aryan supremacy and the direct command of Hitler, to him in the dressing room, to demolish a 'retrograde' African-American. Schmeling's camp was accompanied to New York by a publicity entourage proclaiming Nazi propaganda. A crowd of 70,000 assembled at Yankee Stadium: 60 per cent of America was tuned in on the radio. Louis had admitted beforehand, 'I had personal reasons for victory, but knew the whole country was depending on me.' From the first bell, they only had to wait for two minutes and four seconds. Peter Wilson was unequivocal, 'The greatest fight I ever saw … while it lasted!'

In the preceding furore of nationalistic antagonism, it tended to be overlooked that Schmeling himself was not a Nazi, and was an honourable fighter. Though Schmeling was older by eight years, the two rivals were each supremely fit, aware a lifetime's reputation was on the line for both. It was Schmeling who threw the first meaningful punch, and his last. With undisguised but controlled rage Louis set upon him with an avalanche of blows to the head, Schmeling momentarily remaining upright only because of the sustained punches keeping him off the floor. Gradually, wretchedly, he sank, briefly supported by the ropes, shrieking in pain as Louis delivered a massive blow to his unprotected ribs which allegedly fractured a vertebra. With exceptional courage, Schmeling three times attempted to regain his feet, only to be pounded back on to the canvas, until his trainer, Max Machon, in desperation, threw in the white towel of surrender.

Referee Arthur Donovan never bothered to finish the count with the stricken Schmeling lying twitching on the floor – subsequently to be taken to New York's Polytechnic Hospital and then home on a stretcher. Magnanimously, years later, he was gracious in congratulating the victor. Wilson wrote he had feared 'we might see death in the ring'. It had been a moment beyond sport, as significant as the triumph of Jesse Owens in Berlin two years earlier.

British and European champion Henry Cooper (of whom I write elsewhere), one of the few ever to floor Muhammad Ali in the first of his two losing bouts against Ali, and renowned for his benign opinions, reflected in *The Big Punchers* (written in conjunction with respected author Reg Gutteridge), 'As a kid, I aped being Joe Louis – he was my make-believe, because he was the best left-jabber. He could jab an opponent silly, then hook [from six inches] coming off the jab. Like hundreds of would-be boxers, I was educated on Louis. If Muhammad Ali was the most expansive fighter, Louis was the most economic. I wouldn't attempt to pick a winner between them.'

With Louis's fame secured for all time – not least by having established an affinity with golf and achieving to a degree integration with a 'white' sport for hitherto excluded blacks – he embarked upon a string of further title defences, 13 in succession over two and a half years from 1939 to '41, opponents crudely listed by media as the 'Bum of the Month

Club', though the majority were ranked in the top ten. Some survived for six rounds or so, and in June 1941, the world light-heavyweight champion Billy Conn caught Louis off-guard, his mobility exposing another of the champion's few flaws: a reluctance to chase a retreating opponent. Louis had dismissively forecast 'he can run, but he can't hide', though Conn won several rounds prior to suffering an eventual 13th-round knockout. A magnanimous Louis enlisted in the army in 1942 and fought nearly 100 exhibition bouts to entertain some two million servicemen, a gesture earning him deep approval.

By peacetime in 1946, now 32, Louis again defended against Conn, this time a knockout in the eighth, and in the next two years he retained the title twice more against renowned Jersey Joe Walcott, first on points and then an 11th-round KO. In 1949, Louis announced his retirement yet the financial stress of unforgiving tax demands on his wartime donations – plus handlers' 'untaxed percentages' and family handouts – edged him back into the ring against new champion Ezzard Charles. Louis told the *New York Times*, 'I don't feel this is a comeback, just a short vacation. I'm in the best shape since the war, and expect to win by a knockout.' Though 2/1 on with bookmakers, and having won over 50 interim exhibition bouts, at 36 his was a false optimism. Charles won over 15 rounds, and it was never in doubt. After a further eight bouts and three knockouts, Louis finally met his fighting conclusion against Rocky Marciano, suffering an eighth-round KO in October 1951.

It is too simple to say the end of a legend. In declining old age, well-wishers gave Louis the benevolence and dignity which he had exhibited: a serene celebrity's role greeting guests in a Vegas gambler's palace – the one time I met my once-distant boyhood champion, prior to Ali's painful exit against Larry Holmes with veteran grandee Louis ringside – a year before his death, an iconic symbol of America's social dysfunction.

CHAPTER FOUR

POST-WAR AWAKENING

FANNY BLANKERS-KOEN
Matronly Stardom Had Become Okay

'Hurdled as I never had before'

The founder of the modern Olympic Games, Baron Pierre De Coubertin, did not believe in women as athletes. He was on record as considering, 'An Olympiad with females would be impractical, uninteresting, unaesthetic and improper.' For three decades or more, the International Olympic Committee agreed. Now, in the 21st century, there is sociological concern, politically manipulated, for the issue that 'black lives matter'. For the IOC, for half a century, half the world's population did not matter: women effectively were Petri-dishes, humanity's incubators; competitive sport was certainly no occupation for mothers. Then along came Fanny Blankers-Koen of the Netherlands at London's Olympics, a 30-year-old mother-of-two who dissolved male global prejudice and exclusivity.

Born in April 1918, Blankers-Koen was not formulaic, simply practical evidence: startlingly so, with four gold medals at London in 1948 to equal the achievement of Jesse Owens, whose autograph she had requested when competing at Berlin 12 years previously aged 18. Women had been pressing their case for half a century. There had been no women at the inaugural Athens Games in 1896; a Greek woman, Stanati Revitus, was denied entry for the marathon, demonstrably running the course the next day and refused access to the stadium. At the next Games, four years later in Paris, women were admitted for tennis and golf, and subsequently for archery, gymnastics, figure skating and swimming. Women were not allowed to *run* until Amsterdam in 1928, at 100m and 800m. The sight of Lina Radke of Germany collapsing in triumph when winning the 800m – visible exhaustion being considered honourable for men – meant the event was condemned as unethical, anti-social and banned for the next 34 years.

Blankers-Koen fractured authoritarian male inhibitions not just by winning an inaugural women's 200m, but four of the nine events for women, after having given birth. Here was fulfilment of the fortitude upheld by Alice Milliat of France, the resolute founder of the Feminine Sports International Federation, which for 12 years from 1922 to '34, in the face of IOC and IAAF opposition, had staged rival Women's Olympic Games. Though Babe Didrikson, the phenomenal ball-games all-rounder, had won three track events at Los Angeles in 1932, Blankers-Koen's matriarchal exhibition was the fountain of a tide which would climb to ultimate Olympic gender equality in the 21st century. There was every reason for this Dutch woman to be celebrated by half the human race.

While the supremacy of Blankers-Koen was all but absolute for 12 years, from 1938 to 1950 – five European titles at Oslo in 1946 and Brussels in '50, four Olympic golds,

12 world records improved or equalled, 58 Dutch titles –
it should be reflected that international competition for
women was at that time limited, both numerically and during
the five years of the Second World War, the Netherlands
occasionally close to starvation. Her father, Arnoldus, had
been a thrower, shot and discus; his daughter, alongside the
incentive of four brothers, was multi-talented at swimming,
gymnastics, skating, fencing and running. Aged 17, she had
set a national record at 800m, then soon realised she was
more a sprinter, and was persuaded by her coach, Jan Blankers
– her future husband – to enter trials for the Berlin Games
of 1936. She qualified aged 18 for the high jump and the
sprint relay team. Coincidentally, the two were staged on the
same day: she and the relay squad finished fifth in each, but
more significantly for her, she obtained the autograph of Jesse
Owens – who flatteringly still remembered her when meeting
again at Munich's Games in 1972. Her mounting ambition
in 1936, fuelled by a 100 yards world record of 11 seconds
in 1938, was dampened by the cancellation of the scheduled
Helsinki Olympics in 1940, a week before the Netherlands
had been invaded in May.

Three months later, she married Blankers, now coach
to the national women's team: in 1942, a son, Jan Jr, was
born, but soon she was back in training, setting six world
records over the next two years – 80m hurdles; high jump
(1.71m); 100m (unapproved running against men); long jump
(6.25m), lasting until 1954; 100 yards; 4 x 100m; 4 x 200m.
In 1945, Netherlands' 'hunger-winter', daughter Fanneke was
born, leading to a long track lay-off prior to the European
Championships of 1946. There she fell in the 100m semi-
final, midway through the high jump event, in which, now
bruised, she finished fifth, but the following day she won

the hurdles and anchored a sprint relay victory. Steadily she steeled herself for London's Olympics – regulation-limited to three individual events for women so she chose the 100m, 200m, and 80m hurdles, plus the team sprint relay, thereby eliminating both jumps.

Olympic prospects intensified when early in 1948 she equalled the 100m world record of 11.5s, aged 30, only for severe criticism to gather across the country that it was 'irresponsible for a mother to neglect her children' in pursuit of mere sport. Blankers-Koen recalls, 'I had a tide of negative letters, telling me it was offensive for a mother to be appearing publicly "in knickers". I should stay at home with the children.' Moreover, it was suggested that, at 30, she was too old: this opinion even voiced by Britain's athletics team manager Jack Crump – an inveterate busybody who quietly doubled his income by working for the BBC and a newspaper. Never mind, there was to be no restraining a woman at the peak of her powers – even if Britain, volunteering post-war to rescue the Olympics, was so financially crippled that many visiting teams had to bring some of their own food provisions. Billeted at a school in outer north-west London, Blankers-Koen would have to take the train to Wembley each day.

First up was the 100m, hardly welcoming. When opening the Games, Prime Minister Clement Attlee had hoped 'for fine weather and record-breaking': it was to be predominantly wet and windy on a sludgy track, but Blankers-Koen qualified for the final and then won in a canter with 11.9s ahead of Britain's Dorothy Manley. That evening, she told her husband/ coach that she wished, now an Olympic champion, to return home to her children. There were confusing stories in a later biography of lack of affection towards her family when not on the crest of success: yet here she was, the first Dutch athlete ever to have won an Olympic track title. Her coach talked her into sense.

Anxiety preceded the next target, the 80m hurdles, aware as she was of the talent of Britain's number one, Maureen Gardner, who would also marry her coach, Geoff Dyson, and was conspicuously in prime current form. In my official IOC history books, Blankers-Koen recounted, 'I recall every detail of the heats and the final. On the day of the heats, I went to the warm-up track behind the stadium, already an Olympic winner, yet nobody could have felt less like a champion. I was trembling. I'd never been so nervous before a race, and was even turning away children wanting autographs, who normally didn't bother me. I went through my warm-up but wasn't concentrating properly, waiting for my first glimpse of Maureen, whom I'd never seen before. I was aware she had a best time of 11.2, and although earlier that year I had set a world record of 11.0, I knew how things can go wrong. Maureen arrived by car and made a big impression when I saw that she had brought her own practice hurdles. Someone who does that must be first class, I thought.

'There were no other hurdles available on the training track, so with courage I asked if I could borrow hers before my heat. We shook hands and I noticed she was as nervous as I was. Yet I was to witness just how good she was when she touched a hurdle in her semi-final, lost her balance, but still managed to qualify in third place. People started to tell me it was going to be easy, but Jan was cautious, recognising how dangerous was this rival. I hardly slept that night, turning over in my mind Jan's words of warning.

'For the final, I was drawn in the next lane to Maureen, which was helpful, but on one of the few occasions in my career I made a poor start and was a yard down after ten metres. I then hurdled as I'd never hurdled before, and was almost level with Maureen ... going so fast that I was too close to the fifth hurdle, caught it, and lost my balance. From there it was a struggle again, with my rhythm astray. Even so, I felt I'd passed Maureen before the finish, but was not sure about Shirley Strickland of Australia who seemed level with me at the line. I was then jolted when I heard the British national anthem, supposing Maureen must have won, but the band was playing because the Royal Family had just arrived. In fact, in my lunge for the finish, I had leaned forward enough to get in front of Maureen, so low that the tape cut my neck and the blood trickled on to my vest.' A photo finish declared Blankers-Koen the winner, with the pair timed equally.

Yet again the new double Olympic champion was depressed prior to the 200m semi-finals, in tears in the dressing room and feeling homesick. Jan reassured her: she qualified, then left the field for dead in the final, winning the women's inaugural 200m in 24.4s, 0.7s ahead of Audrey Patterson, the first Afro-American to win an Olympic medal. It was the largest winning margin for 200m by any man or woman.

In celebration that evening, Blankers-Koen headed with colleagues for London's West End and a modest glass of wine. The following day, devoting too long in selecting a raincoat for the local weather, she arrived back at Wembley to find her Dutch colleagues already warming up for the sprint relay final – she was on the anchor leg. By the time she was passed the baton the Netherlands were lying fourth, just behind Australia. With the most devastating run of her career, she hauled back the deficit to squeeze victory and a fourth gold by a tenth of a second.

Back home, the nay-sayers had not merely surrendered but had changed attire: now welcoming her at Amsterdam railway station in a sea of orange, carriage drawn by white stallions awaiting her arrival. Matronly stardom had become okay and for good measure, she was presented with a new bicycle to save her running – to the grocery. Her country's queen gave her the Order of Nassau. Fifty years later, the IAAF – subsequently World Athletics – voted her Female Athlete of the Century. Two years on, she repeated her London quartet in the European Championships at Brussels: gold in 100m, 200m and hurdles, silver in the relay, beaten by the British. Another two years later came her third Olympics, at Helsinki, but she fluffed in both 100m and hurdles. Retirement beckoned at 34.

She later said, 'Looking back, I remember thinking how strange that I had made so many people so happy, but during the war life had been hard, and people were glad of the chance afterwards to celebrate anything. I couldn't have won four golds today. We used to train only twice a week, now they train twice a day. Maybe nowadays I could just make a final, yet every heat nowadays is like a final. Now it is a job. In our time we were amateurs, but I reckon we had more fun then than they have now. There was never a chance in those days to make money for something you did so much just for fun, after the experience of living through the war and Nazi occupation, so that afterwards I was just happy to have the opportunity to travel.'

Motherhood is not necessarily conviction to seclusion.

EMIL ZÁTOPEK
Epitome Of Dignity

'It is an advantage to train under
bad conditions'

It might be reasonably said that the emotional fortitude which Emil Zátopek gave by his athletic deeds to the people of Bohemia/Czechoslovakia, during political crises of the 1950s and '60s, was, say, comparable to the gift of Chopin to the plight of Poland amid of Silesian revolutions of 1830–45. The cultural impact of each individual in perilous times, never mind whether Chopin was composing in Paris in the company of George Sand or Zátopek performing in Gothenburg, would nurture abstract nationalism for them and generations to come.

There is no sports champion in history who has twice voluntarily put his very social existence literally at permanent risk as Zátopek did in 1952, prior to the Helsinki Olympic Games, and then in 1968, in vain support of premier Dubcek's attempted anti-Soviet campaign. Zátopek was monumental on two counts: physically as athlete, morally as political liberal. This latter principle imposed 20 years of social demotion, hard labour, ill health and separation from his wife. Yet his principle never deserted him. When I last spoke to him, just in advance of Sydney's Olympic Games of 2000 and shortly before his death, he reflected, 'I hope this marvellous world event will sustain sport's motivation, the ethic of fair play and the warmth of worldwide friendship.'

Zátopek's aphorisms were many and often: 'An athlete cannot run with money in his pocket. He must run with hope in his heart and dreams in his head'; 'If you want to win something, run a mile. If you want to experience something different in life, run a marathon'; 'It is a great advantage to train under bad conditions, for this difficulty is then a tremendous relief in a race.'

Bad conditions, politically, were to haunt him, the first time when about to depart for Finland and defend his Olympic 10,000m title won in London in 1948. A prominent young middle-distance athlete, Stanislav Jungwirth, was on the verge of an international breakthrough at 1,500m. Helsinki would be a springboard, but his name was missing from the selected squad. This was political discretion: Jungwirth's father was an anti-Communist activist and a political prisoner, his son's exclusion but a reprisal. Immediately Zátopek, his name by now in the world media's headlines, informed the Czech organisers, 'No Jungwirth, no Zátopek.' This demand would provoke a scandal within IOC and international circles. Both athletes remained behind when the Czech squad departed for Helsinki, Zátopek's future as a senior-ranking army officer now in jeopardy. For three days the Moscow-imposed government stalled but eventually, in the face of Zátopek's fame, they relented: he and Jungwirth arrived days late, Zátopek soaring to triple triumph with his young compatriot missing his final, subsequently finishing sixth at Melbourne in 1956 but breaking the 1,500m world record a year later.

Zátopek's next few years were filled with record-breaking extravagance, a sequence of spectacular achievements for this Soviet satellite nation in which he had risen to be a prominent military and sporting figure, until the political hurricane of 1968.

Colonel Zátopek supported the Communist Party's democratic rule, and he was a significant backer of new First Secretary Alexander Dubcek's liberating *Manifesto of 2000 Words*. Shortly before midnight on 20 August 1968, a Soviet-led army of Warsaw Pact forces invaded and outmanoeuvred a surprised Czech army. Protestors swarmed through the streets, student Jan Palac sacrificially set himself alight in defiance of this political abuse, and agitators including Zátopek and wife Dana assembled in famous Wenceslas Square, proclaiming Dubcek's 'socialism with a human face'. Swiftly, the people's uprising was brutally torpedoed, with more than 20 killed, Radio Prague silenced at gunpoint, and Dubcek's Prague Spring corralled by tanks.

Zátopek, having suggested that the Soviet Union should be barred from the upcoming Mexico Olympics, was instantly stripped of rank, expelled from the army and the party, and deported to a labour camp in the Bohemian mines, shovelling with a geological squad, while Dana was left at home. A stream of Western journalists would be informed he was 'not available'. After nine years, by 1977, his health was ailing and his spirit depressed; no longer a political threat, he was permitted to return to Prague and to Dana, with a menial job as a linguist filing foreign publications on development of sports finance, until retiring in the early 1980s. Post-Soviet disintegration in 1990, Zátopek was rehabilitated by liberating Vaclav Havel.

What a litany of glory his athletic career had been: as commentary in *Spectator* magazine observed, 'A hero not just for his time but for all time.' In a nutshell, these are the remarkable, basic statistics:

- Four times Olympic champion: 10,000m 1948; 5,000m, 10,000m, marathon 1952
- Three times European champion: 5,000m, 10,000m 1950; 10,000m 1954
- Undefeated at 10000m from May 1948 to July 1954, 38 consecutive victories
- Eighteen world records (mostly unpaced): 1949– 1955, from 5,000m to 30,000m

Born the seventh child in September 1922, at Koprivnice, Moravia, Emil by 16 had joined the Bata shoe factory (later associated with Stanley Matthews), where he was instructed to run, reluctantly, yet finished second in a race, feeling unexpectedly comfortable and joining a club. There, he embarked on a fitness programme fashioned on legendary Finnish champion Paavo Nurmi of the 1920s. By 1944, Zátopek, aged 22, broke the Czech records for 2,000m, 3,000m and 5,000m, being granted more time by state intervention for his extensive training regime.

A turning point in his career came in the autumn of 1945 with a visit to Prague by Swedish middle-distance record-breaker Arne Andersen. Zátopek was motivated by the training schedule of this eminent rival of famed Swedish compatriot Gunder Haag, recognising that more severe and adjusted preparation was needed: a combination of Finnish and Swedish disciplines, fundamentally the principle of 'interval' training, the alternation of sprinting and jogging phases, which blended a simultaneous capacity for aerobic stamina and brief anaerobic sprints. This was to give Zátopek a remarkable combination of both: notwithstanding that his controversially lolling head and swaying trunk distracted attention from his flawlessly flowing leg rhythm. At the peak of his career, alone, often deliberately wearing heavy soldier's boots, he was covering 1,000 hours a year, at 800km a month and half a marathon a day. His first race at Zlin, home of Bata, was in 1941, over 1,400m, tasting his first victory at the fifth attempt. Drafted into the army, he cycled from Prague to East Berlin in his army boots to compete for Allied occupation troops, gaining momentum that would serve him so well in London two years later. At the European Championships of 1946 in Oslo, he was fifth at 5,000m, breaking his own Czech record with 14:25.8.

When I interviewed him for *The Times* long after his retirement, Zátopek was humorous and wholly without assumption, recalling that his first recognition for speed 'came from fetching sandwiches for his school master, I was a fast messenger!' He laughed at memories of his mother's Chinese geese – bred for the oven – who would enthusiastically follow him out of the garden gate when he went running, gathering speed for take-off and flapping overhead, enjoying the fun – to mother's stern disapproval. Emil left home for Zlin at 14; by 18 he still did not know the precise length of an athletic track, yet by now it had already been observed that he was 'running like Nurmi!'

'I discovered a good club, running had become the centre of my life. After the war and German occupation, I was already Czech record holder at 5,000 and 10,000, and suddenly I became eligible for selection for the Olympics in London. Even at night I was practising interval running, which at that time was an unusual schedule, driven by the knowledge that I would meet the world's best, my motivation not to make a fool of myself. At the European Championships in Oslo, I'd learned that I needed to know *how* to run tactically, how to preserve power for the finish.

'Arriving at Uxbridge, west of London wartime aerodrome converted as makeshift athlete village, I trained, played the guitar, attended the opening ceremony even though the 10,000 was the next day.'

Instructed by coaches to return to the village, he sneaked into the Danish team (marching behind the Czechs), defiantly re-entering the arena. A man with a sense of history. Confronted again by officialdom, he insisted, 'Can't leave now, the King is watching.'

For the 10,000m, semaphore advice was overtly scheduled with his coach in the stands for checking lap time consistency: faster, white flag; slower, red flag. After eight laps came the red flag. Zátopek overtook Finnish world record holder Heino, who retaliated but was drained by seven kilometres. Zátopek irresistibly set a new Olympic record of 29:59.6, Alain Mimoun of France taking silver. In the subsequent 5,000m the threat was from Gaston Reiff of Belgium and Wim Slijkhuis of the Netherlands. The latter two set a severe pace, Zátopek clinging distantly with Reiff 60 metres ahead. Overtaking Slijkhuis on the last lap, Zátopek was unable to close on Reiff, who got home by a metre.

Helsinki in 1952 was the apotheosis, in the wake of the Jungwirth controversy. Opening a triple crown came the 10,000m, surpassing his own Olympic record by 42 seconds. Five days later came the 5,000m final, one of the most dramatic contests of all time, with a formidable contest of four elite contenders: the other three being the gallant Chris Chataway of Britain, and Mimoun and Herbert Schade of West Germany. All four were there at the bell, Chataway accelerating for his bid down the last back straight but critically stumbling on the final bend's kerb, and falling, at which point Zátopek's irresistible finishing kick from fourth place saw him surge into the lead past Schade and Mimoun, having covered the last lap in 57.5s to win in 14:06.6. Mimoun took silver a second behind and Schade claimed bronze, followed by Britain's Gordon Pirie and the unfortunate Chataway. The IAAF's authoritative historian Roberto Quercetani termed Zátopek's victory 'the truest expression of track aggression I have ever seen'. Later that day, Dana became women's champion in the javelin.

The approach for the marathon, Zátopek's first yet with a meticulously planned strategy, was simple: stick with the pre-race favourite, Jim Peters of Britain, the world record holder. After 15 testing kilometres and with 25 still to go, Zátopek asked Peters what he thought of the pace. 'Too slow,' said Peters, intending to disarm a 'novice'. Zátopek promptly accelerated, lost Peters – who did not finish – and, aged 30, set an Olympic record before Reinaldo Gorno of Argentina had entered the stadium. By the following year, Zátopek was being pressed by an upcoming Soviet Ukrainian, Vladimir Kuts, new automaton. Although Zátopek won the European Championship 10,000m at Berne in 1954, with Kuts absent, the Ukrainian dominated the 5,000m, Zátopek finishing third behind Chataway. In this year Zátopek nevertheless ran his fastest ever 10,000m and 5,000m, but age was now calling. He attempted to defend his Olympic marathon title at Melbourne in 1956 but injury and hospitalisation saw him finish sixth behind winner Mimoun. The legend retired the following year.

For the next 11 years, life was prominent in army service and sporting responsibilities for a man globally admired, not least for his generosity. Visited in 1966 by Ron Clarke,

Australia's eminent long-distance record breaker who suffered an exasperating Olympic setback when defeated by unheralded American-Indian Billy Mills, Zátopek's kindness was exemplary. He pressed a small package into Clarke's hand as he boarded the plane on departure. Clarke supposed it was something discreet, something smuggled perhaps? Opening it in mid-flight, he found one of Zátopek's gold medals from 1952.

All those who experienced private life with Zátopek and his wife cherished his quiet bonhomie. 'The merriest home I have been in,' remembered Pirie. A relative non-entity, I was met and entertained with disarming, unpretentious courtesy not long before his death in November 2000, an international congregation attending his funeral at the National Theatre. A statue was unveiled at the Stadium of Youth in Zlin in September 2014. A man who epitomised universal human dignity: an expression of nationalism through spontaneous international friendship.

STANLEY MATTHEWS
A Conjuror's Unfathomable
Sleight of Hand

'It was essential not to panic'

In the closing, frenetic moments of the FA Cup final of 1953, I was incoherently beating the head of the man seated in front of me with my folded newspaper. The rest of Wembley's 100,000 stadium was likewise in near hysteria, all because a balding man of few words and 36 years was about to realise a long-delayed ambition. He had been my boyhood hero from the age of 12: a player revered across the world, prior to keyhole television's exposure, for a wizardry he himself could never explain. There are many proclaimed landmarks in sport: the last-minute 4-3 victory by Blackpool against Bolton Wanderers was an imperishable moment of my youth and for much of England's football fraternity – largely because the magic of Stanley Matthews' footwork had a conjuror's unfathomable sleight of hand.

For defenders, one moment he was *there* – and the next he wasn't. I first saw him, peering beneath the armpits of adults at Portsmouth, unable to comprehend how the ball seemed to be fastened to him by his shoelaces. He was the only player I have known, in over 70 years, who could make a crowd laugh out loud, an ability only matched latterly by Lionel Messi for Barcelona.

Again and again, he mesmerised unfortunate opponents – witness a memorable Wembley defeat of Brazil in 1956 when up against their captain, Nilton Santos, widely regarded as the world's best left-back. He literally toyed with a player regarded back home as a god: by then, Matthews was 41. Simultaneously ordinary-looking yet incomprehensible once he moved from a standing start into a swirling, balletic sprint, he was as unmanageable as mercury. I saw him clinically dismantle a fine Arsenal side at the old Highbury stadium. There was a moment in the second half when for several seconds he stood stationary with his foot on the ball, and not a single Arsenal player had the courage to challenge him. He had had full-back Lionel Smith against him, then they switched Welsh international Wally Barnes across to take him on, Scotsman Alex Forbes had a go, then England midfield skipper Joe Mercer, eventually Don Roper: five players attempting to halt him and nobody able to do a thing. It was the most intriguing performance many there had ever seen, and afterwards, there being thunderous applause from the home terraces as Blackpool left the field 4-1 victors, he just got into the bath as if nothing had happened. Arsenal's manager Tom Whittaker was duly astounded, 'At 40 years of age, a miracle.' Jackie Mudie, Scotland's midfielder, reflected, 'Stan had no understanding of what he had just done.'

Writing a biography of Sir Stanley years later – the only footballer knighted while still playing – he was staying at my home. At dinner my wife Marita, many times a Wembley visitor, asked him how he had learned to control a ball, an opponent, a match, to such a degree. 'I really don't know,' he answered, almost embarrassed. His was a story almost beyond invention. Born in 1915 in the Potteries town of Hanley, third of four sons of Jack, a barber, conventionally patrician for that era, whose reputation was widely enhanced by success as a featherweight boxer defeated only nine times in 350 bouts. Sundays saw the family make the five-mile walk each way to grandmother's house. Such was the boy's own precocious development, in playtime on a rough patch of open ground outside a pottery, that workers on the way home would pause to admire his dexterity. Genetic inheritance enabled Stanley to be playing for Stoke City, and gaining promotion back to the old First Division, at the age of 50: unlikely today, given the physical pace of the game on perfect pitches with synthetic rather than leather balls.

Matthews first played for England aged 19, against Wales at Cardiff in 1934, in a 4-0 victory. Ultimately he made a total of 84 appearances, which would have been many more but for the interruption of the Second World War, during which he played in 26 'friendlies', 14 of them against Scotland. At the age of 42 he was still included in three World Cup qualifiers, against Denmark home and away and the Republic of Ireland, then controversially omitted from the squad to play in Sweden's finals.

Such was his magnetism that seven stadiums, including Manchester City's Maine Road and Glasgow's Hampden Park, the latter with 149,000 present, had their record attendance on account of his involvement. Transferred from Stoke City after 15 years in 1947, experiencing friction with an envious manager, he then spent 14 years with Blackpool. Twice they experienced FA Cup Final defeats, memorably against Manchester United in 1948 and, undistinguished, against Newcastle in 1951, prior to fulfilment two years later.

He transferred back to Stoke in 1961 – the former maximum wage now abolished, for which I had seriously campaigned in the *Daily Telegraph* – on the initiative of manager Tony Waddington, a shrewd utiliser of elderly talent with the veteran Mudie, Dennis Viollet from Manchester United, and Jimmy McIlroy from Burnley. Stoke, low in the Second Division, had been drawing attendances of some 7,000: the night Matthews returned, there were 32,000 present. In permitting his departure from Blackpool, the directors had demanded a transfer fee of £3,500, insisting, '*We* made your reputation.'

The tactical structure of the game in those days was so different, certainly in England, prior to the arrival of European competitions in the late 1950s, and the advent of what was termed Total Football, originating from Hungary and then Holland, though Spurs in the 1950s were notable for their inter-passing possession game under manager Arthur Rowe, who had studied in Hungary and was later to coach Pegasus. Matthews was embedded in the then-rigid 3-4-3 tactical formation: a central defender between two full-backs; two wing-halves and two inside-forwards, the creative midfield, with possibly one of the inside-forwards an occasional additional striker; and three forwards, the centre-forward between two outright wingers. And wingers *were* wingers, as was Matthews; that's where they stayed, utilising wide spaces, intent on getting round the outside of the defence and crossing – preferably backwards – away from defenders, for the centre-forward to score.

Matthews was the ultimate winger: he didn't expect to play *with* colleagues, but to conjure goals for others. There is the clearest definition of this formality in my biography, as related by Stan Cullis, the formidable pre-war England centre-half and later manager of dominant Wolverhampton Wanderers immediately after the conflict, 'There was no national team manager in those days, so the captain had to try and sort out the tactics. Stan would never offer suggestions, just sit there quietly. I remember Raich Carter [renowned contemporary of Matthews] once saying before a game, "*Please*, talk to Stan. He never gives me the ball back!" And I said to him, "Never mind, just give it to him and get into the penalty area." I'd suggest to Stan that he come inside occasionally, which I felt could be dangerous.

'It was remarkable how he would be kicked from pillar to post and never seemed to resent it, just concentrate on destroying his man. I remember playing with him against the Scottish League, and hearing them beforehand talking about how their new left-back "would stop Matthews". Stan went out and ran the fellow dizzy. He really could make people fall over. Once, with this left-back sitting on the ground, having failed to rob him, Stan put his foot on the ball, waited for the fellow to get up, and beat him again. Let's face it, a lot of people went to football for nothing more than to watch Stan.'

It was this conventional concept, 'give Matthews the ball and he'll create the goals', which resulted in England selectors – wholly in command until the transformative appointment of Alf Ramsey as replacement for Walter Winterbottom in 1962 – frequently abandoning Matthews 'to try someone else'. Yet his irresistible threat was recognised across the international game, his capacity to destroy single-handed the opposition. West Germany's World Cup-winning team of 1954 came to Wembley in December and were routed 3-1. So dismembered was their eminent left-back and captain, Kohlmeyer, that he never played again. Germany's inside-left, Jupp Derwall, who would later become the team's manager, recalled, 'I was inside-left, and many times tried to halt Matthews, yet I hadn't a chance. It was wretched for us, it could have been five or six instead of 3-1. Kohlmeyer was saying to me, "What can I do against this man?" In the dressing room afterwards, Kohlmeyer didn't say a word, he just sat on the floor with his head in his hands, and he was still there after the rest of us had dressed, and we had to wait for him in the bus before we could leave. He was in a daze. When Matthews was dribbling, he was never looking at the ball, he was looking at waiting defenders. He was so special.'

The post-war nadir for England, supposed masters and originators of the game, had arrived in 1953 in the form of the Magical Magyars, Hungary's Olympic champions of the previous year. A glittering array of touch players including midfield architects József Bozsik and Nándor Hidegkuti, lethal killers Sándor Kocsis and Ferenc Puskás in attack, slaughtered bewildered England 6-3. Yet the Hungarians acknowledged the wizardry of Matthews. Confronting him was left-back Mihály Lantos, whom I later met in Budapest. 'We respected England as the home of football, and of course we'd heard of Matthews, I'd been told about this right-winger who was 38, assured that his age was irrelevant, that he was a master of dribbling and very quick, but still wondering what I would find. I was fascinated to see such a man and be playing against him. One of our aims at Wembley was to exclude Billy Wright [England's centre-half], to bypass him by interchanging in midfield. But Matthews I found a problem. I'd tried to get to the ball before him, but couldn't, needing others to help challenge him. There was a great similarity in dribbling skills between him and Garrincha of Brazil, the same speed off the mark. Garrincha scored more goals, but I found that Matthews had a much finer awareness of the position of his colleagues.'

This view was echoed by Ted Drake, the memorable Arsenal and England centre-forward, with the all-time English top-flight record of seven goals in a single match, who recalled, 'Matthews never hid, he was always there, wanting the ball. He had fantastic awareness, could read the shape of play with a single glance, and picked the best positioned colleague to give the ball to. I never saw him lob-it-and-hope. As soon as Stan had the ball, I'd go for the near post, not the far post as people expected. On the near post, where Stan was so accurate, I could go for the glancing header.'

A particular distinction of the way that this mastery captivated audiences was that often it would also be a treasured memory of an unfortunate defender who had capitulated. Harry Haddock, Scotland's left-back in a 7-2 thrashing, remembered, 'On the day of the match, Scottish officials were saying to me, "Go at him, he's got no left foot." I tried this the first time, Stan went inside me, and shivered the crossbar with his left foot. With his skill, he had no need to head. I once made three tackles on him between the halfway line and the goal line, and he still went clear and crossed it!

'He'd walk towards you, with the ball on his right foot, feint to his left, you'd go with him to your right, he'd touch the other way, and be gone. You'd see it, and could do nothing. I knew that's what he'd do, wanted him to do it, to force him down the line on the outside, because I thought with my speed, if I was still on the inside, I could stay with him. But he lost me. Once he'd gone past you, it seemed he'd forgotten about you. That day was special for me – although we lost, it's something I treasure, and it was marvellous to discover that he was so brilliant yet still just like any other fellow.'

Perhaps I should dwell on my teenage moment of euphoria at Wembley in 1953. On the morning of the match, Bob

Ferrier, a respected commentator for the *Daily Mirror* and later *The Observer,* had forecast, 'No matter what else happens at Wembley, it will make today probably the most extraordinary cup final of them all. From 100,000 people will come a wave of sympathy for Matthews in his third final in five years such as sport has never known … It may seem to be putting a match and a player on rather a high plane, but it will offer the greatest unspoken tribute to a man who has graced and dignified football for two decades.'

Blackpool, either collectively blissful or blind since losing the final of 1951, were capable with Matthews of defeating any team, any day. By 1953, Matthews was 38, with a thigh injury prior to Wembley and a late fitness test. The man to be marking him for Bolton was Ralph Banks, who wouldn't be frightened: a frontline survivor of the grim battle of Anzio, where his binoculars, placed on the trench ridge in front of him, had been blown to pieces. Bolton's England record sharp-shooter, centre-forward Nat Lofthouse, was anxious about Matthews, 'Everybody in England, except the people of Bolton, wanted Stanley to get his medal … I was thinking beforehand whether our defence could cope with Stanley's accuracy, he was such a perfectionist, always training on his own. You never saw him place a cross inside the six-yard box, where the keeper might reach it, always half a yard outside, tempting. As a forward, his cross was always coming towards *you.* His strength was getting to the byline, which was the key to his game.'

The early phase was gloomy for Blackpool, one down within the first minute through a goalkeeping error, yet soon Bolton themselves were in trouble when Bell, their left-half, pulled a muscle. With no substitutes, they were down to ten-and-a-half men. Blackpool equalised shortly before half-time through an own goal, but another goalkeeping error plus a fortuitous header by Bell saw them go 3-1 down with only 20 minutes to play. All seemed lost but there was a remarkable, emotional transformation. Suddenly, belatedly, Matthews started to turn the game, his diminutive midfielder Ernie Taylor the powder-monkey provider of the ball. Ralph Banks recalled, 'I was now getting cramp, trying to hang on to Stanley. He was phenomenal over ten yards and it was almost impossible to do anything with him once he had the ball … we were in a right state.' Blackpool reduced the lead to 3-2 with Matthews at his most mesmeric. A deft cross to the far post, fumbled by goalkeeper Hanson, allowed England's striker Stan Mortensen to scramble the ball home. The roar was deafening.

There was a quarter of an hour to go in a spell in which Matthews was freezing Bolton's limbs. 'I had no feelings at that stage,' Stanley said. 'I knew it was essential not to panic.' With a bare three minutes remaining, it was still 3-2 to Bolton when Blackpool gained a free kick on the edge of the penalty area. Mortensen, with his rifle-like shooting power, spotted a tiny gap in Bolton's crowded defence in the goal area, then stunned the opposition and the audience with a clinical shot: few could strike a ball so hard as he. In the main stand behind the Royal Box, the Matthews family was equally close to hysteria, his mother-in-law having fainted, his mother silent and intent. According to the referee, with the score 3-3 there was less than a minute of injury time still to go. As Lofthouse would recall of Bolton's panic, 'I spent the time just watching Stanley. He stood there, toes turned inwards, looking like a little old man – until he moved. In that final spell, he *knew* he could do it.'

As the Blackpool players hurried back to the halfway line, Matthews clapped his hands, slowly, three times. 'It's not over.'

From the kick-off the ball once more flew Taylor to Matthews for the climax. On the fringe of the penalty area, with Banks and centre-half Barrass ahead of him, Matthews does what he has done 10,000 times before over the past 21 years: obliges Banks and Barrass to come at him. The usual sway to the left as though coming inside, in an instant gone to the right. Over by the penalty spot, Mortensen is at the ready, but left-winger Perry has moved in behind him. Matthews is cutting in towards the goal area, clear of Banks and Barrass, left behind. An upward glance, and Matthews senses Mortensen will be blocked, so he angles his pass through 40 degrees further back: opportunist Perry smashes the ball home with his right foot, a hooked shot through almost 180 degrees. Pandemonium.

After collecting his medal from the Royal Box, Matthews was about to shake hands with Banks, who amid the celebrations said in an interview, 'I thought it nice when Stan was complimentary, saying, "Ralph doesn't kick you all over the place." I never was a thumper. I'd beaten him a time or two before the cramp came on, but then it was murder.' Lofthouse remembered nostalgically, 'I felt it couldn't have gone to a better man. I don't think a bullet would have stopped Stan in the last 17 minutes. Ernie may have been the man of the match, in a sense, but it still needed Stan's judgement.' England selectors, with characteristic Pavlovian reaction, now promptly recalled the 38-year-old hero, who had been out of the England team for more than two years, for the forthcoming tour of South America.

In a continuing daydream, I spent an hour searching for the schoolmaster who drove me to London, wondering whether, as a winger, I could have made the same kind of cross from the same position as Matthews when winning the match. I was not to know that in two years' time, from exactly the same spot at the same end, I would indeed be crossing the ball, but without achieving the same cacophonous arousal provoked by Stanley – though my parents in the grandstand were amused at my repositioning the foot-square divot that I had created.

Some 30 years later, it was my privilege to be involved in an honour for Matthews in his home town. I was invited by the eminent local sculptor, Colin Melbourne, to provide the inscription for the statue about to be unveiled in Hanley, and this was it: 'His name is symbolic of the beauty of the game, his fame timeless and international, his sportsmanship and modesty universally acclaimed. A magical player, of the people, for the people.' It was a cold and windy day, yet the town precinct was packed with the loyal and the curious. Old ladies who remembered him from when he was a lad – and they were younger and gay – were there in their bonnet hats, calling him 'duck' and shaking hands and crying a bit, and looking happy, and saying it was lovely to see him. Workmen, busy completing some new office block, stopped work and lined the scaffolding in rows of several dozen. The Ceramic City Brass Band played a merry tune to keep minds off the cold, and at 11am Sir Stanley, a little bowed of leg and shoulder, shyly pushed his way through the throng with Lady Mila, to mount the podium for the unveiling. The city council had asked me to make the address, and this is some of what I said:

'Stanley Matthews has been to football in the 20th century what Johan Strauss was to music in the 19th. He has given pleasure and entertainment to millions, who followed him like a Pied Piper wherever he played. He put a dance into a dull life. He was as well known abroad as in Britain.

'Today we are gathered here in honour of a man who is unique in the history of English sport, indeed perhaps unique in the whole world of sport: the only professional footballer knighted while still playing. Stan won no wars, discovered no foreign land, made no scientific invention. What he did was, in its way, bigger than that. He touched the heart of the nation because he was simultaneously exceptional and ordinary, internationally famous yet humble, spectacular yet shy and unpretentious. Most of all, playing this simplest of games, he had a special affinity with ordinary people, with his own roots.

'Never again will football witness such a career, either for endurance or spellbinding entertainment. The public thronged through the turnstiles, during four decades, to enter a life of fantasy, as J.B. Priestley wrote, "Away from clanking machinery and into a splendid kind of life, hurtling with conflict yet passionate and beautiful in its art." It has been Matthews the sorcerer who more than any other in my lifetime has created that fantasy which made fathers take young boys who were almost babes in arms to some of his last matches, so that they, too, might say in later years, "I saw Stan Matthews."'

A shining English representative, globally exported, yet never effectively leaving Stoke-on-Trent. It is impossible to equate Matthews alongside subsequent supreme players because the game became strategically so different, the European Cup so transformative. All I can claim is that visually, though incessantly assaulted more than Maradona, he was incalculable.

LEW HOAD
Unmatchable Peak

'A way of life that had gone forever'

If any particular figures personify the pleasure I was to discover as a sports correspondent – and there have been many contenders – one would be Lew Hoad. The irresistibly handsome Australian tennis champion was, in the opinion of many more experienced in tennis than I, a true phenomenon. So dynamic was his destruction of distinguished compatriot Ashley Cooper in the Wimbledon men's singles final of 1957 that potential drama became irrelevant. It was one of the most extraordinary single hours of my six decades as a professional spectator at many sports.

Dramas have been otherwise abundant. I need to explain the why and how, in my mind, of Hoad's unique status; such a synthesis of power and refinement being unprecedented in the pre-Federer metal-racket era may be on account of ferocious weight training – and consequent recurrent back strain, which curtailed his subsequent professional career by perhaps about ten years. Hoad touched a level at which the later supreme professional arch rival Pancho Gonzalez would declare, 'At his peak, Lew was unplayable.' This concept of ultimate fame had taken root for me some years earlier.

Almost from the first moment I could run, unselfconsciously and spontaneously I was a sports addict. Put simply, it was the shortest path from loneliness to fun: whether it was playing marbles, or furtively rolling pebbles down the primary school's steep bank beside a pavement, to scare old ladies climbing the hill with their shopping. Games escaped emotional boredom. Discipline – the essence of serious sport – was part of the school's curriculum: taught to walk erect carrying a book on your head, never mind that Hitler was only 50 miles distant, fretting in anticipation of a delayed invasion and our annihilation. For failing to divulge finding a three-penny piece on the playing field, I was summarily suspended on sports day from all races bar the team relay.

Happily unaware of impending wartime crises, I was absorbed, out of classroom, in Wilson the Wonder Athlete: an astonishing hermit-like figure of indeterminate age for whom no athletic feat was impossible. A three-minute mile, a seven-foot high jump, whatever. *The Wizard*'s weekly publication came together with the parallel *Champion*'s serialisation of Leader of the Lost Commandos: a heroic, secretive military subterfuge somewhere in Europe, posted to me at school by my mother from somewhere in England, wherever my father was stationed as radar operator.

The magical Wilson thus created an abstract perception in a young, isolated boy of where I imagined life might lead me, so my voracious reading of reality subsequently seized on living heroes and heroines: Don Bradman, heavyweight world boxing champion Joe Louis, or greatest ever Babe Didrikson. Age-wise my contemporary, Hoad's spectacular early summit coincided with my modest emergence into what used to be known as Fleet Street, the hub of national journalism just west of St Paul's, now long dispersed. Glory in any field inevitably invites exaggeration: the beauty of what Hoad bequeathed to one sport, in perfection and modesty, was breathtaking. As close to Wilson, it seemed, as reality could come.

What was more, Hoad possessed the same debonair, unassuming nonchalance as contemporary screen idol Robert Mitchum. Lew was, publicly and privately, wholly without conceit, a working-class Sydney boy born in November 1934. The son of a tramway electrician, his latent genes aged seven – in an echo of Don Bradman endlessly striking a ball against a wall with a cricket stump – was devotedly banging tennis balls against the garage door until neighbours complained of the noise.

A precocious junior alliance was formed with the similarly talented but strategically contrasting Ken Rosewall, who was more measured and less powerful. Individually and together their partnership took the game by storm; in 1953 Rosewall was the first to achieve a major title, the French Open, and the pair commanding instant doubles supremacy with a trio of triumphs aged 19 at Melbourne, Paris and Wimbledon. In an epic Davis Cup Final, the US were defeated thanks to Hoad's five-set victory over supposedly superior Tony Trabert; Hoad consequently being ranked world number one for 1954, the youngest ever at 19 years and 38 days.

His climax as an amateur – a lingering, inherently false concept in full-time mass-audience sports, such as football, rugby, cricket and athletics, doggedly preserved by 19th-century-minded officialdom – was yet to come. Losing at Wimbledon in 1954 to veteran former champion Drobny and in 1955 (as he had in Paris) to American Vic Seixas – evidence of Hoad's sometimes erratic concentration and possibly related to his romance and marriage to Australian finalist Jenny Staley – meant ultimate fame was still pending.

Although in this era three of the four Grand Slam tournaments were on grass – Australia, Wimbledon, US – such was Hoad's fluency and stroke range, his dominance was potentially unlimited. In 1956, he swept to consecutive titles at Melbourne, Paris and Wimbledon, defeating Rosewall at the latter in four sets, also claiming Italian and German hard court championships. Only Rosewall prevented a Grand Slam quartet in New York's final. Following Wimbledon victory, the recurrent back injury caused Hoad to cross the Atlantic by sea for relaxation.

Temptation for the unduly controversial shift, in those days, to professionalism was already evident, professional guru Jack Kramer (Wimbledon winner 1947) hovering enticingly. The loss in New York gave Hoad pause for thought: professionalism offered such a superstar an ensured life security, yet was socially disfavoured. A personal moon-shot was required as a launch. Partnering Hoad to defend Australia's Davis Cup title in late 1956, Rosewall now accepted Kramer's bait. Hoad's injury persisted into early 1957, requiring a body cast for six weeks, but he then enjoyed 11 pain-free months and the most acclaimed pinnacle of his career. And, as we scribes used to claim before 24-hour television, 'I was there.'

Indifferent displays characterised the early months. Hoad was now a father and the Kramer incentive was mounting. His almost benign inconsistency, to the anguish of his millions of followers, remained: the lapses that were part carefree, part impatience, bullseye-or-bust, leaving him more rueful than sardonic. Yet his moment was imminent. For his second Wimbledon final, I had a beginner's yet perfect viewpoint with a press messenger's ticket available in the then standing area. Admission access was available only at midday ahead of the all-night queue and was followed by a sprint courtside and a two-hour wait for play. My wife and I, courtesy of an unwanted additional *Times* pass, were positioned leaning on the spectator waist-high wall mere yards from the service line. Our own private apex.

Hoad himself had a problem, as he related in his autobiography two years later, 'I was far from confident driving out to Wimbledon. Then, knocking up with South African Gordon Forbes, I broke a string in my favourite racket. Jenny immediately took it by car to the nearest sports shop in Wimbledon, but they couldn't do it. She raced on to Kingston, had it repaired and rushed back to Wimbledon, dispatched it on court ... by which time I had won the first set. I changed rackets and now felt assured.'

Assured? Here, in 90-degree temperature and with some spectators fainting, was a display beyond imagination: an onslaught against an exceptional opponent now demolished by a hurricane of power and expertise. The totality of Hoad's stroke play that afternoon may arguably have never been witnessed before or since: winner after winner, volley upon volley, blistering Cooper's vain defence. As someone who had played football twice at Wembley, had run at the White City Stadium, I could hardly credit, as an athlete at close quarters, the perfection of a young man of almost mythological dimension.

Hoad himself was disarmingly modest. 'I served as well as I have ever done,' he wrote, 'and hit many aces ... This was the kind of tennis I had dreamed since boyhood I might one day be able to play. I had had the feeling that somewhere in the future, probably around the age of 22, I would mature, that racket and ball would be, for a short period of time, within my control. This was it ... I relished every stroke, yet I was sorry, as I had been the year before against Rosewall, that such a likeable person had to lose.' In a straight-sets victory, a mere 57 minutes, Cooper, champion the following year, had won only 30 points.

London's *Daily Mirror* reported, 'Hoad served more aces than a crooked gambler.' The *Daily Telegraph*'s doyen considered, 'It was a display of genius and it has to be doubted if such dynamic shot-making was ever sustained with such accuracy. He was super-human.'

An hour after triumphantly holding aloft the trophy for the second time, Hoad had decided to swallow Kramer's hook. It was an emotionally conflicting step. As he recalled, 'I knew it was inevitable that some people would be hurt, that in tennis circles I would be condemned, but I believe that all my critics would have done the same in my position … There was too big a risk that my back injury would recur, there would never be a more opportune moment. The end of big signing-on fees for amateurs turning pro would soon arrive – I should collect Kramer's offer of $125,000 before it was too late.' As he and Jenny boarded the flight to America and a life-changing contract, he further reflected, 'At 22, the battle I fight with myself [for consistency] was on again. Behind was a way of life that had gone forever.'

The feared criticism quickly came. Sir Norman Brookes, Wimbledon's chairman, urged the English Lawn Tennis Association to sue (for what was unknown). The *Sydney Morning Herald* alleged, 'Morally, he cuts a very poor figure. There is much force in Sir Norman's comment that Hoad could not have done this in a shabbier way.' There is no infringement more stinging than that against virtue-blind aristocracy, as many honourable sportsmen were to discover in legitimate conversion to paid employment.

Not that this concerned Kramer, who forecast Hoad's enlistment as 'the greatest attraction of all time … potentially the best player tennis might ever have'. So it would prove, though concern about continuing back strain was sadly well founded. Yet not before Hoad had cast his magic – now lost to an adoring worldwide audience at major venues – before new, as it were anonymous, crowds at comparatively less known, often indoor venues marvelled at the sight. Hoad's professional advent was exhilarating: a grass-court tour in Australia, head-to-head with reigning pro champion Gonzalez which Hoad led 8-5. Continuing in the USA, Hoad led 18-9 by early February, the formidable Gonzalez losing confidence. Yet Hoad's back trials saw him falter, ultimately surrendering the marathon series 36-51; in spite of which he had earned in one year a quarter of a million dollars, at the time a fortune. His stamina, when fit, remained astonishing: in one four-day consecutive-match spell, including overnight flights from Kenya to Pakistan and then India, he survived without a single main meal. Kramer worked you hard for the money.

On the 1959 tour, now including Cooper, Hoad led Gonzalez 15-13 head-to-head in matches, but finished second overall in the professional group, 42 wins to 20 defeats compared with Gonzalez's 47-15. This season might be regarded as Hoad's professional summit, his injury progressively more inhibiting; though in 1961, in the inaugural Kramer Cup (equivalent of the Davis Cup) he defeated Trabert in four sets, Trabert recalling, 'Trying to stop Lew in the final set was like fighting a machine gun with a rubber knife.'

Returning to Wimbledon in the late 1960s, when Open tennis finally arrived – for which I had vigorously campaigned – Hoad was but a shadow of past majesty. For several years I ghosted his Wimbledon column for the *Sunday Telegraph*: prolonged, humorous evenings including Jenny spent dining down Kings Road with a gentle-mannered legend who never wanted to talk about himself. He was to die of leukaemia at his Spanish coaching ranch in 1994.

Let Gonzalez and Rod Laver, twice a Grand Slam quartet champion, spell Lew's epitaph. Gonzalez, twice US (Amateur) champion, a towering presence on Kramer's pro-tour until past 40, wrote for the *New York Times* in 1995, 'At his peak, Lew was unplayable – I think his game was the best ever. At my best, he was better.' Laver, interviewed in 2019, said, 'The best player who ever held a racket. He had every shot in the book and could overpower anyone.'

My own memory: just grateful to have witnessed, and shared, a tiny fraction of this remarkable life – Hoad was a mirror of Australian national pride, a sporting god devoid of vanity.

JOHN CHARLES
The Gentle Giant

'Maybe I wasn't nasty enough'

Wales to win FIFA's World Cup? We were not to know it at the time, but the late 1950s were that country's halcyon era, with four supreme performers in the side. Sport, like life, can hinge on a single error, an injury, an injustice. In Sweden in 1958, Wales possessed in John Charles arguably one of the most complete players the game has ever known: physically, technically, temperamentally, and I have seen most rivals since the Second World War. Backed by the assured Jack Kelsey in goal, the wizardry of Ivor Allchurch in midfield and the electric, elusive Cliff Jones on the wing, Wales rather than either Sweden or ultimate winners Brazil could have been in the final. Charles, adored in two nations – the other being Italy – could have catalysed unheralded triumph. Having attended 14 final tournaments, of that I am convinced.

The Wales FA did not believe so: drawn in the first round against supposedly dextrous Hungary, losing finalists four years earlier, and hosts Sweden, they had booked unexchangeable return tickets for the end of the preliminary round. However, fate – an injury and two inept referees – closed the history book on Wales's sole finals appearance.

John Charles was born in Swansea in 1931, the elder brother of Mel, who was to play alongside him as an able Wales defender. John joined Swansea's ground staff at 14 and his only senior appearance was for the reserves in the Welsh Football League and he was scouted by Leeds United, with a trial in 1948 aged 17. His mother, a naïve local, warned the scout that John couldn't sign because 'he hasn't got a passport yet'. He duly signed, in the wake of all those Swansea-generated talents such as Kelsey, Trevor Ford, Jones, Terry Medwin, Allchurch and Roy Paul.

Arriving in Yorkshire, young Charles was admonished by extrovert Leeds manager Frank Buckley for politely responding under questioning, 'Yes, Sir.' None of that, barked archaic Buckley, who responded, 'Call me Major.' No one ever quite knew when, where or how that title was acquired. Charles was trialled in various positions before his first-team debut at centre-half in a friendly against Dumfries club Queen of the South in April 1949. He was marking centre-forward Billy Houliston, who a week earlier had run rings around England's defence in a 3-1 rout: the Scotsman's verdict on Charles was simple, 'The best centre-half I've played against.'

On one occasion, the eccentric Buckley had the squad ballroom dancing in an attempt to elevate 'cohesion'. A Football League debut shortly followed against Blackburn Rovers, but for two years Charles was often absent for National Service with the 12th Royal Lancashires, oscillating between the Army XI and Leeds. Simultaneously, he earned a reputation as an accomplished heavyweight boxer, winning 11 bouts until banned by the Amateur Boxing Association as a football professional. We must suspect that his innate nature, devoid of aggression, would have limited a ring career.

With his benign courtesy, he ranked alongside renowned American-Indian Olympian all-rounder Jim Thorpe. There is the memory of him in the mid-1950s harassed by aspiring Manchester United midfielder Wilf McGuinness, Charles murmuring approvingly, 'Nice tackle, son.' Only once was anger ever evident after a brutal foul on brother Mel in a World Cup qualifier against Austria in Wrexham. Returning from National Service in 1951, he remained at centre-half until the following year then switched to centre-forward, immediately scoring 11 goals in six matches. He was appointed captain in 1955 and promotion to the First Division was gained with Charles scoring 29 goals in 42 matches; the following season 38 in 40 as Leeds finished in eighth place. In eight years his club tally was 154 goals in 318 appearances. Jimmy Armfield, the celebrated Blackpool and England right-back, recalls a Christmas Day match in 1956 in snow-bound Yorkshire when Charles scored twice in a 5-0 rout, 'An amiable genius … never fouled anyone in his life.' Invited by a club director, in a generous bonus gesture, to 'fill up at my garage', Charles could only respond, 'I don't have a car.'

In the autumn of 1956 I saw Charles play for the first time. As a mere 'Staff Reporter' – no *Times* byline in those unglamorous days – I drove the then interminable 'minor' roads to Cardiff to report on Wales against Scotland in front of a 60,000 Ninian Park crowd, and a 2-2 draw with Wales twice leading through Ford and Medwin. Aged 21, by now familiar as player and regular spectator of the professional game since the age of 15, I had an established sense that outstanding players – such as Matthews, Finney or Haynes of England – were uniformly of medium height, having a low centre of gravity that enhanced an instant change of direction.

While there were defenders such as full-backs Ramsey of Spurs and Byrne of Manchester United who, crucially, imposed coherence from the defence, it was a revelation now suddenly to see Charles, as tall and almost as robust as any hoof-it defender, with a refinement to dream of. I believe it is no exaggeration to suggest he is the most accomplished and graceful *tall* player of all time; ahead of, say, Franz Beckenbauer of then West Germany on account of Charles's prodigious goalscoring.

John Charles was more or less the progenitor of the tide of leading British players who began to be tempted across the Channel following the Second World War – Neil Franklin, the Stoke City and England centre-half, left on the proverbial vain goose-chase to Colombia. Charles's venture in 1957 was a fortune-loaded incentive that set the subsequent pattern for Jimmy Greaves (Chelsea to AC Milan), Denis Law (Manchester City to Torino), Kevin Keegan (Liverpool to Hamburg), Trevor Francis (Nottingham Forest to Sampdoria), Steven Archibald (Tottenham to Barcelona) and Gary Lineker (Everton to Barcelona), among others.

Arsenal and Manchester United were both willing to invest in excess of £40,000 for Charles, yet Juventus of Turin led the bidding and Charles succumbed. Who wouldn't? A £10,000 signing-on fee alongside spectacular win bonus, plus a luxurious apartment. There was a waiting crowd of 20,000 at the airport, fronted by club president Umberto Agnelli, the Fiat supremo; their eagerness not unconnected with the fact that Juventus were languishing at the foot of Serie A, having finished ninth in the previous season and not having won the title for five years. The chemistry was instant: in the opening encounter with Verona, goals from Omar Sívori and Giampiero Boniperti held the game at 2-2 then up came a Charles winner. The following week his was the only goal against Udinese, followed by a third successive winner against Genoa.

The triangular attacking formula, with effervescent Argentinian Sívori and the rapier Boniperti, created an eruption in Italian football. Moreover, Charles's unassuming demeanour, so in contrast to Italian emotions, made him that much more the hero. A negative aspect would be Agnelli's repetitive reluctance to release his new dynamo for international duty with Wales; Charles having caught global attention with a particular performance against then outstanding Austria in a qualifier for the 1954 World Cup.

Spectacularly, Juve's trio combined to lift the club's tenth title in Charles's first season: he would proceed over five seasons to lead them to two more, and also two Italian Cups, scoring 105 goals in 178 matches in the world's most defensive league: *Il Gigante Buono,* the Gentle Giant. In one FIFA poll to elect a global XI, Charles was named as both centre-half and centre-forward! With his habitual understatement, he considered that Alfredo Di Stéfano of Real Madrid was the most exciting opponent, while 'the best I have ever played *with* was Sívori'. Juve fans, retrospectively, rated Charles superior to Michel Platini of France, a hero 20 years later.

Awaiting Wales in the first round of the 1958 World Cup were Mexico, consistent Latin American qualifiers; Hungary, whose Magical Magyars had captivated audiences at Helsinki's Olympic Games of 1952 but had unexpectedly and controversially lost the final of 1954 to West Germany with the famed Puskás unfit; and Sweden, supposedly an unknown quantity because, in a nation with a less than fully professional league, the majority of their top players performed with foreign clubs.

Because most nations enjoy minimum preparatory practice, any World Cup tournament is something of a lottery; dependent either on how well elite players co-ordinate over two or three weeks, or if a coach's strategies in defensive organisation are tellingly effective. Wales would need a bit of both, driven by a personable coach in Jimmy Murphy, deputy to Matt Busby at Old Trafford. He had at his disposal not only Charles, but one of the world's safest keepers in Kelsey, a reliable workhorse wing-half in skipper Dave Bowen, a master schemer in Allchurch and one of the world's most dangerous wingers in Jones, though there was a lack of depth in reserve. As stated, fortune was not to shine on the squad.

For the opener, Hungary – with only three of their former maestros, Grosics in goal, central schemers Hidegkuti and Bozsik, in the wake of disintegration inflicted by Soviet invasion – fell far below expectation. So, though Bozsik's early goal was levelled by Charles's massive header from a corner, a Uruguayan referee miserably failed to curb the rampant physical intimidation of Charles, even if a draw was better than had been forecast.

Next, in Stockholm, underdogs Mexico gained their first finals point in a match Wales should have coasted. Jones was off key while Charles lacked an effective striking partner, lonely and searching for openings in a wandering role. Here was a contrast in styles: Wales's conventional 3-3-4, depending on striking wingers who were not there on the day, was often outrun by Mexico's ten chasers, flinging the ball around in a possession game that had their opponents bewildered. With Charles isolated, a 32nd-minute goal from Allchurch was levelled by Belmonte in the last minute: an expected victory had gone begging. To Hungary's irritation, Sweden, in the wake of two successive wins, played four reserves in their third match, but again Wales underperformed in a goalless draw, Charles playing deep in search of the ball and seldom in range of the net. In an era before goal-aggregate relevance, a play-off against Hungary for a place in the quarter-final now lay ahead.

I missed this Stockholm encounter, sent instead by *The Times* to the play-off against Czechoslovakia by Northern Ireland, who metaphorically had been pulling up trees. With Scotland fallen, Ireland and England each failed in the play-offs, with Wales triumphant against Hungary – at a price. A first-half lead by Tichy, projected inheritor of now faltering Hungarian glamour, was dismissed with second-half goals from Allchurch and Medwin, but a lamentable Soviet referee, Nikolai Latychev, did little to impede repetitive thuggery on Charles by Hungarian defenders. Allchurch's superb volley from a flicked pass from Charles revealed for the first time in the tournament the true Welsh potential, but the damage had been done. With no substitutes allowed, Charles, despite relentless physiotherapy for three days, was obliged to advise Murphy that he should not be risked for the quarter-final against an as yet unconvincing Brazil.

For the first time in four outings, Wales came close to generating authority. Hopkins, a steady left-back from Spurs, commendably subdued the tortuous Garrincha; skipper Dave Bowen in midfield grittily contained flamboyant Zito and Didi; Kelsey was Fort Knox between the posts. Though often on the back foot, Wales remained defensively sound and there was no score with less than 25 minutes remaining. At this moment, 17-year-old Pelé emerged: his deflected shot wrong-footed Kelsey and Brazil were semi-finalists.

The ebullient Cliff Jones, with whom I have shared laughter and arguments across South America and Europe along the years, retains a clear memory of 1958: 'For sure it would have been different with John against Brazil. He was the linchpin at centre-forward – and they were definitely suspect in the air in central defence, vulnerable against his heading power, and with him we certainly might have won. With John in form, you'd fancy that against anyone, psychologically he was such a leader of the team. There was only one John Charles – *everything* was different if he was there.'

Remorseful about his injury, from his Turin treasure chest Charles had promised the entire squad a personal bonus if they won. A semi-final against talented but erratic France or Sweden? Who knows. Would Charles have turned the tide against Brazil? Here was a player who could head the old leather ball from his own penalty area to the halfway line.

For all his infatuation with Italy and Italian football, by the early 1960s the lure of the valleys 'back home' was beckoning. Charles returned to Leeds; the man with the soft baritone voice ever ready with a Welsh song. Yet the balletic touch was fading and he went back briefly to Roma, because he also missed 'the weather, the food, the people', his nature an ever stronger bond than his unique talent. Roma, however, proved at 31 an illusion so he was home again, to Cardiff City, in 1963 for £25,000, with 19 goals in 66 appearances, and onward to non-league Hereford, then Merthyr as player-manager. Self-effacingly, he later recalled, 'I fancied being a manager, but I don't think I was good enough. Maybe I wasn't nasty enough!' As manager he was carefree to the point of casualness, a fault that condemned him likewise in business. He would arrive in the dressing room shortly before kick-off, exclaiming 'right lads, off we go'. Yes, they would say, but who's in the team? When two players died in a car crash, he was later found in the bath in tears. Appointed youth team coach at Swansea after Merthyr, he sometimes could be found painting the grandstand. At his sports shop in Cardiff, he lavishly gave away goods to friends.

Civilian life is not a comfortable switch from stardom. Charles's football fortune diminished, and public-house ventures around Leeds floundered because of that good-natured generosity to guests. He light-heartedly said in retirement that he wasn't envious of modern astronomic wages, 'We were glad of what we got.' Women adored him because he was strong, modest and kind; men because he personified their fantasised dreams yet was never boastful. A living tonic for ordinary folk, the more so in the tribal, melodic environment of Wales.

Giampiero Boniperti, captain of Juve when Charles arrived, said of him, 'John was from another world because of his humane qualities – one of the most loyal and honest people I have ever met. He kept the whole team united – arguments quietened as soon as he appeared in the dressing room or on the pitch.' Jack Charlton, Charles's Leeds colleague, regarded him as 'the most effective player I ever saw, who made the most difference in the performance of the whole team'. International referee Clive Thomas reflected that with 22 players of Charles's calibre, there would be no need for referees, 'just time-keepers'.

Honours were many before his death from a heart attack in 2004: a CBE in 2001, the John Charles Stand at Elland Road, and a bust in the entrance hall. Yet what he gave above all, uniquely in two countries, through his nature and in rare combination with mastery of a ball, was that sense of identity which binds together humanity, whether humble or eloquent.

ALFREDO DI STÉFANO
Introducing 'Total Football'

*'I never saw such a
complete performer'*

It is difficult to compare tenors Luciano Pavarotti and Charles Anthony Caruso. Recordings of the latter more than a century ago are, at best, unflattering. Likewise, any judgement of elite sports performers prior to and after the arrival of television can be misleading. Nonetheless, let me be bold: if there is general agreement that the five most eminent footballers have been three Argentinians, a Dutchman and a Brazilian – namely Di Stéfano, Pelé, Maradona, Cruyff and Messi – I consider the broadest gifts belonged, before television carried to every household, to Di Stéfano.

Earlier than Di Stéfano by 11 years was Stanley Matthews, globally acknowledged in the 1930s as mesmerising, and of whom Pelé himself said 'he showed us the way', but even as someone who idolised Matthews from boyhood, I regard Di Stéfano as the ultimate: not because of exceptional technique, subtlety, goalscoring or physical elegance, but the manner in which he could control like no other the whole pitch from penalty area to penalty area: a capability bordered by Messi.

It is often claimed that the Dutch, through coach Rinus Michels and Johan Cruyff, initiated 'Total Football', though that rightly belonged to Hungary, as revealed in the early 1950s. Simultaneously to Hidegkuti with Hungary, Di Stéfano was introducing the concept with Real Madrid when he arrived hot foot from Millonarios of Bogota, Colombia, in 1954. Yet Di Stéfano was so much more than a master tactician, directing counter-attacks from his own goalkeeper. He was a technical magician, as I witnessed in a World Cup qualifying tie in Cardiff in 1961, when he was aged 35. With the score 2-2, and Wales having a real possibility of reaching the finals for a second time, Di Stéfano scored a winner of extraordinary dexterity. He possessed not only vision broader than 180 degrees around the direction he was facing, but a sixth sense on the flight of a pass coming from behind. An angled, dipping ball from adroit playmaker Suarez was floating over his left shoulder to fall several yards ahead as he sprinted forward towards goal. Somehow, while at full speed, he struck the ball as it overtook him, on the half-volley, steering it through a tiny gap between Wales's formidable goalkeeper Jack Kelsey and the right-hand post. How did he ever judge the ball's split-second bounce? All as effortless as raising a glass of Rioja. I have never seen a similar shot in 14 World Cup tournaments: taken with such aplomb, such lack of flourish, that the majority of the Welsh crowd were barely aware of such genius.

Zinedine Zidane, France's World Cup winner, who would fill Di Stéfano's boots years later at the Bernabéu Stadium, had an apt description of Di Stéfano's control: as though 'he had gloves on his feet'. That eminent critic Geoffrey Green of *The Times*, himself a celebrated centre-half for Corinthians of the 1920s, considered Di Stéfano the most complete player ever: likewise, Bobby Charlton, England's own Aladdin, who as a teenager was mesmerised by the vision: 'Wherever he is on the field, he is in position to take the ball, telling the goalkeeper or the full-backs what to do, influencing everything that happens. I never saw such a complete footballer, could not keep my eyes off him.' This echoes the assessment of Real's coach, Miguel Muñoz, 'His greatness is that with him in your team, you have *two* players in every position.'

The statistics only tell half of it. In his 11 seasons with Real, from 1953 to '64, they won eight La Liga titles with Di Stéfano scoring 218 goals in 282 matches, 27 in his first season for Real's first championship in 21 years. In the first five years of the new European Cup he scored in each of Real's five winning finals. His career total (in three countries) reached almost 500 goals in more than 650 matches (accounts vary). In only six appearances for Argentina when young, he scored six. There were four games for Colombia, while with Millonarios (unregistered by FIFA), and he scored 23 times in 31 appearances for Spain. Yet through irregular FIFA regulations, an Argentinian players' strike, Spain's non-qualification and his injury pre-Chile in 1962, he never played in the World Cup finals. In 1984, during the European Championships in France, I played alongside him in a charity match. At 58, his touch on a pass was still impeccable with barely a glance, and his instruction was incessant, 'Work, English. Work!' I was 49.

Born in July 1926 in Buenos Aires, of first-generation immigrant parents, Di Stéfano joined River Plate aged 18, played in the reserves, made his first-team debut the following year, impressed rivals Huracán and joined them on loan, scoring within ten seconds of his debut – against River Plate. Returning subsequently to his 'home' club in 1947, he strategically switched position from winger to centre-forward, and with 27 goals helped River Plate win the league title. The 1948/49 tournament was suspended due to the players' protests on status and rights. Di Stéfano nonetheless scored 13 in 27 appearances, River Plate finishing third. The intermittent players' strike continued into the following season with many players fleeing abroad, especially to Colombia, then outside FIFA's ambit. Di Stéfano joined flamboyant Millonarios, with whom – beyond FIFA control – he won three league titles in four years, and was the leading goalscorer three times, totalling over 70.

Many foreigners were briefly and disconcertingly tempted by exaggerated Colombian wages, including Charlie Mitten of Manchester United and Stoke City and England centre-half Neil Franklin. The bubble burst when Colombia became affiliated to FIFA in 1953, with most overseas players returning home, but Di Stéfano equivocally to Spain, having caught Real Madrid's eye during a Millonarios tour of Europe. Real attempted to pay Millonarios a fee, and so did Barcelona, but River Plate held his registration, his transfer to Colombia having been illegal. Barcelona agreed a deal with River Plate but the historic Castile–Catalan rivalry saw Real, with clandestine backing from President Franco, negotiating an absurd 'shared' transfer: Di Stéfano was to play for each club in alternate seasons. Amid moderate early displays by Di Stéfano, Barcelona lost faith and surrendered their 50 per cent 'ownership' to Real, whose gross transfer outlay, including match bonus payments, amounted to an alleged third of the club's annual income. It was to prove worthwhile.

Di Stéfano's impact upon his arrival in Madrid in the autumn of 1953, aged 27, could not have been more dramatic with a hat-trick in a 5-0 trouncing of Barcelona. More than goals, he revolutionised the strategy of the team, marshalling every phase of play with an undemonstrative authority which captivated the huge Bernabéu audience of regular six-figure totals. With his contribution of 27 goals in 28 matches, Real were champions for the first time in two decades. The second title, in 1954/55, earned entry to the inaugural European Champion Clubs' Cup. Besides Di Stéfano being La Liga's leading scorer for the third season running – though Bilbao won the title – Real, with talented Uruguayan Héctor Rial now added to the squad, disposed of Partizan Belgrade and AC Milan to reach the European final against Reims, who boasted the formidable Raymond Kopa and Just Fontaine. Real claimed the cup in Paris, coming from behind to win 4-3. For UEFA's first awarded Ballon d'Or, Stanley Matthews was acclaimed three votes ahead of Di Stéfano.

With Real having lost the Liga title, club president Santiago Bernabéu shrewdly negotiated with UEFA for the European Cup winners to be eligible to defend the title: thus Real did so, successively defeating Rapid Vienna, Nice and Manchester United, then Fiorentina 2-0 in the final. Besides this second European prize, Real began a remarkable sequence in La Liga of a consecutive run of home victories totalling 121, from 1956 to 1966, encompassing the domestic title in 1957 – repeated the following with Di Stéfano top scorer on 19, plus a third European Cup triumph over Milan, Di Stéfano having scored ten, including four in the 8-0 rout of Sevilla. Liga runners-up to Barcelona in 1959 – although Di Stéfano was the top scorer – Real, now with Ferenc Puskás aligned alongside Di Stéfano in an explosive attack, took their fourth European Cup, defeating Reims 2-0 after needing three matches to overcome Atlético Madrid in the semi-final.

During the 1959/60 season, Real signed Didi, a superlative midfielder for Brazil when winning the World Cup in Sweden in 1958. There was an inevitable clash of personalities in midfield authority with Didi seeking release from his contract, yet Real were due to unleash a performance never since replicated when scoring seven against Eintracht Frankfurt in their fifth European Cup Final in a row.

I had seen Eintracht destroy an ambitious Glasgow Rangers team in the semi-final, home and away. They were quick and electric in attack but, in front of a 125,000 crowd at Hampden Park in Glasgow, Eintracht themselves were over-run. Di Stéfano scored twice for Real to lead 3-1 at half-time. He scored a third and Puskás recorded four as Real galloped through a seven-goal cavalcade in a display never to be forgotten. For Di Stéfano, now 34, that was Everest: the following season Real lost their European semi-final to Barcelona – who then squandered a spectacular final against Benfica – and in the final of 1962 Benfica successfully defended the trophy against Real in what was the Spanish club's sixth final. The following year brought Di Stéfano's last La Liga title and at the beginning of 1964/65, with Real on tour in Brazil, he was kidnapped by the National Liberation Army of Venezuela from the team hotel. He was released unharmed three days later when the captors realised they could have done nothing more publicly damaging to their own interest.

At the season's end, Di Stéfano left for Espanyol, playing 60 matches and retiring aged 40 in 1966. In a grand gesture, Santiago Bernabéu staged a farewell match against Celtic of Glasgow in honour of the man who had donated memories beyond compare. It was a lasting sadness that, in the Spanish national team – for which Suarez of Barcelona was so long the playmaker – Di Stéfano had never been able to exert the supreme influence he had exercised with Real. Part of the problem arose when the national coach was Helenio Herrera, also from Argentina. If Di Stéfano had a flaw, it was being intolerant of alternative tactical opinion: truly an Einstein of this simple game.

CHAPTER FIVE

TELEVISION EXPANSION

MARIA BUENO
Pearl-Like Elegance

'The moment I have to think,
I cannot play'

A serious regret in my early career was that I floundered on a project of potential professional significance: ghosting an autobiography of one of the best known and most influential figures in tennis – Ted Tinling, player, umpire, fashion couturier, administrator in the women's inaugural professional tour, intellect and wit. Had I not faltered several weeks into the project in 1962, I would have gained more intimate insight into arguably the most glamorous sportswoman of all time: Maria Bueno. Of the many women, in multiple sports, it has been my task to describe, Bueno possessed a pearl-like elegance which in combination with her exquisite balance and timing made her court displays unforgettable. Tinling, creator of Bueno's on-court apparel in an era of sex discrimination when women's appearance for many still mattered as much as their ability – or more – perceptively understood the character behind this public queen.

At Tinling's request – following my writing a sequence of stories for the newly published *Sunday Telegraph* on his spell as youthful confidant of legendary Suzanne Lenglen on the Riviera, and subsequently high society couturier for debutantes – I had begun extended interviews with him, only for my preoccupation with football and the World Cup in 1962 in Chile to obstruct my momentum. In the book concluded by another writer, Tinling revealed the definitive comment by a spontaneous sporting genius, Bueno having told him, 'The moment I have to *think* about my tennis, I cannot play.' Tinling rightly observed that, as with parallel genius Lew Hoad, if you remove unorthodoxy, you take away the glitter. Bueno shone like a galaxy, a joy to behold, which made so many thousands happy to share her triumphs.

As Dan Maskell, the wise and veteran coach and commentator, recalled, 'I cannot remember Maria ever playing an ugly shot, even when under the severest pressure.' That is an exceptional analysis on a player who won 19 out of 35 Grand Slam finals (Australia, France, Wimbledon and US): seven singles (three Wimbledons, four US) and 11 doubles (with Althea Gibson, Sally Moore, Darlene Hard, Billie-Jean Moffitt/King, Nancy Richey and Bob Howe). As Tinling noted, Bueno's flaw was her strategic impracticality: no shot was perceived impossible, refusing to calculate the percentages – which, as anyone can confirm, within 30 or 40 years, had often boringly become the fundamental maxim for the majority of players. Bueno would simply become cross if she wasn't perfect.

Every shot was an attack: she hadn't heard of spin, that would be a compromise. When, seeded number three at

Wimbledon in 1963, she encountered in the women's final the wily Czech spin doctor Vera Sukova, Bueno capsized 6-4, 6-3. Yet three months later, on the then-grass Forest Hills of the US Championships, in the first of five Grand Slam finals with over-powerful Australian Margaret Court, Bueno won 7-5, 6-4: the two best players in the world, each the first Australian or Brazilian to have won at Wimbledon, artistry and grace versus power and athleticism. The following year, Court would have the upper hand on the hard surface at Paris, 5-7, 6-1, 6-2, only for Bueno to triumph at Wimbledon 6-4, 5-7, 6-3. Court won the final pair of the five encounters of the two titans, in Australia and Wimbledon. As a commentator who came to know Court quite closely, going sailing with her husband, I found the contrast in personality fascinating: Bueno was a contained extrovert, a fluent linguist in three or four languages, Court comparatively shy until she stepped on court and unleashed almost masculine ferocity. In terms of public appeal, Bueno was always the more magnetic, never mind Court's unparalleled string of tournament victories. Billie Jean King, who would win in Bueno's third Wimbledon final of 1966, gave fulsome tribute to Bueno's impact on raising awareness of the women's game, 'Maria caught the interest of fans during an era when men held centre-stage. She created the foundation of developments yet to come.'

Maria Esther Bueno was born in October 1939 in Sao Paulo. Both of her parents were tennis members of Clube de Regatas Tiete, and likewise her elder brother, Pedro, who represented Brazil in the Davis Cup before he was 20, and won the US Inter-Collegiate title while at Lamar State College, Texas. While Pedro was a natural baseliner, his sister had the instinct for volleying, attacking the net and searching for winners, modelling her service on former champion Bill Tilden from book illustrations. Most of her youthful opponents were boys as she climbed the ladder of local leagues, yet some were reluctant to confront this exceptional young woman as she took both under-14 and senior national titles simultaneously, revealing already rare potential in exhibition encounters with women already prominent on the international stage. A UK agency – to which I was at a young age willing to contribute, alias freelance, from minor tournaments at £1 a day – recorded that Bueno's daily schedule began at 2am, club practice was from 5.30am, she went to school by 8am, then homework in the afternoon, and bed by 9pm. She qualified to teach at primary school level by the age of 14.

It was not unexpected that in 1957 she should win Florida's Orange Bowl, and the following year, travelling abroad for the first time, she exceptionally took the Italian title in Rome. Suddenly she was already an international celebrity, continuing with titles in Wiesbaden, Dusseldorf and Bristol, then making her Wimbledon debut with four victories prior to losing a quarter-final in straight sets to the slightly more experienced 19-year-old Ann Haydon (subsequently Jones). Unperturbed, Bueno proceeded to rattle the cage of Wimbledon's elite by partnering Althea Gibson, the tournament's first black singles champion, to seize the doubles title with a straight-sets win against America's Margaret duPont and Margaret Varner. These were strictly amateur days: Bueno had been criss-crossing Europe on a second-class rail ticket. Now she was being feted back home in Brazil, drawing international attention to a nation hitherto little recognised, certainly in Europe, as the place 'where the nuts come from'.

Her celebrity had truly blossomed in 1959 when achieving her first Wimbledon title. A quarter-final straight-sets win against Germany's Edda Buding, was followed by a semi-final against Sally Moore for the loss of only six games, then claiming the silver rose bowl in straight sets against America's Darlene Hard, who was described by US journalist icon Budd Collins as 'incomparably balletic and flamboyant'. I agreed. I was there, but insufficiently senior in the journalistic tennis hierarchy to be recording the match.

Bueno would be ranked number one in the world during four of the next seven years – though there was no prize money. With the ladies' final being on a Saturday, friends had to persuade a local dress shop in Wimbledon to open up to acquire an evening dress for the ceremonial ball. Her linguistics were ready for the required speech, from which she sped off to take the US title, defeating the UK's current sweetheart, Christine Truman, for the loss of five games and becoming Associated Press Athlete of the Year ahead of all those baseball/football big guns.

Amid the clamour of fame, it was more than coincidental that Bueno carried Tinling's flag of fashion. In 1962, with Bueno having missed the previous year through illness, Tinling's proffered underskirt and panties, delectable on a supreme model, were in the All-England Club's mauve and green colours, and another in pink. Hide-bound members choked on their G & Ts and urgently instructed 'white clothing only'; over the years, this gender sensitivity would all but disappear.

A name that would be as illustrious in Brazil as later that of Ayrton Senna, Bueno's era was just too early for the professional game, playing only a single tournament in the 1970s yet thereafter being expectedly a permanent feature of media commentary footlights, forever remembered for shimmering athletic beauty. She died aged 79 in 2018, from skin cancer. The Senior Women's Team Championship is named in honour of this sporting orchid who concealed muscularity behind elegance.

BOBBY CHARLTON
A Sense of Duty

'The difference between us being average and being good'

On a grey afternoon, on 6 February 1958, I was on duty as sub-editor at *The Times*, standing beside the chattering Reuters news teleprinter as the National Hunt results from Fakenham or wherever flashed up on the tape. And then, 'Manchester United flight crashes at Munich'. An unimaginable horror was unfolding, for me, for millions of the club's followers, and for a global sporting world already aware of the glamour being created by Matt Busby's so-called 'Babes', among them 20-year-old Bobby Charlton – Busby breaking tradition by the introduction of teenagers into the first team. Many of the side, eight of whom died, were my contemporaries, and were emotionally the inspiration of a burgeoning journalist's career.

My very first published news contribution had been only 18 months earlier from Old Trafford, on the opening day of the 1956/57 season, in which the gifts of Duncan Edwards, Eddie Colman, Dennis Viollet, David Pegg and Charlton had overwhelmed FA Cup winners Manchester City. With his lifelong distinctive courtesy, Busby had left a complimentary grandstand seat and tea ticket for the wife of an unknown

Times man. In my comment on the match, I had written, 'They have everything, a bewildering profusion of talent but, supremely, a surging irrepressible youth … the man who moulds their fortune must indeed be happy at what he sees.'

For some years my wife and I metaphorically lived and breathed in sympathy with United's fortunes in the company of much of England. Unquestionably, the tragedy remained with Charlton thereafter forever, yet such has been his character that no other sportsman has presented publicly such a social ideal: modesty, sense of duty, commitment to hard work rather than grandstanding, club and national loyalty, social discretion, subordination of personal ambition to the team's interest, in an arena too often guilty of individual extravagance. As he recounted, 'I suppose a lot of my old man has rubbed off on my brother Jack and me. Dad was down the mine from the age of 12. We'd go to meet him from the pit, with only his eyes and teeth showing white. He never shirked, never took a day off work. He was frightened to death someone might accuse him of being lazy. He had great pride. You could see his character coming out in Jack when Leeds were losing.' A son of this close-knit mining family from Ashington, Northumberland, Bobby Charlton has epitomised the steadfast nature of our nation, internationally recognised and celebrated in his prime to the remotest corners of Europe, even as I once discovered in a mountain village in then Marxist Albania.

It was fortuitous, having been hurled from the stricken aircraft as it disintegrated on take-off from Munich, and being dragged to safety by heroic Irish goalkeeper Harry Gregg, that Charlton should still have become such an icon of the international game: 249 goals in 768 appearances for United; a then record 49 goals for England in 106 matches; winner of the FA Cup in his third final; two First Division titles; winner of the 1968 European Cup – the first by an English club; 1966 World Cup winner; being a member of four World Cup squads – 1958, '62, '66, '70.

Yet amid this fountain of exhilarating entertainment, he will have been haunted by a forlorn memory. In 1961, on the eve of a World Cup qualifier in Luxembourg – in which England scored ten – my wife and I found him in a bar adjacent to the team hotel, alone with a beer and lost in silent solemnity, emotionally adrift from a potentially exciting but inconsistent England team under a pleasant but distant manager, Walter Winterbottom, for whom Charlton was a technical extravagance.

For United, he was an attacking inside-forward: for England, he was a quicksilver two-footed left-winger, breathtakingly fast and a lethal scorer. 'Not that I liked it much on the wing,' he reflected. 'I was still playing inside for the club, but didn't tell Matt I wasn't happy with England. Mind you, we could beat anybody at Wembley, and I fancied us for the World Cup in Chile.' On the far side of the world, he was internationally voted the best left-winger in the tournament, where England seriously underperformed and were defeated by holders Brazil in the quarter-final, some players all too keen to return home. What drove Charlton, behind the grief, was the foundation of security at Old Trafford from Busby's benevolence. Charlton admitted to me that the time after the crash 'was a nightmare': tailed everywhere by the press, his private life scrutinised, so that matches became a refuge where he was safe from intrusion – and wondering if his best days were gone.

'There's no doubt in my mind, 'he recalled, 'that our pre-Munich side was the best I'd played in. There was this feeling that if we lost, it would be by one; if we won, it could be by ten. The team was special in many ways, the infection from the time you arrived, not playing for wages or bonuses but dedication to the club. What was unique was the *blend* – when we were really going, the balance was perfect. Matt Busby never did a lot in training, except join in. I honestly believe there was little you could teach them. As a youngster, I loved hitting long passes, showing off, but then losing possession to a defender. Jimmy Murphy, Matt's assistant, taught me the importance of the short game, and the value of *effort*. I'd never got that message before.'

Charlton made his senior debut in the 1956/57 season, scoring 12 goals in 14 appearances, with United retaining the title. There was the expectation of the century's first double when facing Aston Villa in the FA Cup Final only to be denied by a scandalous foul. With a Wembley standing ticket, I was a mere 20 yards from the incident when Villa's Ireland outside-left, McParland, jumped face-to-face at goalkeeper Ray Wood, his shoulder fracturing Wood's cheek: it was not even a free kick let alone a red card, there was no substitute, and centre-half Jackie Blanchflower went between the posts as United tumbled. Earlier, as England's first entry into the new European Cup, they had lost to holders Real Madrid in the semi-final. It was now, in their second European sortie, that a successful second leg quarter-final against Red Star Belgrade precipitated the disaster, having won 2-1 at home and then drawn a rough-house second leg in Belgrade 3-3 with Charlton scoring twice.

In the wake of the crash, Charlton returned for an FA Cup tie against Sheffield Wednesday on 1 March. Jimmy Murphy – absent from Belgrade when attending as manager a Wales World Cup qualifier – was unable to name a team until shortly before kick-off, signing in emergency veteran

Ernie Taylor from Blackpool and Stan Crowther from Villa, Wednesday having little stomach for a contest against tearfully dismembered opponents. England's regular captain and left-back Roger Byrne, centre-forward Tommy Taylor, and mighty midfielder Duncan Edwards were among the deceased. In a quarter-final, a similarly less-than-motivated West Bromwich Albion lost in a replay; a semi-final against Fulham, led by England captain Johnny Haynes, was drawn thanks to two goals by Charlton, with the replay won 5-3.

In their second consecutive final, with Busby now in frail recovery and sitting on the bench beside Murphy, United again stumbled. A controversial shoulder charge by Bolton's England centre-forward Lofthouse into goalkeeper Gregg's back was symbolic additional misfortune to a crippled club, which had predictably gone down in the European semi-final to Milan. Charlton recalled, 'Losing to Bolton didn't matter – what did, was that we'd maintained our position in the game, the glamour and identity, of being a top-class club. Matt, who'd just come out of hospital, came to give us a pep talk at Old Trafford beforehand, and just couldn't, he just cried. Those fellows who died were his family – an insight into how much the club meant to him.'

Only ten weeks after Munich came Charlton's international debut, a 4-0 defeat of Scotland with a characteristic volleyed goal from him. Two more followed against Portugal at Wembley, but his lame performance in a 5-0 friendly defeat in Belgrade triggered selectors' loss of faith, omitting him throughout the World Cup finals in Sweden. However, in the British Home Championship Charlton would score a total of 16 goals. He was a paramount cornerstone yet with reservations about the coach, Walter Winterbottom, who was subjected to FA selectors' whims. Charlton once said, 'What made things difficult was that you never played more than a couple of matches with the same players. England had no mental attitude for playing abroad at that time. We never seemed to go anywhere that mattered and win. I was dropped after Belgrade, but as a youngster didn't feel resentment. I was still seeing the World Cup in Sweden and not having to pay for it! I wasn't ready for international football, and Walter probably detected this.'

As he matured in Busby's steady rebuilding, Charlton's reputation with England became institutionalised with a hat-trick in the 8-1 defeat of the USA in 1959 and another in an eight-goal walloping of Mexico. With marriage, he gained a sense of security, but that was absent from England's Chile campaign in 1962, never mind a preparatory rousing run of performances at Wembley, with Jimmy Greaves of Spurs in rampant form. The time had come for a true professional coach in control of selection. Alf Ramsey, appointed by 1963, was unequivocally Charlton's man. 'It was immediately apparent with Alf that he didn't miss a thing. Footballers *need* telling. In his systematic way, it was the same with Alf wherever we went. He made you realise that you have to work for almost everything. I suppose that's why I always got on well with him. The fundamental difference between him and Walter was that Alf talked about the game like a professional. He'd been one. He didn't talk down to you. Although he very rarely coached individual players, he picked you because of what you did for your club, if he thought you could reproduce it at international level. He never tried to change people's style.'

Back home, Busby was spending extravagantly to lift morale, in contrast to the pre-Munich evolution of youth. The arrivals of full-back Cantwell from West Ham, midfielders Crerand and Quixall, Herd and Law, from Torino, in attack, alternately flourished or stuttered, Charlton too, until FA Cup success against Leicester City in 1963 injected new confidence. The ultimate infusion was the arrival from Belfast of flamboyant youngster George Best, simultaneously ally and rival of Charlton's, with equivalent individuality, if not temperamental equilibrium. Together they were to prime three illustrious seasons, within which Charlton and England would win the World Cup. Throughout, Charlton had an equivocal view of Best's brilliance, 'In one of his first games, he gave Angus of Burnley a real roasting. *Nobody* did that to Angus. George was a tremendous young player, he'd run for 90 minutes and was unique in being a forward who was a strong tackler. He became a top man quicker than anyone, the idolatry came so soon. By the time Matt or Jimmy came to say anything to him, maybe he thought they were jealous, though you could never talk about these years without talking about George. He'd drive you mad on the pitch, never pass, but you'd put up with him while he was scoring. People started criticising him when he was only 21, but the public had helped make him what he was, though in my opinion he was not in the same category as great players like Finney, Di Stéfano or Pelé. I just didn't understand him. It's your duty to give your best to the people who come to support you, but he seemed not to have a sense of duty to the public. If he'd played his cards right, he could have had the public in the palms of his hands for a long time.'

Expectation for England in 1966 was, publicly, to a degree muted. England had faltered in a 'trial run' at Rio's mini-World Cup in the summer of 1964; the press at home, especially in the north, were sceptical about Ramsey's tactics, his uncertainty about wingers. For only the third time, England were beaten at home by a foreign side, 3-2 by Austria, early in 1965/66.

The next match, against Northern Ireland, would be the last in which England would employ two conventional wingers, Peter Thompson and John Connelly. Yet all was about to change: profoundly, not only with Ramsey's tactics, but across the game internationally. On a bitterly cold December night, England gained their first victory in Spain with a performance that was doubly innovative and a turning point in Ramsey's career. He introduced for the first time a 4-3-3 formation with Stiles, Charlton and George Eastham in midfield, and Roger Hunt from Liverpool replacing Thompson in attack alongside Alan Ball and Joe Baker, which left no place for Connelly on the other wing. The two-goal victory was a revelation, and when England narrowly defeated Poland at home in January on the eve of the draw for the finals, I was among a minority to forecast World Cup victory, in an ITV documentary edited by Frank Keating of *The Guardian*.

Fast-forward to England's second match of the World Cup first round, following a hugely criticised opening goalless draw against Uruguay. Charlton sent English hopes soaring with one of his most spectacular of all goals in a victory over Mexico. He told the story in my history, *England's Last Glory*, 'I picked up the ball quite deep, no intention of shooting. I thought I'll carry it into their area, see what develops, you might get someone that doesn't mark. I didn't expect them to allow me to keep going. Had someone come at me, I would have laid it off to a colleague, but I just kept going, and all I could see was Roger [Hunt], diving in different directions, pulling their defenders, allowing me to go further and further, and I veered left, thought I'd shift position and have another look, brought it right, thinking I'm over the halfway line, and knowing it's lovely, at Wembley, because the ball runs so smoothly, and if you really whack it you've a fair chance ...

if they let me go another half-a-dozen yards, I'll have a dip, and I brought it to the left-hand side, Roger went off, taking a defender, and it just opened up, and I remember a full-back and thinking if *he* comes at me now, I've had it, but he didn't, and I just knocked the ball to the right and just thought, hit it in the general direction of the goal and let the goalkeeper worry about it, and it came off so sweetly, and when it was on its way, I thought, well *that's* the goal, and I was very pleased.'

With a controversial victory over France – a reckless foul by Stiles on Simon rousing threats from FIFA and demands from the FA that Ramsey discard his defensive midfielder – England progressed to a quarter-final with Argentina, and further controversy when on the half-hour their captain, Antonio Rattin, a supreme performer who was playing every deceptive trick in the book, persistently fouling, protested at the German referee's red card and took eight minutes to depart, with the entire team threatening to leave with him. With ten men, Argentina still remained defensively skilful until ultimately being deflated by 'newcomer' Geoff Hurst's near-post header. Charlton remembers, 'Argentina had the best defence in the competition, their back people were superb, big and strong and confident. *They* believed they were going to win the cup, but they were a bit frightened of us and needed to break us down, intimidating, not allowing us to play. If you pushed the ball past them, they'd always check you, stop you at all costs. Yet they were such good players.' Nonetheless, Charlton had reservations about his liberated midfield role with England, 'When I'd played on the wing, I'd disliked it, because I depended so much on other players to get the ball. In midfield, you're active all the time, you're in the game … the way we played in '66, you have to have discipline as well as skill, you had to have fit players. The legacy was that everyone afterwards thought, "That's the way to play," but overlooked the fact that you need really good players. So subsequently Alf was crucified for our formation, but it wasn't his fault.'

A semi-final against Portugal posed a threat for England as they possessed thus far the tournament's most impressive performer, Eusébio – but Stiles effectively marked him out of the game, and a 2-1 victory carried England to the final. Charlton recalls, 'We had respect for Portugal, but were confident we would win. In fact, they were stronger in the semi-final than we'd expected. I'd felt there was no one who was likely to score against us. I bet none of the teams who played us *enjoyed* it. We made other teams *work*.'

At 28, the final against West Germany was for him both climax and tactical compromise: the subordination of his natural free-flowing instinct so as to accommodate Ramsey's direction of neutralising the danger from the opposition's most accomplished midfielder, playmaker Franz Beckenbauer. In effect, while the match was being won and lost either side of these two, neither of them seriously dictated the tactical structure in their mutual role of shadowing opposing game-changers – an observer rather than a partner in Hurst's match-winning hat-trick. On England's crucial third goal, Germany having snatched extra time at 2-2 very late on, Hurst pivoted to hook Alan Ball's cross against the crossbar, from where it bounced down and was headed behind. Charlton remained equivocal, having watched many re-runs, 'These probably show it wasn't a goal. My inclination at the time was that it was, I'd moved forward in case Geoff turned it square to the left, so I was in a reasonable position to see.' A 'Soviet' linesman from Azerbaijan, who was ill-placed to have judged, consulted with the Swiss referee and, with no shared language, awarded the goal.

Wembley would be Charlton's penultimate reward: across the world he had become to British sport what WG Grace had been to cricket. He was, reflected former England captain Jimmy Armfield, our trump card. Charlton himself recalls that though victory was not the end of his career, there was little now at which to aim, 'I'd like to have won away from home in Mexico, but having said that, everything was an anti-climax after '66. It was the end of any ambition you ever had. The World Cup was the end of the line.' Brother Jack, England's stoic central defender, put his finger on the balance of 1966, 'Bobby was the difference between us being average and being good.'

Regaining the First Division title in 1966/67, United were back in the European Cup. Consecutive victories against Hibernians (Malta), Sarajevo, Górnik Zabrze (Poland) and Real Madrid – a cliff-hanger at the Bernabéu Stadium, coming from 3-1 down in the second leg to earn a draw, with a late goal from Munich survivor Bill Foulkes – setting up a final against Benfica at Wembley. This was, however, no great United side: Law was gone, replaced by bubbling youngster Brian Kidd, up front alongside Best; Charlton and Crerand the midfield brains, Stepney the agile guardian in goal, the aged Foulkes still there. Key to victory was, as in the World Cup semi-final, the commanding restraint of Stiles on Eusébio. In the 55th minute, a rare headed goal by Charlton put United ahead, Benfica levelling ten minutes from time before the save of a lifetime by Stepney from Eusébio ensured extra time. Now came a bonanza from Best, a waltzing showboat solo goal, followed by Kidd's header from Charlton's cross, and a final stab by Charlton for 4-1.

As the final whistle sounded, Charlton collapsed in relief: the debt to Busby honoured, 12 years of unfailing, dedicated commitment to club and country, and a knighthood assured. A cultural pennant forever alongside Robin Hood. There remained the 1970 World Cup in Mexico, this time a thwarted quarter-final against Germany at Leon, losing 3-2 in extra time after surrendering a 2-0 lead with only 20 minutes remaining. Goalkeeper Peter Bonetti, deputy for a suddenly sick Gordon Banks, was at fault with all three goals. With Charlton justifiably substituted following Germany's first, to save him in 100-degree heat for the semi-final, Ramsey had been correct. Charlton's glory had closed at Wembley.

Franz Beckenbauer later admitted to me, 'England threw away a match they had won,' while Bonetti was revealed to have been undermined by a domestic issue leaving him emotionally ill at ease. Ramsey was unaware of this, and the optimum reserve goalkeeper on the day should have been Alex Stepney, club colleague of the maestro who defined sportsmanship across five continents.

JIM BAXTER
Shameless Irreverence

'Everything I did was instinctive'

Where lies the responsibility of a professional footballer: to himself, to the team, to the public? With Jim Baxter, arguably the most gifted player ever to grace a Scotland shirt, you could never really judge. Such was Baxter's character that it could always seem he was playing for himself, yet so sublime were his skills – almost exclusively with his left foot like Ferenc Puskás of Hungary – that his self-indulgence was definitively why the public so adored him. Yet alongside that indulgence, which bewildered opponents, was a shameless irreverence towards the conventional rules of life: escaping from the youthful travails of a miner's life, Baxter joyfully wallowed in readily available pitfalls: drink, gambling and, initially, the lure of a pretty girl. The first strategic move he made on signing for Glasgow Rangers from Raith Rovers, aged 20, for the then-record fee of £17,500, was to buy a Jaguar as metaphoric party-enhancing perfume.

Among the most illustrious players of all time, Baxter had effectively the shortest Rangers career, 1960–65, a glittering spell within which the club won league titles in 1961, '63 and '65, plus three Scottish Cups and four League Cups. Baxter played in all seven finals. In 1961 he was in the side losing 4-1 on aggregate in the inaugural European Cup Winners' Cup Final against Fiorentina. The self-indulgence, on and off the field, led to a crucial trauma in December 1964. Drawn against accomplished Rapid Vienna in the European Cup, the Austrians masterminded by renowned attacking centre-half Ockwirk, Rangers were winning 2-0 with a minute remaining. Baxter had incessantly embarrassed individual Rapid opponents with his provocative juggling of the ball when stationary. An exasperated defender, bent on retribution, broke Baxter's leg in a wild tackle; during four months' recovery, Baxter's drinking obsession became chronic, and he was never again quite the same scintillating force. The pride of a nation intent on its place in political and cultural history, most particularly in relation to its neighbour England as represented on the football field, had been seriously punctured, although there was one instalment yet to come in two years' time.

Not that the football in Vienna had been out of the ordinary. Intended, reckless, intimidating tackles were all part of the game in that era, by no means subliminal, even internationally. Several such players represented England and it was an accepted ethic internationally, as those such as Pelé and Maradona would discover to their cost.

Baxter, a realist, acknowledged the truth: that he owed a debt to brutality which in contrast allowed him to be such an entertainer. In an interview with an avid Rangers supporter, Labour MP Tam Dalyell (otherwise Baronet Sir Thomas Dalyell), Baxter admitted in retirement, in an era of stricter refereeing installed within the laws, 'I would never have made it in today's circumstances. I needed bastards like McNaught [Raith captain 'Iron Man' Willie McNaught], to allow me my reputation. I owed them.' His unwritten ambition had been to exact revenge for England's 9-3 thrashing of Scotland at Wembley in 1961: not for Baxter the erratic, physical, long-ball game which throughout the middle of the 20th century dominated so much of English and Scottish League football. Slim Jim, as he became known, had in mind a smarter cocktail – even if, at a time when England's Football League had abandoned its maximum wage edict of £18 a week, and Johnny Haynes, Fulham and England captain, was earning the first £100, Rangers would permit the hero of Ibrox Park no better than £45.

Although there are tales of exceptional Scotland teams of the 1920s, it is my opinion that the period of the '60s, embracing Baxter alongside John White of Spurs, Paddy Crerand from Celtic and Manchester United, Dave Mackay from Spurs, plus Denis Law with Manchester United, and Ian St John from Liverpool, was the finest ever, and not just because I was fortunate to have witnessed much of that brilliance on the international field. The first such moment came in 1961 when Scotland came within eight minutes of qualifying for the World Cup finals in Chile. They had qualified four years earlier for the finals in Sweden but had underperformed and were outmanoeuvred in the opening round by Yugoslavia in a fortunate draw, and then defeated by Paraguay and France. They were hamstrung like England with 'selection-by-committee', and with 'team manager' Matt Busby still recovering from Manchester United's air crash.

The omens for qualification for 1962 were promising. Czechoslovakia, their main rivals, were defeated 3-2 at Hampden Park in September, with goals from St John and Law (two). Northern Ireland had been routed 6-1 in Belfast in the British Championship: a 3-3-4 formation playing a rhythmic possession game, the midfield of White–Crerand–

Baxter probably the most fluent in Scotland's history, with Crerand – still at Celtic prior to moving to Manchester – the central ball-winner but adroit co-ordinator between two supreme playmakers.

However, with Scotland and Czechoslovakia the joint group leaders, a play-off was necessary at the 1928 Olympic Heysel Stadium in Brussels. Baxter, who had played in all the qualifying matches, floated the perfect cross for St John to head Scotland in front. After intense Czech pressure and three successive corners, right-back Hledik headed them level, only for St John to restore the lead within a minute. Yet reward was stifled: in the 82nd minute by Scherer's equaliser and buried by two goals in extra time. While this was the best Scotland team I saw across 60 years, Czechoslovakia would prove themselves worthy in Chile, narrowly losing the final to defending champions Brazil, who were without an injured Pelé. In the qualifiers for the 1966 World Cup, Baxter would play only twice, and he appeared in none for 1970.

While Baxter was conspicuously instrumental in Scotland turning the tables against England at Hampden in 1962 by winning 2-0, his pinnacle performance came back at Wembley the following year. With Dave Mackay replacing Crerand, he, Baxter and White ran the show, Baxter scoring both in a 2-1 victory, including an opening penalty: the Press Association agency comparing his performance with that of Hungary's playmaker Bozsik a decade earlier at Wembley. That England team contained only three of those who would win the World Cup three years later: Gordon Banks in goal, plus Bobby Moore and Bobby Charlton. In my account for the *Sunday Telegraph*, I wrote, 'Baxter and Mackay were the inspiration, silkily stroking the ball, now urgently, now leisurely, now arrogantly, sometimes as casual as a duchess stroking her pet dog – Baxter often standing still, left foot contemptuously on the ball, then suddenly accelerating out of sight.' Later in the season, Baxter would be among the Rest of the World XI, including Soviet goalkeeper Yashin, Brazilian right-back Djalma Santos, Di Stéfano from Spain, Eusébio of Portugal and Gento from Spain – celebrating the centenary of the Football Association, in a match against an England XI.

Another victory over England followed in 1964, by a single goal, but in the autumn would come the Vienna injury and the consequent alcohol-fuelled deterioration of this man indifferent to discipline in all areas, admitting at one stage, 'Everything I did on the pitch was off the cuff, instinctive. If I'd been a good boy, maybe the extravagant stuff would have been stifled ... the bevvy did my physique in, and the gambling did my brain in. Lots of people offered me advice, including Dave Mackay, but I just loved the booze. I would never have left Rangers [as he did in 1965] if I hadn't gambled away all my money.' The loss was thought to have been in excess of £250,000.

There was to be one last hoorah for Baxter in 1967, the alternate-year visit to Wembley. Transferred to Sunderland in 1965 for a then-record £72,500, he played less than spectacularly across 98 matches, but is remembered, gleefully by any Scot, for helping inflict a first defeat on the new World Cup holders. To behold the tartan hordes dancing before, during and more especially after a 3-2 victory, you might suppose Scotland had themselves just won the trophy: certainly they perceived themselves momentarily as heirs-apparent. What tended to be overlooked was the not irrelevant incident, an injury to Jack Charlton, England's centre-half, after only 11 minutes, leaving him limping up front – there were no substitutions in those days – in a misshapen formation.

Nonetheless, it was a stirring exhibition by 26-year-old Baxter with that magical left foot, taunting England at every turn. As the noted correspondent Geoffrey Green wrote for *The Times*, 'Cool, elegant and arrogant as he put his foot on the ball, reducing the tempo to walking pace while he teased the wounded bull like a matador.' No wonder the clans were chanting 'easy, easy'. Yet his colleague Denis Law, a partner in the destruction, disappointedly reflected that Baxter's lack of urgency – at one stage juggling the ball as if at the training ground while inviting an English challenge – had denied Scotland the possibility to hammer further goals.

Six months later, Baxter had moved again, to Nottingham Forest for £100,000: a grave mutual disappointment, returning after 16 months to Rangers, and retirement in 1970 – a broken meteor, his decline mourned by millions. Beside his elegiac touch, Baxter was respected, and would be remembered by many, for his dismissal of the bigotry, social and religious, existing between Glasgow's rival clubs, Celtic's Catholicism and Protestant Rangers. He had good friends at both clubs. As Dalyell remembered, 'For Jim, all of life was just a ball.' Appropriately, it might be said with irony, in retirement Baxter ran a pub: inevitable transplants saw his premature end aged 60, having epitomised that extravagance of character which Scotland for three centuries contributed to British globalisation.

GEORGE BEST

Rapturous Audience,
Ruptured Opposition

'Utter disregard for physical danger'

When recalling the six years' contribution to football of George Best's glittering entertainment – for that was the true span of his genius prior to decline – I am unsure whether to rejoice or weep. What might this fragile-seeming Northern Ireland wisp have achieved if given the temperamental stability of a Bobby Charlton or a Bobby Moore? His physical resilience against uninhibited defensive thuggery was, in fact, remarkable: a Houdini of the turf beyond the grasp of any jailor, who bewildered rapturous audiences as much as ruptured opposition.

The gifts of this eldest son of six siblings from a dysfunctional Belfast home were majestic, yet emotional equilibrium never matched his mercurial physical fluency. The relative brevity of his brilliance – a three-year peak yet never appearing with Northern Ireland in the World Cup finals – questions Best's inclusion among the 20th century's doyens. A meteor that ignited and then self-destructed within a maelstrom of adulation and Bacchanalian exotic distractions.

Lacking sound advice from an ageing Matt Busby or true friends, his fundamental partner was ultimately loneliness. Plenty were those who accelerated his alcoholic confusion: television's chat-show hosts industrious in pursuit of their own ersatz fame by eager association with the genuinely famous. The overflowing reception for a Beatle-haired sudden superstar, in 1960s pop culture, overwhelmed a teenager once so shy that, when invited by a scout for trials at Old Trafford, he fled home after the first two days. When, all too swiftly, he then surrendered to commercial glamour, to the attention of clambering women, media detailing the number he had bedded, we should better remember the number of full-backs he had buried: an uncontainable parade of dazzling goals scored with such insolent bravery he seemed demonstrably arrogant rather than inwardly insecure.

Yet the departing mother of his infant baby son would later distressingly say that she was 'unable to cope with two babies'. For a player who so vividly lived for the game, and the experience in which he thrived, Best's contradictory conduct was a literal tragedy regretted by all – colleagues, opponents, managers and public. Danny Blanchflower, celebrated prior captain of Northern Ireland and Spurs, reflected, 'George was supreme because he created surprise, to the mind and the eye, a refined and unexpected range with utter disregard for physical danger.' More so than any other maestro, Best could score equally with either foot, with his head, and could tackle like a tiger, despite his slender build.

He did not so much score the goal of the month, but of the year, or indeed the century. I saw one such, against West Bromwich Albion at Old Trafford. Surrounded by defenders 14 yards from goal, Best dribbled *away* from the penalty area, then pivoted through 180 degrees in two strides and flashed an arrow under the crossbar from some 20 yards past an unbelieving goalkeeper. This was his means of expression and it could be poetic. It is sad to say that it was often not representative of how his attitude varied off the field. Announcing his intended, premature retirement – not for the last time – aged only 26 in 1972, amid deteriorating form at Old Trafford in the aftermath of Busby's reign, Best unthinkingly did so via an exclusive news column on a day when Northern Ireland were losing to Scotland: a lack of courtesy to his country and to his club, to colleagues with whom in a team game all are interdependent. Best had come to consider, with Charlton and Denis Law no longer rampant, that United were too dependent upon him. Certainly, there was mounting disillusionment at Old Trafford; Busby's successor, young Wilf McGuinness, briefly, and then Frank O'Farrell struggling to find renewed coherence. Yet Best might have realised he himself was the figure with dynamic presence who might have helped inspire new arrivals to fresh triumph. I had seen this potential in March 1972. In effectively a two-man display at home to relegation-threatened Huddersfield, Best and Ian Storey-Moore, a record transfer from Nottingham Forest, played the opposition off the park. Yet Best's disaffection – and physical fitness deterioration – would continue over the next two years until his departure under the new reign of Tommy Docherty.

Born in May 1946, academically quick-witted, Best passed the 11 plus but soon focused on football, and was then 'discovered' by United's scout Bob Bishop. Following initial hesitancy, he made his first-team debut aged 17 in September 1963, and captained the side that won the FA Youth Cup next spring, having scored six goals in 26 first-team appearances.

The following season, United won the First Division title and reached the FA Cup semi-final, losing to Leeds; Best contributed 14 goals in 59 appearances as United qualified for the next season's European Cup. The latter was to create Best's overnight international aura with two goals in a quarter-final against previous champions Benfica, in Lisbon – Portuguese media labelling him 'the fifth Beatle' and Best returning 'on stage' at Manchester Airport sporting a provocative sombrero. From that moment was his trajectory now shaped, though United would then stutter in the semi-final.

The title was regained in 1966/67, with re-entry to the following season's European Cup quest: Busby's enduring ambition. A daunting semi-final against six-time winners Real Madrid hung in the balance when United trailed in the second leg, Best having scored the lone goal at home. A rare late strike by full-back and Munich survivor Bill Foulkes for a 4-3 aggregate squeezed United into a final at Wembley – against Benfica. Prior to that climax, Best had become the youngest recipient of the annual Football Writers' Association Footballer of the Year award. Wembley witnessed a tilting struggle with the score 1-1 at full time. Three minutes into extra time, a dazzling solo run through Benfica's defence by Best, and a dummied swerve to send the goalkeeper lunging the wrong way, crowned his global reputation, rolling the ball into a deserted net. Further goals by Bobby Charlton and young Brian Kidd sealed Busby's and United's joy. For Best came added honour with UEFA's Player of the Year award. As trophy defenders, United would fall to Milan in the following season's semi-final, a by now declining domestic team dropping to 11th at the season's end.

With McGuinness having succeeded Busby at the helm, form improved to eighth place in 1969/70, Best scoring

23 goals including an FA Cup record six on a mud bath at Fourth Division Northampton. The sixth was a pantomime event in which, stereotypically, he first sent goalkeeper Kim Book diving in the wrong direction. This display, on the one hand earning an invitation by football addict Prime Minister Harold Wilson to 10 Downing Street, had marked Best's return to the team following suspension: emotional jeopardy was already looming.

With O'Farrell having replaced McGuinness, another eighth place in the First Division was adequate; Best's contribution less so, never mind hat-tricks against West Ham and Southampton. In January the errant genius spent a week keeping fit with Carolyn Moore, otherwise Miss Great Britain 1971, rather than training with a ball in Lancashire; his 24 goals in 54 appearances nonetheless made him top scorer for the sixth consecutive and last time. Then followed the first 'retirement' announcement.

His, and United's, decline continued in 1972/73: Best AWOL in December on some romantic jamboree; Docherty replacing O'Farrell; Best again announcing retirement yet reappearing for the start of 1973/74; Best making his final United appearance in January against Queens Park Rangers then failing to appear for training the following week. Relegation was mutual as United dropped to the Second Division. Shared shame. In 361 appearances over 11 seasons, Best had scored 137 goals. He was to spend the next decade hedge-hopping the globe, from Israel to Los Angeles, appearances intermittent among 18 different clubs with diminished acclaim apart from exhibition spells with three emerging American clubs gratified to embrace a status symbol from the real game. On Best's 50th birthday, television pundit Parkinson claimed he was 'a remarkable man'. That had been gloriously true. For a few years with United, otherwise metaphorically and sorrowfully 'off sick', he displayed a kaleidoscope of skills which Northern Ireland had never been privileged to exhibit on the world stage.

KIPCHOGE 'KIP' KEINO
Godfather Of African Achievement

'We were proud of our country'

As African nations negotiated, should one say struggled, to climb post-Second World War towards independence and identity, one window on to a waiting world was the Olympic Games. The statistics are revealing. No African had then been in the final eight of any of the four events, 1,500m to 10,000m including steeplechase, from 1948 to 1960, bar Maryoro Nyandike of Kenya, who was sixth in Rome's 5,000m in 1960. In the seven Games up to Munich '72, there were only ten medal winners from Africa out of 84 in the four events, with only four golds: compared, for instance, with nine medals from the four events within a single Games such as Beijing '08.

Of the four golds in the period of 1948 to '72, two were by that metaphoric godfather of African sporting achievement, Kip Keino of Kenya. Among the Olympians I have known personally, from the 1960s, Keino is still today regarded as a paragon among athletes in both achievement and demeanour. He is among the most benign individuals I have had the chance to meet, as commentator and once fringe competitor, having devoted himself, with his wife Phyllis, to an orphanage for abandoned children. It was overdue when, at Rio's Olympic Games in 2016, the IOC president Thomas Bach awarded Keino with the inaugural Olympic Laurel for services to sport. And to humanity: the kind of person you are glad to know is present when you attend some convention reception around the world.

It was socially a complex path for a 20-year-old black athlete in Kenya's 1960s. I knew Reggie Alexander, Kenya's first white IOC member, elected in 1960 amid the emerging Colonial Protectorate from 1953 to '61, which grappled with Mau Mau terrorism. Alexander slept in an armchair, back to the wall, facing the front door with a rifle across his knees, fearing for his life during the uprising. I cannot be judgemental on his rationale: born a white man on inherited unbalanced colonial scales, but committed to Olympic non-racial ideals, within a newly independent national government from 1964, headed by secessionist Jomo Kenyatta. Against this background of domestic instability, Keino's equanimity through his racing career and with his spell serving Kenya's National Olympic Committee – of which he was chairman until 2017 – while supervising his orphanage and being a savant IOC member, was that much more impressive. Whenever I have met him, he is always conspicuous for being an administrator who has not 'an agenda that can't wait'. Sprint finisher, but always serene.

John Whetton, a prominent UK miler in the 1960s and fifth in Keino's Mexico 1,500m silver medal run remains in awe of Keino to this day. 'A wonderful athlete … and so modest! The way he ran in Mexico was phenomenal. He'd been the first black African to make an impact, at Tokyo in '64 in the 5,000. With 250 metres to go in Mexico, I felt I was on for a medal, but at that altitude I'd never felt so drained. A few years afterwards, I visited his home at Eldoret in the Rift

Valley – such a kind, warm man, and there on the walls were pictures of 28 Olympians from Kenya, who'd all been at his school, under his headmaster, an Irish monk.'

Born in Kipsamo, the Nandi district of Kenya, Keino's parents died when young and he was raised by an aunt, after school joining the Kenya Police. Running was spontaneous, initially at longer distances. Aged 22, he finished 11th at three miles in Perth's Commonwealth Games in 1962; two years later he attended his first Olympics at Tokyo, where he finished tenth and fifth respectively in the 1,500m and 5,000m. It was the year when his ability matured with world records in the 3,000m and 5,000m, plus two titles in the All-Africa Games at Brazzaville. His 13:50.4 in Tokyo's 5,000m final had been nothing special, but in Auckland he improved American Bob Schul's world record with 13:24.2. In August, Belgian Emiel Puttemans's 3,000m record had been lowered – Keino's first attempt at the distance – with 7:39.6. In a blistering year, he had taken both the 5,000m and 1,500m African titles, the 5,000m with 13:34.4, way ahead of compatriot Neftali Temu, and the 1,500m by nearly seven seconds in 3:41.1. Now the athletic world was alert to a Kenyan waiting to challenge the establishment of Europe and America. He did so at the Commonwealth Games of 1966 at Kingston, Jamaica, with three-mile and one-mile victories. The former was a major surprise with his defeat of record-breaking Australian Ron Clarke, Keino's 12:57.4 being a Games record, eight yards clear of Clarke's 12:59.2. In the mile, Keino led almost gun to tape, a challenge by Simpson of Britain round the final bend fading in the home straight for a ten-yard victory in 3:55.3.

Keino's performance at these Olympic Games, at an altitude of over 7,000 feet (2,200 metres) and when demonstrably unwell, was an astonishing achievement; competing in three events and departing with a gold and a silver medal, a triumph of mental and physical willpower. His own words set the scene prior to the 10,000m, 'I'd had some problems back home, serious cramps in my stomach. When I arrived in Mexico, I was taken to see a doctor with the German team, who diagnosed that I had gallstones. He told me that I should not run, that I would be risking my health, yet I had come to Mexico to represent my country, to win a medal for Kenya, and I was determined to do that. In my first race, the final in the 10,000, the pain became really bad, so bad that I stumbled off the track two laps from the finish and fell, but I managed to pick myself up and finish.' In falling off the track into the in-field, Keino was automatically disqualified, never mind that he completed the distance.

That experience would have deterred many from then considering the 5,000m. Not him. 'The next day, I still did not feel so good, but was determined to compete, to win that first Olympic medal. The semi-final had been fairly comfortable, I was running easily again, but in the middle of the final, the pain returned. I think I would have won, but for a mistake which I made together with my colleague Naftali. I had plenty of energy left and should have made my finishing burst earlier, but he and I simultaneously tried to accelerate into the second lane to overtake the leader, Gammoudi of Tunisia, and we collided, giving Gammoudi his chance. It was our mistake, and I was just behind Gammoudi at the line.'

The shock of the race was Clarke's failure, having set four world records at that distance in 1965 and '66, but though he had taken over the lead around the fourth kilometre he was then overtaken by Gammoudi and the two Kenyans, finally to finish fifth. Keino's fractional defeat by the Tunisian was two-tenths of a second.

And so to the 1,500m. Keino recalled, 'My stomach was now really bad again, and both the Kenyan team doctor and the German told me I ought not to run the 1,500, which involved three races, but I told them my name was not to be removed from the starting list. I knew Ryun of the US was the best, because he held the world record, but I still felt I had a chance, because I'd been able to get a measure of him in the semi-final. The pain was there again before the final. The bus from the village to the stadium was caught in traffic, so I jumped out and jogged the last couple of kilometres to the stadium. I was so tense and focused that I put the pain to the back of my mind, trying to look relaxed with gentle exercises in the warm-up, in two minds about how I should run: whether to go with the field, or run from the front. Some said that my colleague Ben Jipcho and I planned to make the pace, so as to extend Ryun, but really I ran my own race after Ben put in a very fast first lap. I wanted to open a big gap ahead of Ryun, and continued fast into the third lap, even though I was now in serious pain. I don't know where I got the strength from to keep going, but we were proud of our country and ready to sacrifice everything for a medal.'

For Ryun, the race would be his worst of disappointments. He was the world record holder at 880 yards, 1,500m and the mile, unbeaten at any distance for more than three years, yet had been undermined a month or so earlier by an attack of mononucleosis. Additionally, although he had been training in Arizona, Ryun was without altitude experience and never calculated that Keino would opt to run from the front, as he did from the second lap. Yet silently Keino was calculating, 'This is the race of my life – if I die, I die here.' With untold courage, he passed the 800m mark in 1:55.3, a pace no watcher considered sustainable, Ryun included. Yet on the final lap

Ryun was unable to draw closer than a dozen strides on the leader, who went on to win by nearly 20 metres, the widest margin in the race's Olympic history. Keino's new personal best lowered the world record by a phenomenal five seconds. 'That evening I was not feeling at all well, and the following day the German doctor gave me tablets that eased things. I continued with medicine for more than two months. I'd done my best in Mexico and was happy with what happened.'

That occasion would have marked Keino for life, and indeed it did. John Boulter of Britain, the eminent half-miler and persuaded against his own wishes to attempt the 1,500m in Mexico where he failed to make the final, reflected, 'Kip was the first of the Kenyan gods – in Mexico he was unassailable.' He still was four years later in Munich where, wholly without experience or any hurdling ability, he competed in the steeplechase: after only four previous races, he proceeded to set an Olympic record of 8:23.6, ahead of Jipcho, saying afterwards, 'I had a lot of fun, even if my style is not so good.'

From there on, his life would be dedicated, with his wife, to humanitarian work at home: their orphanage, a primary school and, opened in 2009, a secondary school. On receipt of the Olympic Laurel from IOC president Bach in 2016, Keino's response was modestly brief, 'Join me, and support the youth of the world to get the basics of humanity: food, shelter and education. Education not only empowers youth to be better citizens and future leaders, but helps the world to make positive changes.' The civilised world needs Keino's generosity.

Charterhouse School boxing team (author flyweight)

Author leads 220 hurdles against Oxford, 1953.

David Brough (third right) scores winning goal (3-2) against Oxford at Wembley, 1954, from author's cross (second left)

Cambridge University, 1955 (author seated far left). Bill Nicholson (back right)

Youthful Lionel Messi at 23 guides Argentina to Olympic title, Beijing '08.

Aiming for gold, Jess Ennis wows London 2012. (Image IOC)

Breaking the segregation mould, Lewis Hamilton's innovative F1 invasion.

Britain's sadly curtailed Olympic heart-throb Lillian Board.

Death symptomatic of life: for Jack Johnson, at the wheel, incensed when rejected by a restaurant.

Jim Thorpe, revered reminder of Native America's genocide.

Assessed by husband and LA Open partner George Zaharias, Babe Didrikson refines one of her nine sports.

Share-cropper's son Jesse Owens, ideologue who shamed Hitler, defined Olympic celebrity at Berlin '36. (Image IOC)

Winifred Brown, dauntless butcher's daughter, who navigated the clouds and the waves.

Joe Louis bridged prejudice: a hero for all Americans.

Trend-breaking Dutch mother, Fanny Blankers-Koen (far right) defies critics, inching past Britain's Maureen Gardner, London '48. (Image IOC)

Incomparable Emil Zatopek enters stadium for third Helsinki gold in his first ever marathon. (Image IOC)

Forever a Potteries man, Stanley Matthews at his statue unveiling.

Wartime charity match, back row (L to R) Rowe (Spurs), Mullen (Man U), Busby (Man City), Ellerson, Carter (Sunderland), Swift (Man City), MacDay Barnes (Arsenal), Mortensen (Blackpool), Welsh (Arsenal), Scott (Arsenal). Front row (L to R): Matthews, Joy (Casuals), Lawton (Chelsea).

Lew Hoad, such modest charm, such volcanic technique. (AELTC)

John Charles (third left) Leeds, Juventus and Wales hero, shares celebration with Wales colleague Trevor Ford (Swansea, Aston Villa), Stanley Matthews (Stoke, Blackpool and England) and Joe Mercer (Everton, Arsenal and England)

Geometric tactical genius, Alfredo di Stefano on parade for Real.

Maria Bueno's feminine grace concealed hunger for perfection. (AELTC)

Edson Arantes do Nascimento - Pelé at an 80th birthday tribute with Sir Bobby Charlton.

Jim Baxter, inspirational Scot, riding high above colleague Billy Bremner and Nobby Stiles, fashions 1967 Wembley victory over the World champions.

Crowning of a star, George Best returning from rout of Benfica, European Cup quarter-final '66.

Defying the doctors, a sick Kip Keino heads the field for record 1,500m Olympic victory at Mexico '68. (Image IOC)

Italy mere spectators at Pelé's apotheosis, World Cup Final 1970

Belfast heroine among friends: (Left to right) Arlene Hunniford, Mary Peters, Lorna McGarvey and Maeve Kyle.

Olga Korbut, the girl who startled the Olympics, Munich '72. (Image IOC)

Unwavering ferret's eye for any chance: Alex Higgins in 1990

CHAPTER SIX

INTERNATIONAL EXTRAVAGANCE

PELÉ
Too Good To Be True

*'I just always feel I must play
well in every match'*

To have had the opportunity, and responsibility, to meet
and to interview Pelé on many occasions during World Cup
tournaments between 1958 and 1998, and to analyse his
career is a daunting task. How not to seem exaggerated or
sycophantic, not to indulge in easy journalists' affectation?
Because, if I can be objectively correct, the simple response
is in five words: too good to be true. Born Edson Arantes
do Nascimento, Brazil's sporting icon was, and will remain,
a representation of life beyond sport – of aspects of human
nature, other than extreme physical attributes, to which many
of us might aspire. Yet only if we could handle the impact of a
million admirers craving to catch our smile, take our picture,
touch the hem of our coat. What I am stating is fact: Pelé

became public property when he was almost still a boy. In a retirement interview with *The Guardian*, he acknowledged, 'Pelé is a name known all over the world, in every nation, in every embassy, every presidential office, but no one remembers Edson – the man with private feelings, with a family, who works hard. Pelé will go on forever, but Edson is the mortal one with his own life, the one who will die.'

What enchanted Pelé's global audience was not just the cascade of extravagant, match-winning goals, whether for Santos or Brazil, but that by the time he retired at 37, and with more than 1,000 career goals, after a couple of years with New York Cosmos, his demeanour on the pitch was still an expectant teenager's: Edson played spontaneous football for *happiness*. The public longed for beauty more than triumph. This is, in my experience, a characteristic almost unique to Brazilians, an ability to find joy in the midst of despair. Pelé was, and is, the personification of a Brazilian dream that became international. There was once talk of the World Cup becoming 'The Pelé Cup', but there was too much corruption on the field and within FIFA for that to become reality.

In his elevated sphere, Pelé was quite different, and in my sense superior, to Diego Maradona. An Argentinian is seeking the matador's exhibitionist fulfilment while Pelé's objective was somehow more ideologically profound, if that is possible within the context of sport. I think there was a glimpse of this with Brazil's opening gold medal in Rio's Olympic Games of 2016, Rafaela Silva's judo title against Mongolia's world champion Suriva Dorjsuren. Favela survivor Silva's right bicep carries the tattoo 'Only God Knows How Much I Have Suffered to Get Here'. From the podium, she reflected, 'If my medal could touch the people who still do not understand the

Olympic spirit, I believe this is what I can convey, to inspire children. This is the objective.'

Pelé's life has been one of unostentatious inspiration for the people of Brazil and for international integration: witness his post-match camaraderie with England in a memorable World Cup first round of Mexico 1970.

My duty has been to have had the excitement of witnessing Pelé's magic many times across four World Cup finals (twice ruptured by injury); then, during a dozen finals through 40 years, being able intermittently to talk with him more about *game* than with most other notable players. Pelé *cared*: not about money (he made plenty), or transfers (he made none), but about the state of the game and the sanctity of sportsmanship. He was the target of incessant assault ignored by referees, crippled in the 1966 World Cup in England. In a long conversation prior to the final between Brazil and France in 1998, Pelé's revolutionary ambition – if newly elected FIFA president Sepp Blatter would listen – was abolition of the penalty shoot-out, by which Brazil had regained the title four years earlier in the USA against Italy: a dramatic but lottery outcome which has no bearing on the previous 120 minutes' play. Pelé's alternative proposals were either a back-count of previous matche results, or a 'moving' shoot-out. 'The latter,' he said, 'is what we used in the US [when playing in retirement with Cosmos] where the player has the option of attempting to dribble round the goalkeeper. This is exciting, but has an unpredictable time factor, which is awkward for television. The alternative is simply to determine the result by which team has lost the fewer earlier matches, or then by goal difference, then by yellow and red cards. This would seem fair to everybody, would encourage teams to be positive rather than defensive, not to commit fouls, not to shut up the game in the negative hope of winning the penalty lottery.' This idea made no progress.

Pelé, symptomatic of his people, knew only how to attack and entertain. Remember the team of 1982, with Falcao, Socrates and Zico, attacking flat out against Italy when needing only a draw to qualify for the next round, and losing to Paolo Rossi's hat-trick? 'We go for the big moment,' Pelé reflects. That's what the public craves: the agony when Neymar and Co. were routed by Germany in the 2014 World Cup in Rio, the exhilaration when they won two years later in their 'home' Olympic Games. Pelé gave to football what Pavarotti gave to song, Gauguin to canvas. I could continue endlessly with the statistics of Pelé's flamboyant career: the Guinness record of 1,279 goals in 1,363 matches (including friendlies); 77 goals in 92 matches for Brazil, including appearing at four World Cups, the only man to win three of these; 643 goals in 656 games for Santos, with the double-double in 1962/63 of Copa Libertadores (South America) and Intercontinental Cup against Benfica and then Milan. Yet what Pelé meant most of all was an *idea*, a *concept*.

It is a mark of his supremacy that his status is acknowledged by every illustrious contemporary, themselves having global reputations. Pelé's prime with Santos preceded blanket television coverage so public perception was not at the same pitch as for Maradona or Messi today. Ferenc Puskás, lethal Hungarian marksman for Real Madrid, was in no doubt. 'The best player was Di Stéfano. I refuse to classify Pelé … he was above that.' Alfredo Di Stéfano, Argentine legend of Madrid's European Cup domination, a man who never used half-a-dozen words when two would do – and once as manager of Valencia gave me a club wristwatch for taking the time to analyse his coaching principles – was succinct,

'Messi and Cristiano Ronaldo are great players … Pelé was better.' Just Fontaine, record scorer at the 1958 World Cup, whose French side was obliterated by Pelé in the semi-final, said the sight of him 'made me feel I should retire'. Johan Cruyff, inspirational playmaker and coach who was happy to discuss Barcelona's tactics with me for an hour, thought Pelé 'exceeded the game's perceived borders'. And this is all about a player who never sought to leave Santos in 18 years. 'Why would I want to leave for more money?' he asked. 'I had offers from all over Europe, from Mexico, but always said I'm okay with Santos, even though many others went abroad. I think to be a family is the most important thing – I never wanted to change.'

Son of Fluminense footballer Dondinho in downbeat depressed Bauru, appropriately – as events proved – named after electric light inventor Edison, Pelé did not own a pair of boots until he was 11. The nickname came from his own mispronunciation of admired Vasco goalkeeper Bilé, and stuck. Early inspiration arrived with indoor football, accentuating balance and reaction time. Precociously talented, introduced at 15 to Santos FC in the port adjacent to Sao Paulo, a year later he signed professional, making his first-team debut a month before his 16th birthday. From there he was a member of the squad for the 1958 World Cup in Sweden – having been leading scorer with 58 goals in winning the domestic championship, a phenomenon to put even England's teenage sensation Jimmy Greaves in the shade. Pelé's sensational deeds over the next four seasons, briefly apparent in Europe with victory by Santos in the Intercontinental Cup against Benfica, received only moderate television notice. At the time of the 1958 World Cup many people in Britain owned no television, including myself. Of Brazil's matches in Sweden, as I was watching Northern Ireland or Wales elsewhere, I saw them mostly on domestic TV clips.

Pelé had arrived in Sweden, the youngest to appear in the tournament at 17, with a knee injury. He missed the first two matches against Austria and England – the latter a goalless draw, the only time Brazil failed to score. He then scored with a deflection in the quarter-final against Wales, followed by a hat-trick in the semi-final against France. He had enjoyed the squad's headquarters on the fringe of Gothenburg, not to mention the eager attention of blonde Swedish girls at the dance hall. 'They loved us, especially the black guys. In the 5-2 semi-final against France, I had become the player I wanted to be, chipping the ball over opponents' heads, full of confidence. In the final, Sweden were ahead within four minutes, the first time in the competition we had been behind, but soon Vava equalised and in the second half we showed our real class, sweeping Sweden aside. I made it 3-1 when I caught a pass on my chest, let the ball drop, then flicked it over a defender, then rounded him, and volleyed home. It was a nice goal, and people had not seen something like that before.'

Pelé also scored the fifth: in one afternoon he had changed the face of the game, against opposition whom many had expected to turn the tables on Brazil on a wet afternoon. The Swedish defender Sigvard Parling reflected that when Pelé scored the fifth goal, 'I felt like applauding.'

If Europe for a while then forgot about Pelé, I was alertly reminded on a pre-World Cup tour in 1962 with Wales – then still a significant international team, though failing to qualify – for warm-up matches for Brazil in Rio and Sao Paulo. Pelé was now in full flow, with Garrincha on the right wing an additional nightmare for any defence. Pelé was twice the instrument of Wales's destruction, the holders seemingly certain of retaining their title in Chile, but with an injury in the opening game against Czechoslovakia he missed the remainder of the tournament. England were overrun by Garrincha in the quarter-final, and with Amarildo a competent replacement for Pelé, Brazil duly defeated the Czechs once more in the final.

Prior to England being World Cup hosts in 1966, I attended Brazil's warm-up rehearsal in Spain and was granted a prolonged interview with the world's number one, who requested no fee, my wife giving him a set of wine glasses on his arrival in London. It is a reflection of Pelé's modesty that for all his eminence, he was in awe of the tournament being staged, as he described, 'in the home of the game'. England until then had only twice been defeated at home by a foreign country, Hungary in 1953 and Austria in 1965, ahead of the tournament.

'You don't realise what this means to us in Brazil,' Pelé said. 'We have more supporters going to England than went across the Andes to Chile. They are even selling their cars to raise the money to be able to say, "I was in England for the World Cup." No other nation would we trust to take our money for tickets in October and not receive the tickets until the next April. Mexico, Germany, nowhere can be the same after England with its wonderful reputation for its sportsmanship and administration.'

I then expressed the hope that injury would not again undermine Pelé: that the tournament would be remembered for his eminence rather than foul tactics in the attempt to stop him. It was a wish in vain. Pelé continued, on the constant provocation, 'I've been sent off three times at home, each time the same referee, always for arguing. Football today has become far too defensive, no longer a show. Many teams do well, not because they are good, but because they are negative.'

Because of his instinctive enjoyment of the game, he never protected himself, shielded himself against injury, taking it easy. 'I just always feel I must play well in every match.'

And this the public had come to take for granted in his 100 or more matches every season; more than 100,000 attending in Madrid to see a friendly practice against Atlético just for the reward of watching Pelé score another three. It was astonishing how he was able to ride the expectation which offered little relief, 'Playing is not the problem, it is the travelling. I can't remember when I last spent a whole week with my family. The only time I get days off is when I'm injured.'

Pelé's foreboding about the game's negativity was to be starkly confirmed. Scoring the opening goal against Bulgaria – the first player to score in three successive World Cups – he was repetitively fouled, missed the second encounter against Hungary, and returned against Portugal at Goodison Park in Liverpool. An atrocious tackle by Joao Morais, worth instant dismissal, gouged Pelé's shin: myopic English referee George McCabe did nothing bar stroke Morais's head as the culprit feigned apologies, leaving Pelé a passenger and Brazil eliminated. That one moment epitomised a sport losing its soul.

I talked with Pelé prior to his departure for home. He was predictably downbeat, 'Ideal football has become impossible. This is terrible for the game and for the spectators, who want a show. This has been obvious with your English crowds. They are not as fanatical as at home, but more discerning; they have appreciated good football, whichever the team. From what I have seen, only two teams have played really attacking football, ourselves and Hungary. Only by allowing the other team to attack can you do so yourself. But the present negative trend chokes all this, and there are only two ways to beat it

– by playing the same way, and by having good referees. We just happened to be unfortunate with the referees this time.'

Having met Pelé at the Palace sports centre, the squad's base following elimination, I fondly remember giving a lift back into central London to eight of the team: three of us on the front bench-seat of an old Ford Consul, three on the back seat and three on their laps, heading for Leicester Square. I assumed they all made it back safely to Rio.

Joao Havelange, president of Brazilian football, threatened that on account of Pelé's butchery they would never again select him for the World Cup, whatever his own inclination. It would have been more to the point had Havelange mounted a campaign to allow footballers to play football, to educate referees and banish the thugs, but he was too preoccupied with an ambition to oust Stanley Rous of England as president of FIFA, and a 'fair play' revolution would have been politically counterproductive. For another two decades, thuggery would thrive, as Diego Maradona and others were to discover. Pelé at first resisted a recall to the national stage but in 1969 he relented, playing in six qualifying ties for the 1970 finals in Mexico, scoring six goals. By now Garrincha and others were retired, replaced by new uninhibited attackers such as Gerson, Tostao, Jairzinho and Rivelino.

The draw cast Brazil in an opening round with Czechoslovakia, Romania and defending champions England. It is not plain patriotism to say that England's technical and tactical balance was possibly superior to that in 1966. With Brazil's defence suspect, they were as much in fear of England as vice versa. In their opening game against the Czechs, Pelé scored for a 2-1 victory. The meeting with England was a tactical seesaw, England's goalkeeper Gordon Banks making the so-called save of the century from a header by Pelé, while the only goal was scored by Jairzinho. The likelihood of a Brazil–England final remained widely forecast. Brazil then coasted through against Peru and Uruguay respectively, while England foundered against West Germany with goalkeeping blunders by a deputy, with Gordon Banks suddenly unwell.

Brazil's final against Italy was the summit of Pelé's career, aged 30. He scored the opening goal with a header – Brazil's 100th in the World Cup – and deftly created the third and fourth for Jairzinho and then full-back Carlos Alberto; the latter a tactical blueprint of intuitive Brazilian attack. The history of the game, of Brazil, of Pelé, so wretchedly corrupted in England, had now turned a memorable page. Edson would continue for a further four years with Santos then came out of retirement to spend two 'exhibitionist' seasons with Cosmos, setting the trend for many prominent Europeans to follow suit, including Bobby Moore, George Best and Cruyff. Such names generated a surge in American interest in the sport; especially for women and young children.

The global lighthouse that Pelé had illuminated for the game would never dim. A household name in any nation, he was engraved forever in storytelling among any games-playing children. A Messi or Ronaldo might emerge, but the debate would always be a comparison with Pelé, later the Brazilian Minister of Sport. Today in his 80s and frail, we thank Edson for his impeccable donation to global culture. If you ever have the opportunity, there is a museum in Santos with several thousand exhibits recording his legacy.

MARY PETERS
Death-Threatened Dame

'No one really expected me to win'

Competitive sport strives for excellence, commentators to describe it, their temptation often exaggeration: that someone 'changed the face' of judo, archery, whatever. In 1972, at the Olympic Games in Munich, an unassuming woman from Lancashire momentarily, and emotionally, lifted the despondency of terror-stressed Belfast. More than that, the personal prestige bestowed by a gold medal in the pentathlon upon Mary Peters enabled this selfless English migrant, hitherto a comparatively anonymous teacher, to help bring enlightenment over the next half-century to an extremist, religiously ravaged British city.

It is characteristic of Mary P, as she is universally known, that she should have written in her autobiography not long after Munich's apotheosis, 'I was fortunate then, and indeed throughout most of my career, that no one really expected me to win.' Were there a gold medal for smiles, Mary P would earn one every day: still in her 80s the most cheerful, charitable soul in all of sport. Taking breakfast with, previously unknown to her, my oldest friend following my 85th birthday party – an old-fashioned fellow of exactitude likely to interject conversations with 'If I may say on a point of order' – irrepressible Mary charmed the pants off him.

Charm was not a constituent of her Munich victory, more the old adage of true grit. The odds against her were massive: both her background of Belfast's IRA-crazed environment in the 1970s – dodging bomb sites on the way to training – and her moderate status as competent shot put competitor, converted by astute coach 'Buster' McShane into a prominent five-event pentathlete. She had won both these events at Edinburgh's Commonwealth Games in 1970.

It was not to be a comfortable preparatory phase prior to Munich. A few weeks before departure, the IRA had detonated more than 20 bombs on Bloody Friday, killing nine and injuring dozens, with mounting hysteria in the streets. The following March, post-Munich, four soldiers would be murdered by the IRA at a contrived 'party', initiated by decoy girls, in the house next door to Mary's. Yet her resolution had, and always, remained unwavering. Today she reflects, 'I had needed to win more than ever, because Northern Ireland was suffering such a terrible time, and I wanted to bring back some good news for all those trying to lead a normal peaceful life.'

Born in Halewood, Lancashire, Mary's family had moved to Belfast when she was 11, her father's employment re-assigned. Dismayed at the prospect, her distress then deepened when her mother died of cancer. Worse followed with her father's almost immediate decision to re-marry with her godmother, her mother's bridesmaid. 'It was very difficult, because they didn't talk about cancer in those days, and I didn't know how seriously ill mum was. Dad asked my godmother if she would come over and live with us in Northern Ireland as housekeeper, with a view to marriage. I couldn't understand how he could be interested in somebody else so soon. Athletics became very important to me, because it took me out of the house where I was finding it very stressful.' Her father aided her teenage training with fitness facilities prior to her professional coaching, while she qualified as a teacher.

Mary's athletic progress was, viewed objectively, less than meteoric. The tempo sharpened when liaison was established with a new man in town: energetic, ambitious, irrepressible, working-class Terence McShane, a gymnasium manager who brought intellect to physical culture in depressed Belfast. Not only did Mary eagerly come under his wing, but she accepted additional part-time employment assisting administration in the gym, thereby becoming, under avowed, archaic regulations of the International Amateur Athletic Federation (now World Athletics), and the International Olympic Committee, an ineligible professional. Notwithstanding that she effectively was being paid pence rather than pounds. Even without her hand on the Bible, her repetitive competitor's signature of honourable amateur status would not have shaken any juror's acceptance. McShane was to become the all but manically driven coach behind an initially unspectacular but wilful youngster whose motivation in life was as much social as personal, more concerned with others than herself.

By degrees, Mary's impact on international events prospered: fifth in shot put in the European Championships of 1962 aged 23. Parallel with improvement was a developing friendship with a compatriot international star of the day, fellow pentathlete and supreme all-rounder Mary Rand. It can be fairly said that self-admitted humdrum Mary was fascinated though in no way envious of ritzy, always ogled, born-to-win Mary. It was workaholic Mary's delight, in the captivating surroundings of Tokyo's Olympic Games of 1966, to partner her twice-married colleague who took pentathlon silver behind the Soviet Union's powerhouse Irena Press, Mary P a distant fourth, a split-second behind bronze medal winner Galina Bystrova (this was the event's Olympic inauguration, by the time of which I had left on my exploratory rail return journey across Siberia back to London's Liverpool Street).

With pentathlon yet to be included in the Commonwealth Games, Mary P was guided by McShane to go for the solo shot put at Kingston, Jamaica, in 1966. She embarked on a bulk-building diet she found, emotionally, repulsive but effective. McShane's strategy was that it was a necessary development to counter the alleged – as yet untested – steroid exploitation widely prevalent in eastern Europe and the US. Refinements measured in millimetres and split seconds were now at stake. Even less acceptable, for Peters and all women, was an introduced manual sex test, now begun at Kingston, to verify women were not masquerading men. A medical adjudication was subsequently replaced by more tolerable gene testing. On account of bulk-building, Mary became widely rumoured to be a steroid cheat – a prospect she abhorred. However, notwithstanding her increased power, Kingston was a flop as she finished a disappointing seventh. So too, with an injured ankle, was her Olympic sortie to Mexico City's Olympics in 1968, finishing ninth, at a time I was working as midnight news editor for ATV in London, summarising David Hemery's triumph in 400m hurdles and favourite Lillian Board's disappointment in the 400m flat.

Onward now for Mary P: Edmonton's Commonwealth Games as preparatory for Munich's Olympics in 1972. The first bolstered Mary's burning, lingering ambition – now aged 31 – for the all-important second: pentathlon gold at Meadowbank Stadium with the UK and Commonwealth record of 5,148 points plus added gold in separate shot put and the finals of the individual high hurdles, some seven events. What might finally clinch the ultimate Olympic objective? Exclusive, warm-weather training is the common factor for any elite athlete. But where, and at what cost? The Churchill Trust Charity might help. Of these preoccupations, I was unaware at the time, being immersed in the tribulations of Alf Ramsey's now slightly ailing England football squad.

An uncomfortable interview with the trust questioned Mary's age and qualification for such a venture, grudgingly donating a modest £800; nonetheless a golden handshake, granting three months in Californian sunshine, facilities at Pasadena City College. While Mary was out of sight in this training idyll, British media regularly regaled readers with speculation – legitimate it might be admitted – on the vainly promised 10,000m showcase by record-beater David Bedford. Such are the ill omens of fate, as Lillian had discovered in Mexico; and now, too, Mary Rand, breaking down in a last-gasp attempt to qualify for third-spot inclusion in the British team, as she lived in America and having missed out on Mexico City. Silently, Mary P regretted her friend's disappointment, being equivocal about loss of opportunity to beat her for the first time, but conscious that her own ambition was now perhaps strengthened.

My own expectations heading for Munich for the *Sunday Telegraph* were multiple. Here was a panoply of extravagant new stadia in a city and nation anxious to demonstrate to a global audience of a billion people that West Germany, like Japan eight years earlier, was now an epicentre of cultural, industrial and social hegemony. Arrival substantiated the reality of Germany's escape from earlier opprobrium. Further, beyond wondering if Hemery could defend his title against Uganda's explosive John Aki-Bua, I hoped to see evidence that emerging African football, with increased Olympic access, might demonstrate its claim for expanded World Cup qualification. Mary P, I supposed, was a possible podium decoration alongside West German favourite Heide Rosendahl.

While it was to become apparent over two days of the pentathlon that the 80,000 predominantly German crowd was fair-minded and appreciative of tense rival competition, stadium officialdom was without camouflage of its blatant coincidental bias behind home contenders. Firstly, officials unaccountably queried the legality of the shoe design which Mary P was wearing – a devious, unavailing ploy, following the opening 100m hurdles, in which Mary snapped into her second fastest time, 13.29s – only four-hundredths behind GDR's second-ranker Christine Bodner. However, 27 of the 29 competitors were then delayed in the stadium tunnel en route to the shot put arena, a key discipline for Mary. Oddly missing were the two West Germans, Rosendahl and Karen Mack, siphoned away to a warm-up area. A complaint by the British team leader quickly resolved this scam.

In her strongest discipline, Mary was looking for something big within her three throws. Disappointed with the first, up came 53ft 1.75in, her best in the pentathlon, at the second attempt for an overall points lead with Burglinde Pollak (GDR) lying second and Rosendahl third.

For the day's third discipline, the high jump, Mary twice critically failed at 5ft 7.25in. Fortunately a distant view of McShane in the grandstand, working his elbows to indicate run-up speed, helped motivate a life-saving successful third attempt. The bar three times rose, three clearances. The technical switch to the revolutionary Fosbury Flop, introduced by American Dick Fosbury in Mexico and recently adopted by Mary, was paying dividends. Now late evening, the full-house stadium was riveted by two lone surviving athletes, jumpers at opposite ends of the stadium: sole surviving GDR pole-vaulter Wolfgang Nordwig, a Leipzig engineer, and Mary. The dense crowd's emotional applause of every successful jump by Mary, in challenge to their Rosendahl favourite now eliminated in the jumping, remains a cherished Olympic memory..

Twice more rose the bar, twice more over, Nordwig and Mary dutifully waiting in turn for each other's attempted clearance. Finally, at 6ft 0.5in, Mary failed: yet she was retiring for the night with nearly a 100-point lead over Pollak, with Rosendahl some 300 points adrift in fifth place, but with her best two events to come, long jump and 200m.

After one of the longest, all but sleepless nights of her life, Mary re-engaged with an opening no jump (overlapping the take-off board), while watching Rosendahl soar to 22ft 5in, almost her world record. The heat was truly on. Mary then leapt 19ft 7.5in, the best she could have hoped for. A medal was now assured, but gold? With Rosendahl the known fastest in the field at 200m, the odds for Mary were paper thin. Aged 33, she was going to need to run quicker than ever before, that being 24.2s.

There followed an agonising scheduled interval, Mary losing contact with McShane and returning to the village in a panic, a colleague finally locating McShane who was, reassuringly, a picture of calm. Reunited at the stadium, he simply said, 'This is it. Go.' Inwardly torn between ambition and anxiety, Mary made the perfect start, flung herself round the bend, clinging to Pollak, with Rosendahl beyond reach. Mentally senseless, legs seemingly failing, Mary crossed the line in 24.08s. Rosendahl? Up flashed 22.96, her *personal best*. But the points? Mary tottered in an uncomprehending daze. An arm embraced her. Rosendahl's congratulation! Mary had won the title by ten points, a world record of 4,801 to Rosendahl's 4,791, just by a mere one tenth of a second in her achieved time over the 200m. For Rosendahl, she had been a new world record holder for a mere 1.2 seconds. Pollok took bronze.

The Olympics had not changed, but life for Mary P had. Half a century of public acclaim, and her unwavering public service lay ahead. Yet instant fame was about to be darkened, temporarily, by infamy.

As she and McShane were tearfully enveloped in each other's arms, amid a sea of clamouring media cameras, suddenly Mary learned that there in the grandstand was her father. Not wishing to divert her focus, he had travelled incognito with business colleagues from home in Australia without advising relatives, quietly anticipating this unforgettable climax. Yet this moment of sporting history was darkened: within the stadium hubbub, Mary found father and coach in agitated debate, so she demanded an explanation. A crisis? Indeed there was.

The BBC had received that morning an anonymous death threat: that the IRA would bomb the house of a Protestant champion should she return home. Scotland Yard and the British Olympic Association had been notified, so security now surrounded every step of Northern Ireland's glorious heroine. Arthur, her father, demanded she never return.

At the climax of her life, incredibly, Mary was solemnly absolute. 'Of course I'm going back to my home.' Necessarily now cloaked in secrecy by armed police, Mary unhesitatingly returned to a now ecstatic guerrilla city: celebrations, gifts and champagne a cascading fountain, she was barely able to comprehend what she had just abandoned – an Olympic scenario in which, while she had blissfully slept a first night clutching her gold medal, Black September Arab terrorists had begun assassination of the Israeli team. An apocalyptic conjunction with which Mary, enmeshed in euphoria, could hardly relate (my observation of this horror comes in a later chapter).

All these years later, she is smilingly emphatic in her reflection, 'Here was my chance to give something back to the city, to the generous, ordinary people who seek a regular life – an era when society didn't respect women as it does today, individually to represent them in any way. I had hesitated at one point about attending a Woman of the Year function at London's Dorchester. A woman barrister, the first ever in Belfast, insisted to me, "Indeed you must go, stand up and be counted!" For sure Munich changed my life.'

In many ways. For a start, a renovated synthetic track at Queens University, Belfast, was funded by an £80,000 charity fund; a trust for support of youth, able-bodied and disabled, to expand their potential, known as The Mary Peters Trust, aiding countless athletes. Subsequent honours had been showered upon her: MBE (1973), CBE (1990), Dame Commander (2000), Companion of Honour (2015), Lady Companion of the Garter (2019). Astonishing, the consequence of a tenth of a second in a single race, on the welfare of an individual and a city. Here was a Belfast princess, acclaimed through the catalyst of running and jumping, who was too precious to be a target for religious/political assassins.

OLGA KORBUT
Unprecedented Extravagance

'Gymnastics is all about expression'

I have previously mentioned the tendency of sports commentators to exaggerate, to suggest that a performer 'changed the
face' of their sport. Yet in one unforgettable instance this was
abundantly true. There we were, at Munich's Olympic Games
in 1972, duly impressed with West Germany's modern new
stadia – track and field, swimming, basketball – with our
expectations preoccupied with the sprinting of Soviet cheetah
Valery Borzov, Finland's defending track phenomenon Lasse
Virén, US dolphin Mark Spitz, all of us unaware of impending
terrorist doom. Suddenly we were assailed by frantic office
telex messages from back home – ancient communication! –
demanding, 'What about Olga??' To which for most of us the
answer was, 'Olga who?'

'Revelation' is another epithet overused, but not here.
While the majority of correspondents habitually covering
a Games are necessarily multi-tasked amid 30 sports,
gymnastics was then widely regarded as an esoteric exercise
that had been – and continued to be – dominated across 30
years by largely expressionless Soviet automatons, assembled
at gymnastic factories in a mood of social/political ideology.

The Olympics, surely, were more about dramatic triumph or spectacular failure, were they not? But no: diminutive, sparrow-like Olga Korbut, a 17-year-old from satellite Belarus, as supple as an elastic band, was transforming her sport, and a vast television audience, with an unprecedented extravagance which overturned preconceived principles of gymnastics.

To such a degree did Korbut seize attention, both of existing aficionados and the suddenly addicted, that there was some lingering scepticism. My late, esteemed fellow commentator, John Rodda of *The Guardian*, more a track specialist, was moved to write dismissively of Korbut 24 years later, in the IOC's six-language official centenary history of 1996, 'Television ruthlessly now distorted the very basic measure of sporting excellence.' Not for Joe Public, it didn't. Often smiling, sometimes tearful at errors, athletically experimental and occasionally alarming, Korbut gave the Olympics a new dimension, even if sections of establishment international federation officialdom remained unimpressed at the time. Eleven months after Munich, Korbut's backward somersault on the beam was for a while banned, supposedly considered dangerous. To this accusation, Korbut, threatening to quit the sport, declared, 'Gymnasts are not immune to injury ... people don't ask my opinion ... gymnastics is all about expression.'

Olga Valentinovna Korbut was born in May 1955 in Hrodna, Belarus, and as a teenager was a mere 4ft 11in (1.50m) and six stone. Aged nine, she was assigned to one of the USSR's exclusive gymnastics schools, initially coached by Yelene Volchestskaya, herself an Olympic medal winner in 1964, prior to Olga switching aged 12 to head coach Renald Knysh: a man with imaginative ambition for the sport and for Korbut. History, and controversy, awaited them.

Aged 14, Korbut made her first conspicuous appearance at the Soviet National Championships of 1969, a year younger than the normal admission and finishing fifth, yet already losing marks for an 'unconventional' style. In the next two years, winning the individual vault at 15, she was fourth in the all-round; at 17 her precocity overrode the judges with victory over her two main rivals, each winner of the European Championships in the last two years. Olympic qualification became automatic after five years of relentless training under Knysh, whose conduct she described as 'a loner, a despot … and a genius'. She accepted his ferocious regime, often concluded late in the evening after countless hours of repetition – and originality.

Arriving in Munich, few as yet knew her internationally. Her first individual discipline was the beam, a surface little more than four inches wide, sufficient to rest a teacup. Knysh's foresight had been to convert the intellectual concept of a wooden tightrope into the reality of an airborne floor: utterly dependent on the courage of a whirling, compliant schoolgirl with unimaginable balance. Miraculously, Korbut had possessed the intellect and a physique to match a coach's theoretical geometry which abandoned normal balletic symmetry. An astonished audience, live and on television, was now spellbound as Korbut performed her 'backward flip' somersault, common on a floor exercise. Gold on the beam had been followed by another with a peerless performance of tumbling on the genuine floor discipline. It seemed that Korbut was in line to win the all-round individual title, but several errors on the uneven bars reduced her to tears, though the Soviets nonetheless retained the individual all-round title through Tourischeva – Korbut a dejected seventh.

However, returning to the individual medal discipline of uneven bars the following day, Korbut revealed her masterpiece, an unimagined jewel: another backward flip from the upper bar, but with hands transferring blind behind her from one bar to the other. An 11,000 crowd gasped in amazement: uncomprehending, niggardly judges awarded her 9.8 points rather than 10.0. The audience whistled disapprovingly; judges' ears remained closed; competition was paused. Korbut took silver. Yet in one moment, a tiny girl's metaphoric Aladdin's Lamp had transformed her sport, the Olympic Games, and her.

Paul Ziet, publisher of *International Gymnastics* magazine, analysed Korbut's impact, emphasising the contrast, temperamentally, between her revolutionary routine and regular Soviet performers: Korbut emotional, turbulent, unpredictable and charismatic, rather than staid and formulaic. We hadn't supposed until now that the Soviets had any ability to show emotion the way Korbut did. They had been simply poker-faced but commanding the prizes.

On Munich momentum, the Soviet team financially exploited Korbut's sudden fame with global tours but, sadly, her brilliance, so arduously achieved, comparatively rapidly declined. She soon expanded her career as a modestly rewarded instructor – notwithstanding that on tour she was a celebrity guest target by the likes of US president Richard Nixon. By the time of Montreal's Games of 1976, hampered by inevitable injuries, her star, if not in eclipse, was now clouded. Though fancied once again as champion, she could match in Montreal neither her team colleague Nellie Kim nor the new sensation from Romania, teenage Nadia Comaneci, the latter first to score a perfect ten.

Within a year, Korbut retired from competition. Her consolation had been Montreal's more anonymous team gold. Nixon's earlier flattering assertion, that Korbut's international personality had done more to help thaw Cold War antagonisms than any ambassador's dialogue, began to sound hollow to the young woman from a poor home, where her working mother had been unaware of her daughter's teenage occupation until she first saw her on television.

Korbut graduated from college in 1977, becoming a teacher and marrying musician Leonard Bortkevich, son Richard being born in 1979. Living in the capital Minsk, Korbut worked to aid climate casualties in Belarus from the Chernobyl nuclear disaster in 1986, commuting to and from the USA then finally emigrating to New Jersey in 1991. Subsequently she divorced and became a US citizen in 2000, moving again to Arizona in 2002 and being appointed as head coach at Scottsdale Gymnastics. While there, she reflected that her sport had changed again, having by now become obsessed with muscular power. 'I'm waiting for maybe another Olga to arrive, and revert gymnastics back to being more graceful. It's now become like robots, nobody smiling.'

We can never know how profound an influence on Korbut's life has been the alleged sexual abuse she endured in those early years from Knysh, her fanatical coach: the kind of abuse which would become an international issue in the 21st century with the #MeToo movement, and parallel allegations of abuse of young girls in national gymnastic federations of both Britain and the USA. In 1999, Korbut had publicly spoken for the first time, with accusations of rape before and after Munich, which elicited similar accusations against Knysh from two fellow former Belarus teenagers, Halina Karchenskaya and Lyudmila Rekova. Knysh, now in his late 80s, had been investigated by Soviet officials in 1981, following the attempted suicide by a young gymnast in Hrodno, she leaving a note citing Knysh as the cause of her trauma. The coach persistently denied all testimonies of habitual abuse, as related by Belarus media.

Olga Korbut's enduring salvation is that she is forever remembered as a joyful exponent of a basic, common form of physical pleasure, which can be shared with an audience irrespective of technical sophistry in a more immediate way than, say, a sculpture. Without being presumptuous, Korbut donated something beyond sport.

ALEX HIGGINS
Intoxicated Audience

'I'm playing from memory'

Down the years, I have known more than a few to fall foul of the bottle. My father, having post-war quit his expertise as a West End actor, for some years ran a pub, often overrun by boisterous French-Canadian army recruits still stationed in Hampshire. Military police would arrive to hurl them head first on to the steel floor of waiting trucks. My adventure into daily journalism, with its 24-hour 'availability' shift, exposed the susceptibility of writers to the lure of the bar while awaiting breaking news, or interviews with those who control or direct our institutions, whether they be business, politics, culture or sport. The bar becomes a haven, for professionals as much as leisure-seekers. And there have been notorious fallen sportsmen. The most conspicuous during my career that wizard of the baize, Alex Higgins, calculated to have spectacularly won, and lost, approaching £4m in his career.

We all have weaknesses. 'Hurricane' Higgins lucklessly had almost more than his 27 tournament titles; a combination of addictive tobacco, alcohol, a short fuse, gambling, cocaine, then cancer, creating an erratic personality which confused his unique technique with a cue. Thus he was simultaneously

218

charming, vain, angrily hostile, insecure and vulnerable. The spectre of flawed genius was manna for a ravenous media, while a fascination, until later degenerative years, for an enraptured and mostly sympathetic audience. So often distraught was the career of Higgins that he himself once aptly summarised it in fewer than 20 words. Asked by biographer Bill Borrows in *Hurricane: The Turbulent Life of Alex Higgins* whether he had enjoyed his life, Higgins retorted, 'I haven't really had much to do with my life. All I've done is take part in it.' As I had discovered the first time I met him, he was not without a sardonic sense of humour.

It was back in the late 1970s. Higgins had already startled the phlegmatic snooker world – transformed only latterly by the conversion to colour television from monochrome – by winning the World Championships in 1972, aged 23, and then being the runner-up four years later. The *Daily Express* suggested I go and have a look at what all the fuss was about. I joined Higgins, all bonhomie, one evening in Birmingham for an exhibition bout at a private hall. There was more beer than there was furniture, the smoke as dense as Dover fog. The picture of Higgins was like catching a fox in your headlights on a dark night. Cunning, alert, anxious, alone. The eyes constantly moving, like a flurry of reds on the table, his slight body never relaxed, rippling hither and thither, barely pausing for stationary balls between one shot and the next. A regular smile, as much one of self-appreciation, as he potted into pockets seemingly the size of saucepans, as for intoxication of a spellbound audience.

Off-table in his chair, he drew so deeply on his cigarette he could be swallowing his tongue, the smoke still being exhaled as he took the next sip of his drink. A vodka and orange? With intervals, we were there until nearly midnight. You could instantly sense the magnetism of this shortish, sandy-haired figure from Belfast, now slipping away into the night. For the next decade, he seemed personally to find my intermittent presence at tournaments agreeable. I, of course, was recording his prime.

Born in 1949, Higgins had begun playing at 11, habitué of Belfast's Jampot Club and later at the YMCA. There was an abortive attempt in England to become a jockey and by 16 he had achieved his first maximum break, within three years winning the Northern Ireland Amateur title, the youngest to do so, and then the All-Ireland event. The rise was exceptional, turning professional at 22 and a year later taking the World Championship at his first attempt, defeating John Spencer – the youngest to do so until 21-year-old Stephen Hendry's victory in 1990. There is the story that, on the way to winning the world title again in 1982, in the semi-final against new young rival Jimmy White, Higgins played a shot so difficult that it had a one-in-100 chance to sustain a break when trailing 59-0. He swerved the cue ball off a side cushion to sink the blue so as to leave him in position on pink and black. In between the two world titles, he had won the Masters in 1978 and 1981, and would take the UK Championship in 1983, becoming one of 11 players to achieve the so-called Triple Crown.

To watch Higgins in a championship was for me almost a recreation: a comfy indoor hall, a contemplative silence between applause, the exact, geometric but ever-changing alignment of the balls inviting one's own judgement of what the man with the cue might next attempt. And such a variety of characters: the bookish Cliff Thorburn, cheeky Jimmy White, porcelain-like Steve Davis, Welsh intimate Terry Griffiths, and the so often volcanic Hurricane, with his unpredictable narrative. It was well worth the entrance fee I wasn't paying.

I saw Higgins several times vying for the Benson & Hedges Masters title at Wembley (another invasive tobacco incentive). On one occasion there was a tense finishing duel against Griffiths, Higgins lamenting, 'I'm playing from memory.' Two years Griffiths' junior, and leading by several frames with his usual flamboyance, he was always on edge beneath the surface. 'There are so many tournaments nowadays, that travelling from one to another there's no time to practise. The game's so different from when I started. Out there this afternoon, I was going for shots I've made in the past, but now just couldn't be sure they would work.' Well, who would be with hardly a pause for the balls to halt? That boldness, the willingness to risk all, which endeared him to the crowd, would never desert him, while the gentlemanly Griffiths kept the contest and the record near-3,000 crowd expectantly alive with an all-time Masters record break of 136 in the 12th frame, ultimately conceding in the 15th. Yet Higgins always as anxious away from the table as a relay runner waiting to receive the baton. A perfect theatrical drama.

Extravagant conduct from Higgins was ever present. Wanting to play afternoon golf following a morning's snooker session in Inverness, he took a £200 taxi ride to Manchester. Yet when bidding to regain the Embassy world title at 33, the fawn-like nerves had not been banished. While serene experts such as Ray Reardon or Steve Davis would survey the table with the air of consultant architects on site, loftily intent on perfection, Higgins still had more the air of the hunted. If you were not one of those many women of all ages for whom he induced a rather different Saturday night fever, the emotion tended to be of wanting a wild animal to escape: as if both performer and audience expected a trap. The emotion was almost mutual, provoking a trunkful of supporters' good luck charms arrayed alongside him.

Higgins duly won in 1982, confirmation of his mastery, but it was not a comfortable journey off stage. There was a midnight row with a conscientious electrician wishing to turn out the lights on a practice table, plus a due appointment with a socially alarmed tournament committee for inappropriate use of an ornamental flowerpot when inconvenienced by other facilities being locked up for the night. Yet the magic of his cue lingered, a few years on and he contested the now established reign of Davis in Coral's UK Championship at Preston, a performance regarded by the cognoscenti as without parallel – now the opposite of his Formula 1 impersonation, with a studied, intense defence play, coming from seven frames behind to level the match at 11-11. Regulars on the snooker tour could not recall Davis, by now the acknowledged sovereign, being forced into such errors, by an opponent enmeshed in a divorce dispute. Davis, it was said, had reached that point where financially he probably never needed to play again, but he possessed unshakeable pride. Yet by the time he missed a crucial blue in the final frame, he knew it was not his night, never mind his charitable gentility – gently taking a sip of water while Higgins puffed smoke, quaffed his Guinness, and repeatedly scanned his assortment of well-wishers' cards. The Hurricane had twice swept the table with that rapid poacher's pad. He could still occasionally deliver.

Such a recurrence of flair became increasingly infrequent, the temperamental excesses more embarrassing. In 1986 he headbutted the UK Championship tournament director, was subsequently fined £12,000 and banned from five tournaments, and convicted for assault; in 1990 he was banned for the rest of the season for punching an official at the World Championships. Yet the willpower had remained: in 1989 came his last professional tournament victory in the Irish Masters, aged 40, defeating young Hendry. Thereafter, Higgins was inelegantly hustling for penury sums in one-night exhibitions, two attempted professional comebacks in Ireland ending dismally. Marriages in 1975 and 1980 had come and gone, with the birth of a son and two daughters. The toll of 80 cigarettes a day led to mouth and throat cancer by 1998, and major surgery, with intensive radiotherapy, despite which he continued to smoke and drink to the bitter end. His weight fell to six stone and he was dependent on a disability allowance until his death in July 2010.

Few illustrious careers embrace such decline, his sublime skills ultimately condemned in self-destruction, yet a lasting inspiration to such successors as Jimmy White and contemporary Ronnie O'Sullivan. In a television documentary, Steve Davis described him as 'the one true genius': a player who would electrify the game and its audiences. In his funeral address at St Anne's Cathedral, the Dean of Belfast, Houston McKelvey, intoned, 'Alex encountered two of the greatest temptations, fame and fortune, and found it difficult to cope with both.'

It is not recorded whether the Hurricane achieved his alleged death wish – a greater number of mourners lining the street for his passing cortège than that for rival Belfast hero George Best. It is a sad social contradiction that his inherent inner inner frailties were part of the fascination that trailed his fame. Both Davis and O'Sullivan attribute to Higgins – vulnerable genius gambling on his extravagant risk-all style rather than traditional safety – the magnetism which rivetted public appeal in the 70s and 80s.

FILBERT BAYI
Trojan African

'Nobody took much notice of me'

In the 20th-century emancipation of Africa as it strove for freedom from colonial fragmentation, it was unfortunate that more of its emerging political leaders were not as noble as were many heroic figures in sport. These were initially north of the Sahara in football, then increasingly in track and field led by barefoot Ethiopian marathon winner Abebe Bikila at Rome in 1960 and subsequently a tide of high-altitude east Africans. I was privileged to have been present for one of the milestones – almost literal – in athletic history: by a man from Tanzania, then Tanganyika, a nation still ravaged in the 1970s by evolving post-Portuguese turmoil. The first European to invade had been Vasco Da Gama in 1498, followed by Omani Arabs and a flourishing ivory and slave trade, which in turn became subsumed by German East Africa in 1887; overtaken by British/Belgian occupation in 1916, becoming British mandate in 1919, governed by Julius Nyerere, independent in 1961, reinvaded by Ugandan terrorist Amin in 1978, liberated the following year. Try becoming a world record-breaker within that fraught national background.

The sudden, meteoric impact of Filbert Bayi, born in 1953, upon the sporting world in 1974 was beyond experience. His presence had begun moderately: ranked 46th and 31st respectively in 1,500m and 3,000m steeplechase heats at Munich's Olympics two years earlier, then leapfrogging rivals in 1973 at Lagos, Nigeria, to win the All-Africa Games 1,500m in 3:37.23. He was not a contender on my preview list for the *Daily Express* when making the three-day stop-start fuel-crisis trip to Christchurch, New Zealand, for the Commonwealth Games of 1974. Four stops – Brussels, Athens, Sri Lanka, Singapore – searching for airlines with some gas, plus a booking for speeding at the first roundabout outside Christchurch Airport. Much British expectation was, as in Munich two years earlier, on David Bedford for the 10,000m – another disappointment – and on home favourite John Walker or Ben Jipcho from Kenya for the 1,500m.

Underrated Bayi had other ideas, 'When I arrived in Christchurch, nobody took much notice of me. John was a Kiwi hero, so the money was on him. Many of us sensed something special might happen: there were outstanding Kenyans, Jipcho and Mike Boit, also in the field. I was already with a race plan, following Lagos, and again intending to run from the front.' Was he kidding? Few had done that in tactical record breaking, though the neutral wartime Swedes Gunder Haag and Arne Anderson, lacking opposition, had often been their own pacemakers, as had formidable Australian Herb Elliott a decade earlier. And here was Bayi, little known from an even less-known nation.

Today, I remember the event as vividly as though it were yesterday: three and a half minutes, reckoning for all but the last 15 seconds or so 'he cannot sustain this, Walker will catch him'. But Walker couldn't, and didn't.

Twenty years earlier, I had missed a supreme moment – Roger Bannister's four-minute mile. Several of us at Cambridge had rented a car – a fiver in those days – to head for Oxford, but with the sky overcast, doubtful if a record was 'on', we had pulled out. Equally unsure were Bannister and the pacemakers, until shortly beforehand the skies cleared, and the wind dropped. Now in Christchurch, we were ready for something special – but not what was about to happen.

Bayi's route to eminence had been along a path many were treading – physiologically symbolic. Schooldays had been spent running barefoot five miles each way to and from the village of Karratu, 6,000ft up the foothills of Mount Kilimanjaro, with another two miles each way for lunch in the heat of midday. Sea level would always be an exhilarating pleasure. He had only been running seriously since joining the army as an aircraft fitter.

A measure of what to judge as, thus far, one of the most impressive middle-distance races ever – and still considered so today – stems from the recollection of Bannister. Prior to Helsinki's Olympic Games of 1952, Bannister had run a three-lap trial, 1,200m, in 2:52 – nearly four seconds faster than the then world record by Anderson. That was now Bayi's three-lap time with a *further* 300 metres in 40 seconds for a world record of 3:32.2, to bust the six-year-old time of American Jim Ryun.

There was only one word, either for the time or for the manner of its achievement. Astonishing. With two laps (800m) remaining, Bayi was sustaining his intended lead from the gun, by now some 20 metres ahead of Kenyans Boit and Jipcho, who were clustered with pursuing New Zealanders Walker and Rod Dixon. At the bell, Boit had closed to ten metres, Jipcho third ahead of the Kiwis. On the final back straight Jipcho made his effort, but both Walker and Dixon surged past, Jipcho momentarily boxed. Into the home straight, Walker was closing, but 40 metres out Bayi again surged. Both beat Ryun's record, Jipcho overhauling Dixon. The first seven men all improved their own best times, with Brendan Foster of Britain coming *seventh*, lowering the British record.

Walker's verdict: 'Filbert ran an extraordinary race, I was never going to catch him. He went off straight from the gun – this was never heard of before.' Bayi had achieved, dramatically, what he had planned. 'Many watching, and those chasing, thought they would catch me over the last 200. When John closed in the final 100, I accelerated. Glancing back with 50 to go, I glimpsed the black shirt, and gave all I had left. Though I'd felt with half a lap remaining that I was okay.' Was there ever a point at which he sensed he might have misjudged? 'Just take a look at the video. My knees are still high, the arms are pumping.'

Bayi's place in history was engraved, yet there was more to come. A year later in Kingston, Jamaica, he was to break Ryun's eight-year-old mile record, blistering the field from the front with a 20-metre lead at halfway, narrowed at the bell but again pulling away to win in 3:51.3. This honour would be short-lived and months later Walker would achieve the first sub-3:50 with 3:49.4. All was set for a titanic rematch between the pair at Montreal's Olympic Games of 1976, only for the first of three successive boycotts to erupt. Prominent African politicians, incensed by 'illegal' New Zealand rugby union involvement with apartheid South Africa – notwithstanding that rugby was not an Olympic sport – provoked the withdrawal of African nations, led by Tanzania.

'It was sad for me,' Bayi recalls. 'I was ready, training for four years for this following Munich. I'd suffered malaria in the months beforehand, but reckoned I was still good for a medal. The way John won in Montreal, with 3:39, I knew I would have been close, even winning, watching on television.'

The last hurrah could have been at Moscow's Olympics of 1980. Now 27, Bayi rightly judged that he would be unlikely to mount a challenge to either of the record-breaking Steve Ovett and Sebastian Coe, so he switched his target to the steeplechase; desperate to achieve Tanzania's first Olympic gold medal. Opposition would be Bronisław Malinowski of Poland, fourth in Munich and winner of a silver medal in Montreal, the European champion of 1974 and '78. Malinowski, with a Scottish mother, might have opted to run for Britain. Come the summer, inexperienced hurdler Bayi defeated Malinowski on a summer circuit 'warm-up'. In Moscow's humid stadium, the trojan African, driven by patriotism, yet once more led the field by 30 metres after two kilometres and by five metres at the bell. I can truthfully say I was all but moved to tears on his behalf as Malinowski remorselessly overtook with 200 metres remaining, leaving Bayi with silver. A year later, Malinowsi would die in a car crash.

In retirement, an industrious Bayi created an education foundation, based in Mkuza, 50km from Dar es Salaam, consisting of primary and secondary schools, each aimed at lifting children out of poverty and in the late 20th century to be familiar with the threat of AIDS. He still has mooted regret at omission from the World Athletics Hall of Fame. 'I feel it's been forgotten,' Bayi reflected during an interview at Glasgow's Commonwealth Games of 2014. 'Maybe there's something wrong with the athletic family – a 1,500 metres was once a slow start and then a sprint. I changed all that!

Subsequently, world records again needed pacemakers. I think a world record should come when someone does it by themselves ... 40 years on, I'm still being interviewed by a few from Australia, New Zealand and the UK.' And worth the memory, a man who valued his country as much as his pride in himself.

JOHAN CRUYFF
Evolutionary Architect

*'Football without artistry is
not worth watching'*

Attempting to tell the absorbing story of Johan Cruyff, the most exceptional European footballer of all time, it is difficult to know whether to dwell on his performance as player, as elusive as a fox, or as manager/coach, as intellectual as some evolutionary architect. No elite player has ever been a top-flight coach, nor an eminent coach previously been a box-office star on the field. The working-class boy, born of greengrocer parents a stone's throw from the old De Meer Stadion in Amsterdam, did not so much change the game in the 1970s – in a nation belatedly grappling with full-time professionalism – as re-invent strategic concepts. Cruyff was a nominal centre-forward yet mastermind tactician for Ajax, Barcelona and Holland; subsequently a formative strategic coach for the two clubs. His intellect infected many followers, and can be said to have helped fashion not merely three consecutive European Cup titles with Ajax from 1971 to '73 but also 11 trophies in eight golden years as coach of Barcelona in the 1990s, thereby establishing the template for dominance by that club and the Spanish national team in the 2000s.

The lone blight upon Cruyff's exemplary influence within the global game came from the simple, agonising aberration at the climax of the World Cup of 1974 in West Germany.

Across three decades, it was my fortunate intermittent task to listen to Cruyff expounding on the principles of Total Football – the concept expanded from the example of Hungary's interpassing in the 1950s and then the all-field monopoly of Di Stéfano with Real Madrid, suffused through Cruyff by coach Rinus Michels. Several times Cruyff admitted the conundrum, 'Football without artistry is not worth watching, but playing only for the result is boring.' With calamitous emotional lapse, Cruyff and his Dutch colleagues effectively lost the final of 1974 in the opening 90 seconds of the match.

Holland had arrived in Germany as soar-away favourites, compiling in the opening rounds a goal aggregate of 14-1. They trounced Argentina during an evening thunderstorm which the team emulated with four goals, then outplaying shamelessly brutal title defenders Brazil in the semi-final. Unsettled Germany, embarrassingly defeated in the opening round by their GDR neighbours from the East, were short on consistency if not character. Holland kicked off in the final and with stylish nonchalance they danced elusively through 15 consecutive passes, Cruyff finally gliding clear of jailer Berti Vogts before being felled two yards into the penalty area. English referee Jack Taylor, a butcher from Wolverhampton, nervelessly awarded a penalty against the hosts, and Neeskens scored. Germany had yet to touch the ball.

This abrupt, dramatic advantage misguidedly persuaded Cruyff and colleagues that they could now bury the opposition, settling some old scores from 1940–45, and make them look foolish. Cruyff himself forgot that Germany, of all teams, would never surrender in the remaining 88 minutes. Attempts to toy with Germany foundered, and the day was lost as Breitner and Müller put West Germany ahead before half-time. Holland dominated the second half, Cruyff being unable to free himself from the tentacles of the rugged Vogts, now playing the match of his life.

The outcome was inadvertently complex for me: I was commissioned to write the English edition of West Germany's official, four-language book on the finals. How tactfully to write that the result was justified by events yet perverted the judgement of history? Rudi Krol, Holland's sumptuous full-back, was philosophical, 'You can score too quickly, and start thinking about the result instead of about the game. It's probably true to say that it was better for Germany that we scored so quickly than for us. It made them realise just what they now had to do. We woke up too late.'

Of the dozen or more times I saw Cruyff play, that was his only uncharacteristic performance. The revelation that was emerging in Holland came at a time when England's national side was fading at the unexpected conclusion of the reign of Alf Ramsey and had failed to qualify for the finals of 1974. The impact of Cruyff, aged 23, was already raising eyebrows as Ajax had galloped to three consecutive victories in the European Cup, with many minds across Europe as yet unaware of the Total Football syndrome being fashioned by coach Michels around the blossoming genius of Cruyff.

The germ of some of the principles had originally emerged in Amsterdam when Vic Buckingham arrived, an imaginative manager to a degree disregarded in England when working with West Bromwich Albion and Fulham – touch play at odds in the Football League with the conventional long-ball game.

As a teenager, Cruyff responded to Buckingham, the more so when inspired, at the European final of 1962 in Amsterdam between Benfica and Real Madrid, by the orchestral co-ordination of every phase of the match by intuitive Alfredo Di Stéfano. Although Real lost, here was a demonstration of Total Football's 'architecture' governed by a player on the pitch. With Michels replacing Buckingham, Cruyff now had the ideal mentor for rattling the bars of Europe's conventional football cage. Cruyff had joined the Ajax academy when ten, and left school at 13 to work in a sports clothing store after morning training. His father dying when he was 12 and his mother re-marrying, as a boy he understood the value of labour, often being engaged on stadium jobs. When, later, he had learned that Netherlands FA directors had travel insurance on foreign trips but not the players, he was swift in demanding correction.

Insular England tended to be unaware of foreign trends in European football if British clubs were uninvolved, or playing distant opposition. 'Where the hell's Kiev, old boy?' asked the *Telegraph* sports editor when I tentatively suggested we should cover Celtic's first-round defence as European Cup holders in 1967: they lost, unreported in England. Nobody much knew that Ajax were beaten European finalists in 1969 – Cruyff to the fore – and even when they defeated Panathinaikos in the 1970 final at Wembley, coverage had been non-committal: the Greeks were better known, the British went there on holiday, didn't they? Victory for Ajax in 1972 over Inter Milan came courtesy of two unspectacular goals by Cruyff. By 1973, a European semi-final involving Ajax drew attention in the UK because the opposition was Real Madrid. Awareness of Cruyff had now crossed the North Sea, and I was dispatched to Amsterdam where a 2-1 first-leg victory, with Cruyff less than fit, seemed probably inadequate. The return, at the Bernabéu, was the ultimate exposition by the orchestra conductor: Cruyff directed the game from penalty area to penalty area, effectively a coach on the field, and Ajax were never threatened, though they scored only once. A third title victory followed against Juventus, central defender Barry Hulshoff reflecting, 'The team had its own kind of architecture, where every player knew when and where to run, where to find space, how to understand the geometry of the team over the entire pitch, a collective awareness.' This symmetry was currency for Cruyff and a $2m transfer to Barcelona followed. Would Total Football's 3-1-4-2 formation enliven indifferent rivals to arch enemies Real?

What was frustrating for Cruyff's by now global audience was that he never came to be summoned by the Dutch federation formally to handle the national team – given that he had done so, informally, on the pitch as player, in conjunction with Michels, as roving adjudicator. I had repetitively witnessed this dual function: in the 1973 semi-final against Real, central defenders Hulshoff and Horst Blankenburg would often be found within shooting range of Real's goal. Conversely, when England met Holland in 1977, England's central defenders Watson and Doyle were perplexed: for 90 minutes in a two-goal defeat they had no one to mark, the Dutch jigsaw having a mercurial six-man midfield and no apparent designated striker.

That is not to say that Cruyff was always conciliatory. There had often been dressing-room frictions within Ajax or the national team, perhaps explaining hesitancy by the national federation in granting Cruyff international control. Prior to a European Championship qualifier against Poland in 1975, goalkeeper Jan van Beveren and striker Willy van der Kuijlen had deserted the squad in defiance of Cruyff's on-field authority.

It would be presumptuous to claim that I knew Cruyff well during his 25 years of eminence: it was a journalistic bonus that many of the multi-lingual Dutch were readily available to discuss events and attitudes, none more than Cruyff, his ideas a tap that was never dry. Three times during his heady years as Barcelona's coach from 1988 to '96 I was audience to his philosophy; the first occasion when, having terminated three years at the tiller of Ajax, he was assembling disjointed threads back in Catalonia, while simultaneously Sepp Blatter, FIFA's general secretary, was randomly blaming coaches for negative football. Cruyff's explanation was unequivocal, 'Declining emphasis on technical skill, over-emphasis on tactics rather than simple possession – you can only score if you have the ball! – and the inability of referees to stifle negative play, for instance passing back to the goalkeeper. So much of the game has become a fight with muscle rather than with the ball.'

Gradually, over his eight years at Camp Nou, Cruyff would institute a cycle of development, from the youth academy to the first team, that would not only immediately harvest trophies but would transform Spain's football concept for two decades, embracing the 21st century emergence of Messi, Xavi and Iniesta. Cruyff's years as Camp Nou *generalissimo* were a landmark in football history, although were strangely forgotten in time by Holland, the nation from where the ideas emanated. I only wish that what I learned from Cruyff at the age of 60 I had known at 20, and might not then have retired as a player in 1957 to become a scribbler! These are the maxims of the gospel from my last conversation with the 'Pythagoras in Boots':

- Midfield controls the game, so a 3-5-2 formation should be used to control midfield
- Keep the defence trio *deep* – this lures opposition attackers forward, increasing the distance, and connection, among your opposing players
- Use your sweeper *in front* of the defence as interceptor and link with the midfield
- All ten players operate as a collective group, attacking or defending, attempting to maintain possession. You can only score *with* the ball
- Touch-and-go, yes, but where? Every pass should have a measured intention. Group-passing creates space elsewhere, while isolating opponents
- In training, play six against four, in a space the size of the penalty area, with two players regularly swapping sides to join the 'four' who have just gained possession, so that the 'six' have more options: the heart of the midfield principle
- In passing, the passer mostly has a better view of the receiver's possibility than does the receiver, probably with his back to goal. The passer's positioning of the pass is therefore crucial to the receiver's turning capability
- Learning these fundamentals, alongside ball control, must be established by the age of 12 if a player is to become elite

Following that moral thrashing of Real Madrid by Ajax in the European Cup semi-final of 1973, my 11-year-old son happened to be with me when I went to interview Sunderland manager Bob Stokoe prior to the FA Cup Final against Leeds (a memorable underdog victory). While we were at Roker Park, the former Sunderland idol Len Shackleton had paid a chance visit. Who was he, my son asked. I made a comparison with Cruyff: a player so unorthodox, so insolently clever on the ball, so affectionately popular, that his mesmerising skill alone had justified the price of a ticket. Sceptical England selectors had confined his war-curtailed career to five caps. 'Shack' had needed a Cruyff to direct his art.

ARTHUR ASHE
Global Racial Campaigner

'Being black is the greatest burden'

If fortunate we may encounter, in life, beyond husband or wife and our immediate family, someone whose company leaves us feeling emotionally enlightened and improved simply for knowing them. Such a person was Arthur Ashe. It is genuine for me to say I would have valued his friendship and wisdom – in his abruptly curtailed but illuminated years as a Wimbledon and Davis Cup sporting icon and expansive racial integration campaigner – irrespective of his origins. In conversation, we were mutually and affectionately socially colour-blind.

It used to be termed, in the armed forces, 'lack of moral fibre' until medical perception identified this as 'post-traumatic stress disorder'. Nowhere is the regard for colloquial 'guts' more evident than in sport. I have watched and written about thousands of performers, been friendly with many, known a handful intimately, particularly when writing their biographies: Matt Busby, Trevor Francis, Stanley Matthews, Sebastian Coe, Juan Antonio Samaranch and Kim Un-yong. Yet none has exposed, behind that immaculate calm exterior, the tensions and indeed torment that life and fame imposed upon the urbane Ashe. As experienced by 'outsider' heavyweight boxing

238

champion Jack Johnson, later Joe Louis and Muhammad Ali, and in between times Olympic legend Jesse Owens – plus the host of audible African-American racial sporting agitators of today – every moment of Ashe's exceptional life, notwithstanding his international and domestic recognition and acclaim, was clouded by ambient racial overtones.

Of this I was well aware through our intermittent discussion between matches. And it was wholly coincidental that, just as he was composing his premature farewell memoir, I was attempting to explain, inadequately, to his six-year-old daughter Camera, in an open letter in *The Times*, her father's unique will to rationalise humanity's confused social history. Arthur's words were so appropriately titled 'Days of Grace'. I have never encountered in sport a more gracious man or woman – he reluctantly acknowledging the imminence of death from an HIV-infected blood transfusion during a scheduled hospital operation. He was devoting his fading energy to a beloved daughter, expounding to an infant a summary of his communal philosophy, for philosopher he truly was.

It was characteristic of Arthur that he made light in his memoir of the most dramatic and spectacular event of all, his victory in 1975 against the overwhelming Wimbledon favourite, defending champion Jimmy Connors, the anvil-hardened left-hander who was widely expected to torpedo a compatriot ten years his senior at 32. Wimbledon has always reserved a special affection for the old guy who keeps coming back. It was symptomatic that Wimbledon's Christmas card six months earlier had depicted not champion Connors but evergreen runner-up Ken Rosewall. For all the lingering idolatry still surrounding past champion Bjorn Borg, in a quarter-final now against Ashe the crowd was predominantly behind the refined yet, from his demeanour, seemingly unambitious American. Next, in the semi-final, perhaps crucial to his consequent confrontation with Connors, Ashe demolished another left-hander, Australian Tony Roche, two years his junior and runner-up to inimitable Rod Laver back in 1968. For the *Daily Express*, I wrote that this semi-final 'had strengthened Ashe's altruistic attempt to bridge the barriers still oppressing the world's coloured people'. That bridge had been previously crossed, somewhat unavailingly, by Althea Gibson, the first Afro-American to appear at Wimbledon, winning successively in 1956 and '57 and then subsequently by Aborigine champion Evonne Goolagong in 1971 and, as a mother, in 1980.

I had been an avid advocate behind Arthur since he first appeared in England at Beckenham in 1966, lithe and with whiplash speed. In that early Beckenham appearance, when Ashe was already the US number two, an early-round English opponent, Geoff Bluett, had observed, 'I can't remember a more purposeful serve since Neale Fraser.'

Attempting to capture for young Camera a concept of the occasion, for her later years, of an astonishing Wimbledon triumph, I related the story for *The Times* in 1993. Her father did not merely win the crown he so deserved, I suggested, delighting millions and restoring to the tournament much of its historic tradition of dignity in the wake of recent controversial bouts, but had joined that select band of champions, in any sport, whose triumphs were distinguished by the cool clarity of sports intellect rather than the raw aggression of physical skills: those such as Olympic track champions Jack Lovelock and Herb Elliott or golfer Peter Thomson, whose performances had so often floated on a private cloud. Ashe's was a triumph of the mind of meticulous planning, of resolute tactical self-discipline against the exceptional and seemingly irresistible physical attributes of the defending, odds-on young champion. 'Arthur is so cool he is almost cold,' observed one of the game's most astute judges, commentator Dan Maskell, the day before the final. The fundamental warmth of the man was clearly revealed in his gently self-mocking but humorous speech at the evening's Wimbledon ball, recalling Kipling's celebrated verse, scrolled on the club's honours board, 'If you can trust yourself when all men doubt you.'

Ashe was a sculptor's dream, with that noble head and inscrutable gaze, and now he had won every psychological round against his demonstrative but demoralised opponent. Never would Ashe begin his silky yet ferocious serve until Connors was already emotionally taut and muscularly crouched in preparation to receive. Yet when Ashe was himself receiving, he would casually stand, racket head limp, looking at Connors across the net as though he was watching the match rather than playing it, obliging Connors to be the one to begin motion on the next point. When Ashe gratuitously would toss an unused service ball back over the net after winning a service game, the gesture carried a mental superiority more telling than any earlier aggression by Connors in declining to represent the US in the Davis Cup. When asked afterwards if this was his finest moment, Ashe answered, 'No, the second greatest. Winning the Davis Cup in 1967 comes first – winning for your country must always be the best. Wimbledon is equal second with winning Forest Hills, our own championship.'

Sensitivity was always there. In his memoir, Arthur recalled one of his journeys to South Africa, including controversially participating in the South African Open during the era of apartheid, which for him was an arena of exploration and education. He recalled being followed around Johannesburg's

Ellis Park, the hallowed rugby site but also home for the tennis, by a 14-year-old boy, watchful but shy, as though he were trailing Ashe to gain some mystical possession. When confronted, the boy answered, 'You are the first one I have ever seen.' The first what, Ashe enquired. 'You are the first truly free black man I have ever seen,' claimed the boy. It gave the American a distinct chill: no one had so captured as poignantly the abyss of inhumanity that was apartheid. Yet this was a burden with which he was familiar at home. The burden had not been lessened by the advent of his later perilous disease. Asked by a reporter from *People* magazine whether AIDS was the heaviest penalty he had had to bear, he answered, 'No, being black is the greatest burden – having to live as a minority in America, even now, feels like an extra weight tied around me.'

In his final chapter to Camera, he pleads for her to trust in family, that whatever her direction when she becomes an adult she must be fighting for morally justifiable ends, upholding the family tree going back ten generations to their time as slaves. He warns here that black demagogues, spawned by the poor conditions under which many Afro-Americans were still forced to live, would try to advance their own narrow political careers by fomenting, artificially, deeper schisms among ethnic minorities in fact bearing goodwill. Lastly, like he himself, Camera should be moved by art and poetry. 'Don't let anyone tell you that either is frivolous or expendable or inferior to making money. Without either, and music, life would be dry and without feeling. Art comes from an urge as primal as that of survival itself.'

In my 'open letter' I told Camera, that though I was white, 'For your father that was not something to separate us but a starting point for closer communication and friendship, what he attempted to encourage among millions with the fundamentals for humanity of tolerance, understanding and generosity.' I said that there were three reasons why an ordinary writer on sport should presume to try to tell her something about her own father: firstly, on almost every page of his memoir, evidence of his special love for her and her mother; that he strove to make sport a vehicle for wider communication, keeping his own fame in perspective while he tried to utilise the common language of sport to break barriers in the way it had broken them for him; lastly, that her father, as a sportsman, had the truest philosophy about sport, with an Olympian concept about the attitudes to competition, and especially the difficulty for women: to winning and losing and how we should conduct ourselves in attitudes towards others, especially when we do not like them, in case in our judgement we may have misunderstood them.

The lessons of sport, he decreed, could not be duplicated easily. We should remember that he had experience over 20 years of tournament play, from 1959 to '79. His unceasing work to confront America's social divide was universally recognised. Richmond, in his home state Virginia, in 1982 built the Arthur Ashe Athletics Center, housing 6,000. Upon his untimely death in 1993, there were 5,000 mourners at his funeral, conducted by Andrew Young, an arch disciple of Martin Luther King who had also officiated at his marriage in 1977. Ashe instituted the Foundation for the Defeat of AIDS; he was posthumously honoured in 1993 with the Jefferson Award for Greatest Public Service; the Presidential Medal of Freedom, presented by Bill Clinton; and the Humanitarian Award of the Year by the Association of Tennis Professionals – on court an intellectual hero, off court a social emblem.

MUHAMMAD ALI
A Friend of Bertrand Russell

*'I'd become an important part of a
movement I hardly knew existed'*

If sport really does matter, and equally thereby those
participating or compulsively watching, then an audience of
three and a half billion being enraptured by the sight of an
ageing, ailing monolith hero, is verification of the concept.
With a darkened Atlanta Stadium being the focus of half the
world's population, the silhouette of a white-clad Muhammad
Ali, cultural and sporting legend now barely able to hold
steady the torch with which he will ignite the cauldron for the
opening of the Centenary Olympic Games, is an emotional
moment in history. Wrought by Parkinson's stranglehold, Ali
is still at heart the wilful, flamboyant ambassador of civil
rights and Afro-American integration, here in the heart of the
former Deep South: not to mention three times heavyweight
world champion with 21 knockouts in 56 victories during 61
bouts.

There have been those – whites – on Atlanta's organising
committee who have not approved of this Muslim convert, a
1960s Vietnam alleged draft dodger, being nominated to open
ceremoniously Georgia's door to the Olympic world's 200-plus

nations, and whose personal liberty objection cost three prime years in the ring and, equally divisive, respect or disapproval. Sane influence, however, including that of overriding sponsor NBC television's Dick Ebersol, navigated the essential, only choice. America's humanitarian principles had yet to be re-written – and still have 25 years later – but Ali, with courage, language, wit, generosity and fraternity had illuminated the runway, his personal launchpad the Olympic Games of Rome in 1960 as light-heavyweight boxing champion. Now on this night of union among past and would-be champions, Ali was the final torch-bearer; in succession to Al Oerter, four times discus winner who entered the stadium; passing on to local boy Evander Holyfield, Olympic heavyweight champion of 1984; Voula Patoulidou, Greek hurdler of 1992; and Janet Evans, US swimming icon.

The vision of Ali, the most famous figure on the planet, touched America's conscience in multiple ways, some ordinary. Linda Kelly, CEO of the UK's Parkinson's Disease Society, knew Ali offered a global message, 'of hope to everyone affected, the image of him standing alone, with the tremor in his hands, was truly unforgettable'. Daley Thompson, Moscow decathlon champion, acclaimed Ali's lifetime example, 'He proved it was possible for the poor, uneducated and disenfranchised to fulfil their dreams. He showed if it was possible for him, others could follow their path and succeed. He is not perfect, not unbeatable, but he is the greatest.' Pragmatic boxing promoter Bob Arum, admitting he had been wrong when disapproving of the 'Louisville Lip' deciding to oppose army recruitment, was fulsome, 'Ali's exploits in the ring pale in comparison with his impact on the world.'

Cassius Clay, as was his birth name, was born in January 1942, in Louisville, Kentucky, son of Cassius Marcellus

Clay, himself named after a 19th-century abolitionist and descendant of African slaves. Clay's maternal great-grandfather emigrated from Ireland, DNA testing in 2018 revealing that his paternal grandmother was a descendant of Archie Alexander, a central figure of an abolitionist history, *From Slavery to Freedom*. Young Clay was guided into boxing aged 12 by a local police officer and boxing coach, Joe Martin, subsequently by trainer Fred Stoner, with a debut bout in 1954. Six Kentucky Golden Glove titles, two national titles and an AAU championship were followed by light-heavyweight gold at Rome's Olympics in 1960: an amateur match record of 100 wins and five defeats. His tossing of his medal into a river back home when refused service at a white gas station is thought to be an inaccurate anecdote, but already he was acquiring the label of the 'Lip' by his uninhibited wit at the expense of ring opponents: a style initiated in conversation with professional wrestler 'Gorgeous George' Wagner in 1961. Magazine editor Emil Wilbekin noted Clay as 'lyricist and wordsmith, using language to spar with opponents and engage the media', Clay already in league with cornerman Angelo Dundee, minder for the next 20 years.

Hugh McIlvanney, a perceptive UK journalist who addictively followed Clay's career, observed, 'There was troubling contradiction in his public persona, when supporting Black Muslim doctrine [adopted by him in the mid-1960s], and cruel when belittling opponents, seeming contrived for effect, but at the core of his nature was warm humanity, a vibrant love of life and people, with wit and intellect never obscured by lack of education.' Clay's professional debut was a six-round defeat of Tunney Hunsaker, in the wake of the Olympics, with a 19-0 success run including 15 knockouts by 1963; among them former champion and his part-time trainer

Archie Moore, and UK hopeful Henry Cooper – Clay floored by the latter in the fourth round but saved by the bell. Cooper later recalled, 'He was very unorthodox [in his comments], if we'd tried that, we'd have been hammered, but he got away with it, which made him special. He was the fastest thing on two legs. When he scorned opponents, they became angry, which paid off as he was Mr Cool. Whenever I see him now, he always gives me a bear hug.'

By late 1963, Clay was leading contender to challenge Sonny Liston for the heavyweight title: a supposed ominous prospect against a former mobster who had twice disposed of past champion Floyd Patterson in first-round knockouts. Clay, at 22, was a gambler's rank outsider, yet provocatively asserting, 'After I beat him I'll donate him to the zoo.' Yet by the third round of the February 1964 bout, Clay was outmanoeuvring the champion, inflicting on him a cut eye for the first time in his career having him groggy. Weeping eyes, infliction unidentified – possibly ointment on Liston's face – temporarily impeded Clay, but his unceasing assault found Liston failing to answer the bell for the seventh round, claiming a shoulder injury, Clay becoming the youngest person to defeat a reigning holder. Almost immediately, Clay changed his name to Cassius X, because of his affiliation to Malcolm X, then again to Muhammad Ali in sympathy to the Nation of Islam. A rematch a year later saw Liston sink to the canvas in the first round from an unapparent blow, referee and former champion Jersey Joe Walcott delaying the count until advised by timekeepers that Liston had failed it.

With two successive defences, the first against Floyd Patterson, Ali was now scheduled for a second bout with Cooper in London in May 1966. Simultaneously, he had refused, in March, the US Army's notification of his draft for Vietnam, while declining an affiliation to Nation of Islam, and adhering to Sunni Islam. He pronounced, 'I am American. I am the part you won't recognise. Get used to me. Black, confident, cocky. My name, not yours. My religion, not yours, my goals, my own.' Widespread fury lashed out at him from across America with a torrent of hate mail, and unremitting phone calls of resentment and abuse. He rode them all, steadfast in his conviction. 'Without planning, I'd become an important part of a movement I hardly knew existed.'

One call intrigued him: an English voice. The caller asked if he had been quoted correctly. Yes, Ali responded, but why did everyone want to know what he thought about Vietnam? Well, said the caller, the war was more barbaric than any other, and because of Ali's lifestyle, there was curiosity about the world champion's opinion. Ali explained he would soon be in England to fight Cooper again, so asked what the caller expected of the outcome. 'I'd pick you,' was the response. 'You're not as dumb as you look,' joked Ali. The caller was unable to attend the fight – a six-round KO by Ali, but they exchanged postcards. The name Bertrand Russell meant little to a Louisville lad, until he noticed it in an encyclopaedia – a foremost mathematician and philosopher of the 20th century. An immediate apology for 'not so dumb'. Russell could not make the fight, but wrote, 'I read your letter with admiration and personal respect. There is no doubt that the men who rule Washington will try to damage you in every way open to them, but I am sure you know that you spoke for your people and for the oppressed everywhere in the courageous defiance of American power. They will try to break you because you are a symbol of a force they are unable to destroy, namely, the aroused consciousness of a whole people determined no longer to be butchered and debased with fear and oppression. You have my wholehearted support. Call me when you come to England. Yours sincerely, Bertrand Russell.' The gesture was never possible.

Following victory against Cooper, there were five successive title defences with four knockouts before Ali's boxing licence was terminated, and a prison conviction stalled pending appeals. He had forfeited over three years of his prime for his principles. Ultimately he returned for an undisputed title fight with Joe Frazier in March 1971 at Madison Square Garden. His share of the purse was $2.5m, which after a national tax and that by New York City and New York State would be some $600,000. In a torturous 15 rounds, in which Ali's jaw was broken, Frazier earned a unanimous verdict, afterwards coming to Ali's dressing room to concede, 'You put up a great fight.'

Over the next three years, Ali accumulated ten victories, including six knockouts, by now his 32 years beginning to limit his physical extravagance if not his emotional flamboyance, with another swift defeat of Patterson. In March 1973 came confrontation with iron-fisted Ken Norton at San Diego. A split decision in a fluctuating bout narrowly went to Norton, with Ali's jaw again fractured and his watching wife, Belinda, collapsing in hysteria. A 'friendly' visit by Norton to the loser's dressing room was a furtive means to enable a photographer to obtain shots of a crushed Ali and triumphant Norton, which duly went viral. America's foremost commentator Howard Cosell announced that Ali 'was finished'. Not quite. Six months later in LA, he reversed the outcome over 12 rounds.

Four months on, Ali was digging deep, out on the road, preparing for another shot at Frazier back in New York, scene of the defeat three years earlier. Ali reflected, 'Prize fights are not so much decided over the 15 rounds, but like a war, the real part is away from witnesses, behind the lines, in the gymnasium, on the road, long before you dance under the lights.' That quote is taken from Ali's impeccable, revealing autobiography, *The Greatest*, written in collaboration with Richard Durham. Those hours on the road would bestow a unanimous points decision over 12 rounds.

Ali's commercial drawing power was now astronomic and a duel in Zaire against the formidable George Foreman, at Kinshasa in October 1974, would earn him $5.5m. He received a pre-fight warning from veteran champion Archie Moore, 'Foreman is the most improved heavyweight since Joe Louis – much of your pressure is time-worn.' Ali himself was wondering, 'Am I too old?' A training partner of Foreman, Bossman Jones, was persuaded to visit Ali's training camp: what was Foreman's condition, who did Jones predict as winner? The answer was intimidating, 'Foreman's training harder than ever, I expect him to win.' Anxiety in Ali's camp. On an overbearingly humid night, he discovered George 'was the first constantly to cut me off', as Ali attempted his renowned defensive shuffle, yet he defied the odds for an eighth-round knockout to regain the heavyweight title, taunting Foreman near the end with, 'Is that all you've got, George?'

Onwards another year to a third encounter with Frazier, who was reluctant to face possible further nemesis but finding irresistible a $2m purse – compared to Ali's $6m. Ali meanwhile considered if he should give Foreman another chance, but lawyers steered him towards Frazier, whom he continued to tease. 'Trouble with you, Joe, is you can't dance. But if you win, I'll give you a million from my share.' Frazier bit. Ali would recall of the 'Thrilla in Manila', 'The most destructive battle I ever had, I gave it everything I could, and he wouldn't go down.' In his corner, Ali, near collapse, wondered if he himself could make the 15th round off his stool, barely able to discern that Frazier could not rise from his. Frazier later admitted, 'I hit you with blows that would ordinarily knock down a wall, and you still stood up.' From such punishment does Parkinson's arise: between the two of them over three bouts, 41 blood-curdled rounds. At dinner that evening, Philippines president Ferdinand Marcos joked about a financial pre-fight bet between the two. 'We owe each other nothing,' Ali replied. 'We're both free now.'

Whatever the motivation, driven only by some sense of universal destiny, Ali continued. I was there for his unnecessary, sad, penultimate fight, a futile challenge to defending champion Larry Holmes, his former sparring partner, who was intent on not diminishing the legend opposing him: an icon with four wives, nine children and several billion admirers. Before the bout in Las Vegas, I wrote for the *Daily Express*, 'Ali's chance is as remote as when that other legend, the classic Joe Louis, at 37 unwisely tried to turn back the clock against Rocky Marciano. One imponderable overrides all others – whether Holmes, former $500-a-week sparring partner of Ali, has the mental resolution not to be psyched out of the 15-round points decision which must otherwise unquestionably be his.'

On the inevitable outcome of the non-fight, I dejectedly reported, 'The Americans are accustomed to paying expensively for antiques. The millions they paid at Caesars Palace parking lot was for a dud reproduction of the real, revered original. It was billed as The Last Hurrah, but, heartrendingly, all it could ever be was The Last Post. Muhammad Ali climbed through the ropes last night still a universal idol. He was hustled out an hour later a discredited, dejected, broken old man. Immortal

Joe Louis was one of the celebrities present, an ailing figure in a wheelchair, Stetson and carpet slippers. Ali's trainer, Angelo Dundee, humanely halted the slaughter after ten rounds to avoid his man requiring the same transport. As Larry Holmes was declared undisputed world heavyweight champion, the heavenly choir of some Hollywood film score filled the air like a requiem, while search lights split the night sky illuminating the real winner – Caesars Palace Hotel … At the first bell, Holmes whirled in ferociously, jabbing through the taunts of "C'mon, c'mon fight, sucker". There was to be only one sucker inside the ring. Ali backed off, eyes marvellously alive, but body sluggish, swaying and weaving. There was no attempt to fight, only to make Holmes look stupid. Holmes wasn't buying … By the sixth round, the crowd was now booing the static figure, a sound never known before. The Lip was silent now.'

A later autobiography, *The Soul of a Butterfly*, written in conjunction with daughter Hana, portrayed Ali's abiding generosity towards the world towards to which he had given so much: moral support, generosity, religious beliefs. As Hana herself said, 'He's my father first, but also my hero. He took stands for his religious beliefs, which meant a lot to black Americans at a time when they were being lynched. He stood up for what he believed in: he was outspoken and confident. His titles weren't for himself, but so he could go out on the road and show black people that they could achieve anything at a time when people were following the crowd and it was hard to be true to yourself. And the world loved him for that … he was, and is, always there for us.'

In a signing-off, Ali reflected, 'I would like to be remembered as a man who won the heavyweight title three times, who was humorous and who treated everyone right. As a man who never looked down on those who looked up to him, and who helped as many people as he could. As a man who stood up for his beliefs, no matter what. As a man who tried to unite all humankind through faith and love. And if all that's too much, then I guess I'd settle for being remembered only as a great boxer who became a leader and a champion of his people. And I wouldn't even mind if folks forgot how pretty I was.'

It is estimated that Ali's gifts to charity will have contributed to the feeding of 22 million people over the course of his lifetime. Another estimate is that across the world 60 million people will have viewed his edition of the BBC programme *This Is Your Life*. In 1967, he donated $10,000 to the United Negro College Fund. In 1984, he backed President Ronald Reagan's election 'for keeping God in schools'. He was an active campaigner for Rwandan Aid in 1994. In 2000, he contributed substantially to the Michael J. Fox Foundation for Parkinson's Disease Research. Early in life, Ali was granted a global passport without frontiers.

BILLIE JEAN KING
The Gibraltar of Gender Equality

'When you lose, you don't
play the next day!'

A tennis novice at junior school, being small I soon discovered the tactical winning ruse of the drop-volley against the big hitters, and was immediately regarded as underhand and non-sporting. Imagine the satisfaction, therefore, of encountering, as a novice journalist at Beckenham's Kent Championship in 1961, the most accomplished women's low volleyer (struck from below net level) there has probably ever been: teenager Billie Jean Moffitt, equally adroit with the drop-volley. I can truthfully say that for 60 years ever since, I have been thrilled by the recollection of Billie Jean King – as she became a few years later – along with many men and, it has to be said, even more women.

Leaving aside elements of her charm or inoffensive questions of her sexuality, King became a role model for millions of women way beyond the conventional dimensions of 20th-century feminism. King was, or became, a champion of gender equality irrespective of how women looked or behaved, yet while herself maintaining an outwardly upbeat demeanour. A matter of 'like me because of what I *do*, and the way I do it' rather than her perceived gender. There were those who still objected to her, men and women, as her fame rocketed.

So, first, the 24-year statistics of this exceptional sportswoman, famously described by NBC commentator Bud Collins as 'a firefighter's inextinguishable daughter', in reference to fireman Bill Moffitt from Long Beach, California. Moffitt-King was to win 39 Grand Slam tournaments: 12 singles, 16 doubles and 11 mixed doubles, also victorious for the United States in seven Federation Cups and nine Wightman Cups. She had a record 20 titles at Wimbledon – six, ten and four respectively – and 129 career titles. Her Federation Cup match record was 54-9, winning successively the last 30; in the Wightman Cup it was 22-4. She played in 51 Grand Slam events from 1959 to '83, reaching at least the semi-final 27 times, and is one of five women to have won all four Grand Slams. In the Wightman Cup, her singles results were 6-1 against Ann Jones, 4-0 against Virginia Wade, and 1-1 against Christine Truman. How's that for willpower from a girl of only 5ft 4in (1.64m), who later survived multiple knee operations while maintaining major tournament form. The fame began the year I first witnessed her extravagance aged 17, progressing from Beckenham to win Wimbledon's doubles in partnership with 18-year-old Karen Hantze, the youngest ever pair. Her 1970 Wimbledon final against Margaret Court, a match of 46 games in which King fought off repeated match points before going down 14-12, 11-9, was considered the most riveting exhibition witnessed for a generation.

What has distinguished King, not merely during her prime years on court, has been her resonance with young women seeking emotional as much as employment and promotional equality. While essentially jovial – though bordering on aggressive if feeling administratively threatened, off court – throughout her years King has been demonstratively a battler, that characteristic creating a rare brand of feminist idol. This streak in her nature obliged her to revise her instinctive attitude to tennis. 'When I first started, I preferred to play artistically rather than just to win, there was more satisfaction. But when you lose, however artistically, you don't play the next day! That was the hardest thing to learn.'

It was not the only lesson, driven home within her irrepressible passion for life and instinct for gender equality. 'Being a girl was not the only thing I had to fight. I was brought up to be competent in general, yet not to put myself on the line. At some point I wondered why should one not be specialised, that I could really try.' Not being tall, slim and conventionally glamorous, King was determined to demonstrate that a short, non-Hollywood female with willpower and a ready smile could be just as successful as ungracious men with a big serve, regardless of their looks. It worked. There came a time when, in a survey by the US women's magazine *Seventeen*, nearly 40 per cent of girls listed King as the world's most admired woman. Consider that, Jane Fonda (with whom I once went camping together with her husband Ted Turner, up a mountain in Siberia when reconnoitring Krasnoyarsk as host city for the then Goodwill Games with Russia).

An essential leaf of the King image was created, aged 29, with her 'Battle of the Sexes' in 1973 against overt chauvinist Bobby Riggs, Wimbledon champion of 1939, by now 55 and boasting he would triumph against any of the current leading women. This he did by defeating multiple champion Margaret Court of Australia in straight sets. King, previously having rejected his challenge, now agreed to face him in a $100,000 winner-take-all contest. In front of a record 30,492 crowd at Houston Astrodome, with 50 million watching worldwide, King saw him off in straight sets. Estimates have American women's tennis participation soaring by six figures. King the icon was established. 'I thought it would set women back years if I didn't beat him, it would ruin our tour and women's esteem. The thrill was not winning, but experiencing new people coming into tennis.'

Her parents, father Bill and mother Betty, were doubtless not surprised. Aged 13, and asked by the minister of Long Beach's Church of the Brethren – former Olympic pole vault champion Bob Richards – what was her ambition, an assertive Moffitt had simply said, 'To be the world's best tennis player.' She had saved pocket money to buy her first $8 racket, getting her eye in at public courts with free lessons from professional Clyde Walker at facilities subsequently re-titled Billie Jean Moffitt-King Tennis Courts. Attending Long Beach Polytechnic and then California State University, Moffitt left early to focus on tennis. It was while at CSLA that she met Larry King, marrying aged 21 in 1965.

Marriage for Moffitt was an equivocal relationship. She and King were emotionally loyal, and he was studiously devoted to her interests throughout several decades until ultimate divorce and his re-marriage, thereafter remaining friends. A commendable aspect of Billie Jean's lifelong campaign for gender equality – if not uniformly admired – has been the irrelevance, for her, of her own sexuality. She is said to have had an abortion, then survived an ill-advised brief relationship with a woman who infamously and unsuccessfully sued for 'maintenance' in 1981 – damned by the judge in the process – a hiatus nobly endured by Larry. Yet so positive has Billie Jean's conviction remained about her life's professional

objectives on behalf of other women, that her personal prestige
has thankfully continued secure. An educated attitude that
her private life is her own, though there were times when
controversy clouded this self-confidence.

Ilana Kloss, a former doubles partner and close friend
in old age, once confided in Bud Collins, 'The only place
Billie Jean can find real peace is the tennis court, immersed
in what she loves best.' Evidence of that was apparent late in
King's Grand Slam career. After three months recovering from
continuing knee surgery in 1977, she played Maria Bueno,
in Wimbledon's third round, for the last time, winning in
straight sets1, then losing to Chris Evert in the quarter-final for
the first time in any Grand Slam event, admitting, 'No excuse.
Forget the injuries, she just played beautiful tennis. Maybe I
can be happy being number eight instead of number one. At
this stage, just *playing*, that's enough for me. Retire? You've
got to be kidding.' King continued that season with a 31-3
match record, winning five of the tournaments she entered,
and including four defeats of Martina Navratilova and two of
Wimbledon champion Virginia Wade. Resolute?

While she and Larry were actively collaborating, King
had founded the Women's Tennis Association – creating the
first women's professional group prior to 'Open' Wimbledon
– and subsequently the Women's Sports Foundation, cajoling
Virginia Slims to sponsor the women's tour in the 1970s. The
ultimate acclaim for this Gibraltar of gender independence
was bestowed in January 2021: the renaming of the Federation
Cup as the Billie Jean King Cup – the first major global team
competition to be named after a woman (the Wightman
Cup simply for two nations). The timing marked the 50th
anniversary of King's launch of the women's professional
circuit. David Haggerty, president of the International Tennis

Federation, stated, 'We feel the decision is long overdue. All major team competitions, including Davis Cup, are named after men. And we think it's fitting that the women's world cup of tennis would be named after someone as iconic as Billie Jean King, who changed the face of women's sports.'

In acceptance of the announcement, King said, 'Today, the players are living our dream, women's tennis is a leader in women's sports. We are also leaders in the fight for justice and equality. I remember the inaugural Federation Cup when I was 19, forced indoors at Queen's Club in London because of rain, and being match points down with Darlene Hard in the second set against Australians Margaret Smith and Lesley Turner, before we recovered to win the set 13-11, and then the match. I'd like to get more countries competing – we have 116, the men have 142. Cultures are different in many countries, so we're going to have work ahead of us to break things down … No one likes to be discounted, whether it's by gender, race or sexual orientation. We need to make it acceptable when somebody is their authentic self, to break down barriers.'

The finals, scheduled for April 2021 in Budapest, were delayed by COVID, King promising to be present whenever: the ultimate climax to an honourable life, conducted on the platform of sport, yet driven by convictions of gender equality and individuals being more important than the set score.

CHAPTER SEVEN

ESCALATION

BRASHER'S LONDON MARATHON
Greatest Folk Festival

'Hospitality to welcome the world'

If the government, and equally any regional or city council, needs convincing that sport matters, in 2019 there were certainly forty thousand souls who would have told them so. Just for starters. That was the number of applicants for entry to the London Marathon, and that is without all the others who play Sunday golf or irresponsibly swear at volunteer referees on unkempt council football pitches – those that have not been sold off for new housing developments. We are, Dear Boris, a paramount sporting nation, though to be generous to the Prime Minister, he did put heart and soul as Mayor into London's splendid Olympic Games. About one-fifth of marathon applicants, initially nearly 8,000, are accepted for the race: the evidence of the occasion, launched in 1981, being just one rung in the ladder for preserving national health – that being in decline through obesity – and is coincidentally a partial justification for my professional existence, a career devoted to the exposition of sporting events and their news, a mutual joy – mostly! – together with the participants.

As a vehicle for this particular passage of my story, I am wrapping this tale around the personalities of three elite specialists in the athletic arena: their initiatives have served to drive the impetus of a great national event, even though their respective individual experiences were on the one hand exhilarating, on the other, relatively disappointing: Chris Brasher, John Disley and Dave Bedford, each a distinguished runner, with Bedford a generation apart, Brasher and Disley initially instigators of the event, and Bedford later the race director.

As personally a moderate athlete – Cambridge freshman javelin thrower and hurdler in the relay team – I missed witnessing two of the conspicuous performances in Brasher's career: his pacing of the first two laps in Roger Bannister's epic breaking of the four-minute mile in 1954 and then the chance to have seen his Olympic steeplechase triumph at Melbourne in 1956 – in the wake of his own successful appeal against disqualification – because I was dropped from the GB football squad. Brasher was temperamentally robust as both athlete and then journalist for *The Observer*, and it was via his imagination when working in Fleet Street that the London Marathon project coalesced. His Melbourne victory had been iconoclastic. Close to the climax of a three-way tussle, Brasher had detected his chance to accelerate between rivals Rozsnyoi of Hungary and Norway's Larsen, Brasher's elbow bumping Larsen as they cleared a hurdle. Winning by over two seconds in an Olympic record of 8:41.2, Brasher found himself disqualified for obstruction. Unsupported by British officialdom, he lodged an appeal, neither of his opponents supporting the disqualification. Three hours later, he was reinstated: extended celebrations with British media prior to a medal ceremony delayed overnight saw Brasher all but legless on the medal podium.

Dave Bedford was as forthright a personality as Brasher: hugely committed, often when young impulsive and/or erratic, with a behavioural attitude not dissimilar to comedian/ magician Tommy Cooper's conjuring exclamation 'Just like that!' Bedford, a long-distance specialist ferociously over-training at some 200 miles a week, gave almost regular race forecasts of the 'watch me win' genre that were newsworthy but occasionally unfulfilled: notably for the Olympic 10,000m at Munich in 1972. Tall with angular limbs, Bedford's single tactic was to impose ferocious, intimidating pace, yet was without a finishing kick: in the strategies of championship racing, subtle pace-changes could unhinge his rhythm, as in Munich. In his heat, Bedford had discussed, impromptu, with joint leader Emiel Puttemans of Belgium, after eight kilometres, whether they should 'go for the world record'. Puttemans declined. The final was more complex, including the Olympic debut of Lasse Virén of Finland, who had recently beaten Bedford over two miles in Stockholm. Though Bedford now led after five kilometres, he was soon overhauled by accelerating Virén – who had instantly recovered from an early fall – and several others jockeying for the lead. The remarkable Virén, who in successive Games would achieve the double-double gold of 5,000m and 10,000m, now broke the world record of Australian Ron Clarke with 27:38.4. Bedford finished a jaded sixth.

Duly chastened, Bedford majestically reasserted his credentials a year later at home at Crystal Palace – without any prediction and in front of a modest crowd of 3,500. He lowered Virén's record by over seven seconds, with 27:30.8, his searing pace over the first five kilometres, 13:39.4, being itself world record quality a dozen years earlier. He was the first Brit to hold the 10,000m record since Alf Shrubb in 1904. The Commonwealth Games of 1974 in Christchurch, New Zealand, supposed a Bedford 10,000m summit but sadly it was to be a repeat of Munich, a disfigured race in which three Kenyans physically jostled their rivals, inviting unforthcoming disqualification, while unheralded Dick Tayler of New Zealand ran off with the prize. Bedford languished a disconsolate fourth, 44 seconds outside his record. 'I lost my cool, I was tempted to take a swing at the Kenyans, they were all at it. I just forgot about the outcome.' Renowned coach Arthur Lydiard, who had masterminded Tayler's shock result, asserted that correct coaching could transform Bedford, 'I guarantee I could change his style in one season, balance his preparation instead of that huge mileage.' Yet glory was now gone, a different satisfaction lay ahead; Bedford would never himself become the marathon runner many had predicted on his behalf.

Chris Brasher and track colleague Disley, winner of bronze in the steeplechase in Helsinki's Olympics of 1952, had in due course met in the pub close by Richmond Park in south-west London, the social home of Raneleigh Harriers. The talk was of the vibrant New York Marathon, a spectacular event attracting streets crowded with a clamorous audience, the ambience having been experienced by several from Raneleigh, and a stark contrast to bleak cross-country marathons by the dedicated in Britain. Could London emulate the Yanks? Bedford and Disley subsequently raised their training and set off for America. Their discovery was transformative: an ecstatic mass city conglomeration. Returning home, Brasher wrote for *The Observer* in 1979,

'To believe this story, you must accept that the human race can be one joyous family, working together, laughing together, achieving the impossible. Last Sunday, 11,532 men and women from 40 countries in the world, assisted by over a million people, laughed, cheered and suffered during the greatest folk festival the world has seen … We have a magnificent course around the Thames in London, but do we have the heart and hospitality to welcome the world?'

The Observer hosted lunch for relevant authorities. Disley mapped a course using the Thames as route map, closing only two bridges, one being Tower Bridge which was often closed on a Sunday anyway, and embracing London landmarks such as Big Ben and Buckingham Palace. Brasher inspirationally negotiated a £50,000 sponsorship with Gillette – the company having just relinquished cricket's Gillette Cup – and with the police and fire brigade onside, the London Marathon of 1981 was born with the provision that the event support charities. These donations would vary year by year and for the 39th race in 2019, the sum raised was £66 million. In the name of sport, the goodwill generated extended to some 1,500 attendant volunteers from St John's Ambulance, organising 50 first aid posts, with 150 doctors on duty, emergency ambulances, and the invaluable courtesy of BBC TV coverage.

The inspiration of Brasher and Disley has been a social legacy of immeasurable significance, the event expanding to embrace wheelchair competitors, emotionally enhancing the dignity of the disabled in society; in my youth, limited to a disregarded minority at Stoke Mandeville Hospital for the Disabled. London's launching in effect replaced the Polytechnic Marathon, which had endured from 1909 to 1961; Disley's function as vice-chairman of the then UK Sports Council had been another lever of persuasion in convincing City bureaucracy that they might be on to something culturally worthwhile. The subsequent involvement of Bedford, ultimately disappointed would-be track icon but retaining his extrovert personality, bestowed valuable recognition for the event as race director, negotiating entry for more than two decades of prominent elite global figures who would successively establish record times, thereby promoting the occasion's magnetism.

In co-ordination from the 1990s with race CEO Nick Bitel, Bedford transformed a marathon in the renowned capital from a specialist event for an elite clique of lean-boned extroverts into a global extravagance, rivalling if not exceeding that in New York: developing the charity involvement and creating not merely a spectacular athletic occasion, but a festival for everybody, measuring many thousands, and no longer exclusively male. Moreover, with Bedford having corralled the world's leading runners, records tumbled: in 1983 to Grete Waitz of Norway, the nine-time New York winner; subsequently compatriot Ingrid Kristiansen, in 1985, at one time simultaneous world record holder of 5,000m, 10,000m and marathon; Moroccan American Khalid Khannouchi; headline-grabbing Paula Radcliffe in 2003; the most recent Olympic champion Eliud Kipchoge of Kenya in 2019, with 2:02:37. The world – hopefully London – awaits the first sub-two-hour marathon as expectantly as Bannister's mile.

JAHANGIR KHAN
Beyond Anything Ever Achieved

'Discipline and determination ...
cannot be bought'

Squash racquets – the shortest path to arthritic knees in old age – belatedly tumbled into my life by a roundabout route, which so often determines our future. Playing for Pegasus FC in the Cambridgeshire Invitation Cup against Cambridge City, the old amateur days, I was seriously fouled by the left-back – he was never cautioned by referees on account of his father being the all-controlling general secretary of the Cambridgeshire FA. A team colleague recommended I take my crippled knee to Bill Tucker, the eminent London orthopaedic surgeon and former rugby international, who cared for Denis Compton, among others. He happened to be a member of the International Sportsmen's Club, just off Grosvenor Square, and sent me there to use the swimming pool for repair. Living in the suburbs, I needed a London-based recreation facility so became a member; the club was shortly folded in a property deal and my wife and I switched – in then sex-dichotomous London – to the mixed-member Lansdowne Club, often the venue of the British Open Squash Championship, where the resident coach was Nazrullah Khan, mentor of multiple champion Jonah Barrington and uncle of little-known Jahangir Khan. Thus, did I fortuitously become acquainted with the legendary, as yet aspiring but subsequently one of the foremost champions in the whole history of sport.

Nazrullah, an elegant perfectionist, taught me much about mental discipline in sport – in conversation rather than on court – and I regularly attended when free the tiny, cramped gallery where a minuscule audience would intermittently, in the era before glass courts, watch the sport's most spectacular players. I was later eager to see, in April 1981, the young phenomenon, nicknamed 'The Sphinx' by Barrington – an expressionless Pakistani teenager with apparent Martian mobility. The vision of 17-year-old Jahangir in the Audi British Open, the event now in an 'open' court at Bromley in Kent, was something rare: a mere boy up against Australian Geoff Hunt, twice his age and global commander of the sport for the past 14 years. Yet now his authority was confronted by a mini typhoon. In the semi-final, Jahangir had destroyed the number two seed Qamar Zaman. Would Hunt, six times British Open champion, likewise crumble against this kid, son of former Open champion Roshan, the boy having already claimed the world amateur title, aged 15, as an unseeded qualifier? Hunt had been supreme: he shared with Jahangir's other uncle, Hashim, the prestige of being a six-time champion, yet had recently lost to Jahangir at Chichester over 130 ferocious minutes. Now, in Bromley, Hunt would survive 9-2, 9-7, 5-9, 9-7, only for precocious Jahangir to steal the world crown from him in Toronto with steely revenge: 7-9, 9-10, 9-1, 9-2, 9-2.

That world title was the launch of the most historic sequence by any champion in any sport – 555 matches unbeaten, beyond anything ever achieved in tennis or other racquet sports, or by any track athlete. Ed Moses, the American 400m hurdler, may have recorded over 100 races undefeated, but how many such hurdlers are there in the world, compared with those of squash challengers? Jahangir became the first player to win the World Open without dropping a game, and even won a major event, the International Squash Players Association Championship in 1982, without dropping a point. In one sense, within a couple of years, Jahangir's supremacy became counterproductive for the advance of squash as such was the inevitability of his victory that some tournament promoters were reluctant to seek his entry, spectacular though he might be for crowds yet to witness such incredible stamina and variety of shot, such as fading drop shots or lobs in which a soft ball fell as dead as a pancake. All this in a sport which had only tentatively acquired a professional circuit in the early 1970s, and the state of an 'open' sport in 1979. Within his developing Muslim belief, Jahangir became accused by some of being devoid of character, of public appeal, introverted, with a killjoy demeanour which would only gradually be relaxed following the sudden death due to a heart attack during competition of his elder and also accomplished brother, Torsan.

Jahangir, born in December 1963, had inherited relevant genes. His father, Roshan, had won the British Open in 1957, also losing another two finals, as well as winning five US and Canadian titles. Jahangir was eight when he began playing. He once recounted, 'Everyone in the family played, it was very much a "family business". Yet I had been told I would never be a champion – I was the youngest, smallest, feeblest and most sick in the family. Neither the doctor nor my father believed I had a chance of succeeding. I had two hernia operations by the age of 12, yet that in fact strengthened my determination. In Pakistan we believe in respect for our elders, and that helps discipline. It might sound strange to Western ears, but discipline and determination can take you a long way. Most people can acquire these if they resolve: they are not expensive, they cannot be bought. I came from a poor family, yet my father and my brother, Torsan, whom I loved and who died, had both been world-class players. My story can offer hope to millions all over the world who are poor, bereaved or sick. At different times, I have been all three. I wanted to continue my family's legacy.'

Torsan was to die ranked 13 in the world, the same year that Jahangir had won the World Amateur Open, aged 17. The impact on the younger brother was traumatic, 'I was really close to Torsan, and he had always encouraged me. I considered quitting, but decided to continue and live out *his* dream. His passing gave me added strength.' Crucial to Jahangir's continuation was a selfless decision by his cousin Rehmat Khan, a top-20 player, who decided to retire and devote himself to coaching and caring for Jahangir, having him to live as lodger at his home in Wembley, north London, together with Rehmat's wife and daughter. With exemplary mental resolve, Jahangir adopted a life of exclusive self-denial and training. I witnessed this at the Audi British Open at Birmingham in November 1982, with the 'old' Jahangir now 18.

Already he was threatening the sport with total dominance. I watched him devour Australian Dean Williams with an anaesthetising mastery which surpassed that in other sports I followed: the exclusive levels, say, of Joe Davis in snooker – admittedly non-physical – or Jack Nicklaus or Bjorn Borg. Glen Brumby, another Australian victim, annihilated in the Birmingham semi-final, exclaimed, 'He's almost impossible to play, because he hits a devastating perfect length from *any* position. Even in a rally where you hit a good shot, his *retrieving* shot is again perfect. You know you can only beat him by getting in front of him to take the ball early – and he never allows you to get there.' This is in a duel when players are hitting four times as many strokes in an hour as would, say, Borg or McEnroe, yet in a physical environment where endurance can approach the proportion of a marathon, and losing a 50-stroke rally can make it seem your legs have been amputated.

For Jahangir to ride the crest of the surf for more than five years was past belief, technically and physically. Ten consecutive British Opens, the equivalent of tennis's Wimbledon, plus six World Championships between 1981 and '88 (with losing appearances in the finals of 1986 and '87), could surely never be surpassed. The end had to arrive some day: Ross Norman achieved it in the semi-final in the World Championship in 1986. He had bided his time, awaiting Jahangir's ultimate lapse. Yet I was there in Zurich in November 1986 when Jahangir took revenge – an 'old man' of 23 – by defeating Norman in a titanic encounter. That earlier semi-final had been Norman's first victory over him in 31 encounters, and now Jahangir summoned his power in the 32nd. The match was level at one game all with the third memorably tense, Jahangir drop-shotting and volleying more than in the earlier defeat, forcing Norman back and forth from front court to back wall, and switching angles with every stroke. Four times service changed without a point scored. One interminable rally passed 50 strokes, Jahangir then leading 4-0, Norman then recovering to 4-4, until finally Jahangir drained him: 9-4, 9-10, 9-4, 9-4.

By now there was another name looming: Jansher Khan. Jahangir won their early encounters, but by 1987 Jansher had an edge, winning the World Open. Jahangir's response?

Victory over Jansher in the 1988 World Open in straight games. In a sustained rivalry the pair met 37 times, Jansher winning 19 matches and Jahangir 18, but Jahangir claiming 79 games to Jansher's 74.

Jahangir's decade of fame predictably helped sustain the global expansion of squash, with ever increasing availability of 'viewing' courts, alongside his almost circus-like entertainment and publicity. Simultaneously Pakistan was experiencing a worsening social, political and economic unrest, these negative elements reflected in declining emergence of prominent squash performers, never mind Jahangir's elevation as president of the International Federation from 2002 to '08; his restrained personality more avuncular once relieved of competitive stress.

Alarmed that no Pakistan player had won World or British Open Championships since 1997, Jahangir collaborated in a campaign, CHIPS – Champion Hunt Initiative Programme for Squash – backed by entrepreneur/philanthropist Kazim Anwar. The campaign funds promising juniors and participation in overseas tournaments.

Depressing for the World Association, and for the whole game, has been the 2020 decision by the International Olympic Committee to add breakdancing to the programme for the 2024 Games in Paris – a promotion denied to squash for the past two decades in repeated endeavours. To many it seems nonsense to accept another arbitrarily judged vogue leisure exercise, ahead of a global sport in which the winner is the winner. As commentator/historian I supported every attempt by squash to woo the IOC, but in vain; just as I campaigned for Jonah Barrington to become chairman of the British Federation in the 1990s. Barrington was bidding to replace Sir Michael Edwardes, the motor manufacturer whose leadership of squash was, shall we say, equivocal. Barrington won the election. Sir Michael – who died in 2019 – had disliked my quotes from Barrington in *The Times*, and sued. The judge commended Barrington as a High Court witness but the jury, transparently anti-Rupert Murdoch, found for the plaintiff. It is regrettable that the IOC has not found in favour of squash, which beyond epic performers such as Barrington and Khan, provides a leisure elixir which so widely lubricates society.

JOHN BERTRAND
Surrendered Kingdom

'Trained all my life for
moments like this'

Dateline: 25 September 1983

There is nowhere quite like where I stand beside the harbour at
Newport, Rhode Island, the wealthy venue for over a century
of the successful defence by New York Yacht Club of that
elite America's Cup, a bauble for millionaire-funded yachts
prized above any trophy in sport since first contested in 1851.
I am here because this year's contest has reached a climax
unimagined during summer months of elimination races
between contending foreign challengers, and now the seventh
decisive Trophy race as *Australia II*, from Perth, attempts the
ultimate: standing level at three wins each against NYYC's
Liberty, to wrest the cup from its bolted plinth at West 44th
Street. I am here with what seems like half the population
of Australia: nearly 2,000 spectator craft have headed out to
the six-leg, 30-mile course. This is like D-Day but playtime
with sleek 12-metre rivals, 13-men crew and 20-strong
supporting technical teams relying on maybe $7m each in
sponsors' pocket money. Rhode Island's hospitality trade has
long thrived on the America's Cup cycle.

The drama of today's seventh race is that it should never have happened. Ben Lexcen, an unorthodox Australian marine architect, has designed an innovative fin keel on *Australia II*: upside down, so to speak, with the bulk weight at the bottom with two wings, plus a trim tab, which enables the boat to tack (switch from port to starboard, or vice versa, into a headwind) some 15 seconds faster than with a conventional design. All foreign rivals striving to challenge, and the defending NYYC, dispute Lexcen's legality under 12-metre regulations, but in vain, the charter legally upheld. *Australia II* has out-performed every rival prior to the defender series. Even with a skipper as experienced as Dennis Conner, every expert has forecast *Liberty* to have no chance, but John Bertrand, no novice on *Australia II*'s helm, has underperformed, allowing *Liberty* to establish a 3-1 lead. All over?

But no. *Liberty*'s mast rigging fracture in Race 4 has enabled Bertrand to claw back to 3-2 – the first challenger ever to win two races – then level the series in Race 6 in wind conditions favouring the Australians, with the largest margin by a challenger in any race since 1871. There are allegations that Conner unethically but legitimately threatened tactically to ram *Australia II* on a tack, in a port-and-starboard relationship in which the leading boat is then obliged under regulations to give way. So here we are, with all to play for today; Conner knowing Lexcen's design is technically unbeatable in all but slender winds, Bertrand emotionally aware that back home the entire nation is riding on his shoulders – that he cannot afford a fourth tactical misjudgement on critical manoeuvres in the minutes and final seconds approaching the starting gun. In match racing, as opposed to fleet racing, it is imperative to 'cover' at close quarters every shift made by the opponent on any wind change so as not to be left stranded.

The tension in Newport's now throbbing community, more intense though friendly than anything I have ever experienced prior to any other sporting occasion, makes the heartbeat of every neutral accelerate. Following Race 6, there is a rest lay-day, then Conner requests, regulation permitted, a further day's rest, possibly sensing preferential quieter winds. Psychological warfare in the America's Cup is paramount. The emotional stresses within a crew, physical or temperamental, can be more volatile than with 50 musicians in a symphony orchestra.

In his ghosted autobiography, *Born to Win*, Bertrand will write, 'I've been trained all my life for moments like this. It's my trade. I have spent years perfecting it. I'm the man with the background of two Olympic Games and three previous America's Cups. Not only has Alan Bond [the England-born sponsor] seen fit to invest in me the dreams of the entire nation, but I'm in command of a project that has cost him enough nearly to wipe out the Australian national debt. Truthfully, at the moment, I feel that I have the cares of the world on my shoulders. I know it's only a boat race, but to me it's my whole existence. I am witnessing what appeared to be the culmination of my life's work go down the tube.'

Yet, for a fifth time in the series, Conner now wins the starting manoeuvre and leads by 20 seconds. Bertrand fails to cover, so Conner increases the lead. Slowly, with superior boat-speed, Bertrand claws back on the gap on the second head-wind leg. On their viewing launch, NYYC committee members in their peak caps, blue blazers and white slacks, steel their nerves in anxiety: so confident have they been when congratulating Conner on his seemingly unassailable 3-1 lead. Yet Conner knows, then and now, he is nursing a technically inferior vessel.

In a desperate final gamble, on the penultimate of six legs, downwind, Conner goes in search of a breeze; instead, he strikes a lull, and at the final mark, turning for the four-mile head-wind leg to the finishing line, Bertrand now has an unsurpassable lead in the superior craft. Conner, belligerent to the last, drives his weary crew into 47 herculean, threatening tacks. Though *Liberty* cannot be faster through the turns than *Australia II*, they may just cause the Australians physically to founder on the winch-grinding, or for their rigging inadvertently to fail. It's not to be. Even when Conner makes a huge diversionary tack off-course a mile from the finish, Bertrand covers, then turns for a triumphant dash to the line. By 41 seconds *Australia II* sweeps to history. Back home, Australia goes catatonic, and Rhode Island Sound is drowned in a cacophony of horns from the massive spectator fleet. NYYC caps bow in dismay but courteous approval: their unique aura is no more.

Back on Newport's quayside, as *Australia II* is towed against the fading remains of a crimson sky to her mooring, there is literally barely room to breathe in the hubbub of celebration for the crew which so nearly failed the boat. The dockside groans under the weight of the thousands of spectators whom Newport may never see again, after 25 previous unsuccessful challenges. A forlorn Conner, unaccompanied by any consoling NYYC official, makes his way red-eyed through the throng to the media conference: the perfectionist winner of 1980 whose memoir has been *No Excuse to Lose*, yet who now makes, by the narrowest but for all that colossal margin, the singular error which neutralises the earlier ones by Bertrand. Conner suggests there is no shame in defeat: none seek to question him.

In turn, Bertrand arrives, to rousing media acclaim. He is given a transcript of Conner's brief comments: simply that

Australia II 'is the better boat, no excuses'. Bertrand thinks to himself: were we not also the better crew? In fulfilment of his and his nation's vibrant, living dream, Bertrand needs to believe he and his crew deserve it. He and Conner have for months been riding the face of a sporting precipice, minutely scrutinised by unsparing public analysis. On the penultimate leg of a contest psychologically as much as physically fraught, Bertrand in the revolutionary boat today has trailed the acknowledged master helmsman, with a matter of maybe only six miles out of 30 still to go. In one of sport's torturous, life-shaping moments, Conner has in an instant surrendered the kingdom: in mountaineering terms, for want of a belay. There are those who consider that, for a helmsman who blew three out of seven starting manoeuvres in Ben Lexcen's *Lightning*, John Bertrand should privately feel blessed.

JANE TORVILL AND
CHRISTOPHER DEAN
Hypnotic Trance

'The audience were our judges'

The Winter Olympic Games, launched in 1924, had never held too serious attention in Britain. We knew about phenomenon Sonja Henie, the Norwegian who was junior figure skating champion at nine, won ten world championships, six European and three Olympic titles between 1928 and '36, and ran up a subsequent fortune including three husbands. Jeanette Altwegg, junior Wimbledon tennis champion, alternately gained Olympic figures distinction for Britain at Oslo in 1952, general domestic anonymity remaining until the men's figure skating triumphs of John Curry and Robin Cousins respectively at Innsbruck in 1976 and Lake Placid four years later. My journalistic involvement thus far was negligible: praise for Franz Klammer's heroic downhill for Austria in 1976, and defensive intervention for Curry when his sexuality was publicly mocked by a guest speaker at a Sports Writers' Association annual function. It was in the late 1970s, hearing beguiling news of a couple of youngsters in Nottingham, that my wife Marita and I took a private evening out to investigate.

The relative novelty of ice dancing, controversially introduced to the Olympics in 1976, in contrast to long-standing pairs figure skating, was only marginally different, but was it sport? As a teenage ballet dancer – derailed by her father's terminated support – my wife's opinion would be relevant. We discovered an instant Newton-esque exposé.

This anonymous pair, a demure office clerk and a handsome, rather reserved policeman cadet, were already defying gravity in a synchronised collaboration which was self-evidently special. Jane Torvill and Christopher Dean, from modest suburban households, were, we mutually deduced, heading for the metaphoric stars. So it would prove: winning that year the British Figure Skating Championship, doing so for the next six winters and simultaneously ascending the staircase of international acclaim. If sublime, frictionless athleticism can lyrically co-ordinate with melody under competitive, albeit arbitrary judgement, and captively command an audience of millions, why should it not be termed sport?

I was professionally hooked. Moreover, while I was actively experienced with training and coaching at an elevated level in both football and athletics, the rhythmic perfection of skating was an unknown science. I twice went to observe – following their first European and world titles in 1980 and '81, and prior to their second Olympics in 1984 – a phase of the relentless thousands of hours spent searching for perfection: a never-endingly adjusted formula of mind, body and music, every bit as profound as that of Fonteyne and Nureyev. Assisting Dean's choreography were experienced ice dancing coach Betty Calloway and stage maestro advisor Michael Crawford. When I travelled for an interview in summer to an isolated village in the Savoy Alps, the pair's tight budget on Nottinghamshire County Council sponsorship was eased by free accommodation in exchange for Calloway's joint coaching of French skaters.

The music had been selected and programmed, to within seconds of International Skating Union regulations, at Nottingham Public Library. Two months are then spent synchronising music with elaborate steps, Torvill reflecting, 'We work from between four to seven hours a day in summer … of course it will be difficult to string along every move, but I don't think we have explored all areas yet.' Dean added, 'Neither of us studied ballet, but we work out the ballet sequence between us. Ideas come easily, because we work well together. Jane knows instinctively what steps she wants to do to accommodate the ideas. It has to be creative, happening spontaneously.' When working at home in Nottingham, parental houses just a couple of streets apart, rink practice was late at night or early morning when not open to the public. Amateur regulations restricted the permitted sums deducted for expenses from any exhibition performances, i.e. excellence by economy. Mutual MBE honours in 1981 did not pay for air fares.

Music, as stated, was central to the formula. In 1982, they utilised the overture from the musical *Mack & Mabel*; a year later for the World Championship, the circus number from *Barnum*. For their fifth place at Lake Placid in 1980, it had been 'Puttin' On The Ritz', following which Crawford had begun collaboration on theatricality. The masterpiece, it can definitively be claimed, was Ravel's *Boléro*, the portrait of doomed love, for the European, world and Sarajevo Olympic summits of 1984. The composition lasts for 17 minutes; Olympic regulations for the conclusive free-dance discipline permit four minutes plus or minus ten seconds. An arranger contracted the score to 4:28, excessive by 18 seconds. However, regulation stipulates that timing begins only when the skate blades first touch the ice; Dean conjured choreography that began with both kneeling.

To be both ordinary and at the same moment spectacularly unique is a rare capability. Jane Torvill and Christopher Dean each possessed this gift, individually and united. They were wholly without vanity, as though, when it arrived, they were oblivious of their fame. Standing on Sarajevo's rink, overwhelming favourites as reigning European and world champions, the start was delayed by a tiny girl skater removing litter from the ice. At this pinnacle of their public existence they patiently smiled. Being there that evening, and having watched a replay a dozen times or more over the next 35 years, I still quiver internally at their portrayal of Ravel's lyrical, anguished fatality. The fusillade of maximum marks from judges was a lifetime memorial, irrespective of what might still lie ahead. Occasionally sport touches beauty: a Grand National horse and mount, a rowing eight, a high-board diver, a slalom skier. Here was such a moment. On the podium, Torvill gave the innocent teenage smile which would last her lifetime; Dean thoughtfully smelt the ceremonial girl's gift of a flower bouquet.

I regretted Marita's absence from this memorable climax. The symmetry of their embraced movement indeed touched the heart, carrying the audience's emotion beyond the realm of sport, the mauve of their costume against the backdrop of frozen white ice lifting the sense of impending tragedy. Marita would be there ten years later in Lillehammer for a more bureaucratic brand of calamity.

In Sarajevo there would be a telegram of congratulation from Queen Elizabeth II. *Boléro* tells of vanquished love. Was the dance on ice actually testimony to a living love affair?

The speculation circled globally, so exotic was this perceived artistic integration. The pair gently and politely denied it was so, bar an inconsequential teenage kiss years ago. Both would later separately marry. In a biography by John Hennessey of *The Times*, published a year earlier, they had each addressed the speculation of romance. 'We were once very close,' Torvill admitted, 'but that situation is hard to maintain when you work as intensely as we do ... where does deep affection end and love start? I just do not know.' Dean, ever the pragmatist, voiced the same, 'A romantic commitment would interfere with all we have worked for. That is in cold storage ... neither of us will know what we shall find inside, when the time comes to unlock the door ... it is a strange relationship we have, a mystery to most people, ourselves included.' On Valentine's Day in Sarajevo, Dean gave his Olympic partner an orchid. We cannot know of what it spoke beyond a shared brilliance, and he admitted in interview, 'We weren't with the audience last night, we were with each other ... a sort of hypnotic trance.'

Now they were about to step into the unknown world of professionalism, following their imminent final World Championship victory in Ottawa, with there being no established commercial ice dance arena, such as that occupied by former figures champions Curry and Cousins. They were indeed to discover commercial success. Meanwhile, the fantasy of the love nest encircled the world: the down-to-earth reality was irrelevant.

Whatever the new adventures of Torvill and Dean, on account of the varied regulation adjustments by the IOC and International Federations in acceptance of professionalism, by the time of the Winter Olympics at Lillehammer in 1994 it had become possible for the former champions to return to the scene as 'amateurs'. To re-install their credibility they were entered into the European Championships at Copenhagen; a training adjustment costing some £100,000. A class apart ten years earlier, they transparently remained so back in competition. Their 'History of Love' rumba was beyond challenge; seemingly likewise their free dance 'Let's Face The Music', a winning partnership as riveted, in their mid-30s, as Redgrave and Pinsent, Barry John and Gareth Edwards, or Rogers and Astaire. Their years on the theatrical stage had if anything advanced the dramatic presentation of the British couple, threatened as they now were by two Russian pairs. A question mark was whether technical elaborations of extreme balance in their free programme came within the judges' interpretation of restrictive 'lifts' above the shoulder. To this 'outsider', it nonetheless looked like no contest for the Brits, who had departed to Norway for training preparation having experienced no disapproval in Copenhagen.

Come the evening in Hamar, gold and silver went to the two Russian pairs, bronze to the Brits, and a tin medal for the judges, who were jeered by the predominantly Norwegian audience for their inexcusable prejudice for winners Oksana Grishuk and Evgeni Platov. Technically there had been no 'illegal' lift, with Dean at one point horizontally wrapped around Torvill, who was sustaining the weight of both. The Russian pairs had been all zip and little precision. It was time for the Brits to return to commercial entertainment. 'We can get on with our lives again,' reflected Torvill, Dean disparagingly observing, 'We like to think the audience tonight were our judges.'

Arbitrary judgement – boxing, gymnastics, diving, artistic ski-ing – is often in question, and the IOC was now moved to ask whether ice dancing, under ISU governance, was worth its inclusion. Cat-calling of judges is not compelling television. Hans Kutscherer of Austria, head of the judging panel, refused to concede misapplication of assessment, though it emerged three of the judges had had previous suspension. Neutral observers considered Torvill and Dean superior now to their victory in Copenhagen. IOC president Juan Antonio Samaranch expressed 'severe doubt about ice dancing future comparable to boxing's irregularities at Seoul in 1988'. Alex Zhulin, Soviet silver winner with Miya Usova, agreed about the chaos, 'It's all very algebra.' Torvill and Dean could turn their back on the mathematics and return to their world of more cushioned acclaim: ITV's *Dancing on Ice* and a return to Sarajevo in 2014 to re-enact *Boléro* on the 30th anniversary of a moment when sport was transcended through music by humanity's basic emotions.

VIRGINIA LENG
A Pedestal Beyond Imagination

*'You need three years to reach
a mutual peak'*

Horses matter, too. They have long shared planet Earth with us. Think Nero's charioteers, the charge of the Light Brigade, pre-mechanical transport, the sacrifice of millions in winning the First World War, or Hugh Grant's emergency association with *Horse & Hound* in *Notting Hill*. Horses are often more majestic in demeanour than we are, as anyone who has ever been gently 'inspected' by an enquiring, quizzical four-legged friend five times as big and twice as handsome, will know. In childhood I envied horse owners, and the mutual discipline and respect. Often separated from parents in wartime and short on affection, I appreciated the occasional serene warmth in a stable of a welcoming muzzle. This chapter is about an equestrian relationship without parallel among men or women.

Entering sports journalism, I was preoccupied with ball games yet when the opportunity arose intermittently to canter into the commentator's paddock, it was a joy. The appeal was greater from complex eventing than the monied arena of racing and gambling; for the long-term shared horse and rider duet in the three disciplines of dressage, cross-country and show-jumping. Nowhere was this more elaborately evident than in the career of Virginia Leng (nee Holgate, now Ginny Elliott), with her galaxy of 17 championship medals, a pedestal beyond the imagination of any millionaire footballer, including being the first woman to win an individual Olympic medal. To fortify her unique disposition was an attitude unfailingly to put the interest of her horses first and foremost, an integrated selflessness that made her appeal to an international audience, and certainly to naturalists, more compelling.

I first met Holgate, as she then was, in 1983 at the Badminton Horse Trials, the largest garden party in Britain outside the beaches of Blackpool or Southend. Possessing zero expertise, I could offer only enthusiasm – always appreciated – for a sport so unrelentingly demanding. The hazards of any world, European or Olympic course are consistently severe, sometimes dangerous, yet everyone is, so to speak, on the same side; competitive yet respectful. Yes, there can be discord back at the stables, but the public ethic is one of mutual support within rivalry. Seldom are there fractious disputes which discolour some professional sport: long ago there was a boisterous Harvey Smith, but his affectations became duly submerged.

Born in 1955 in Malta, her father a Royal Marine, Holgate's life shuttled across continents, moving from Singapore to the Philippines then on to Canada and latterly Cyprus. She started riding from the age of three, having her first horse, Dubonnet, aged 13, winning a junior European title at 18 and experiencing her Badminton baptism a year later. Potential calamity prevented her involvement in Montreal's Olympic Games in 1976. She was pinned beneath her horse Jason in a fall provoked by a spectator running on to the course; her arm fractured in 23 places, amputation threatened but averted. Misfortune dogged her survival: a missed jump at Burghley trials on Tio Pepe, who broke down in 1977. Fortune smiled with the purchase of two reliable steeds, Priceless and Nite Cap. The former, she believed, was her turning point.

Finance, however, dried up with the death of her father in 1981. A sponsor became essential, as Mrs Elliott now relates from Oxfordshire, 'For six months I took the train to London once a week, trailing around from one office to the next selected from *Yellow Pages*, embarrassed by continuous rejections, until a recommendation for the British National Bank found interest – the chairman's wife enjoyed equestrian events.' The company evolved, and the ultimate Citibank Savings sustained her career. Immediately after BNB had stepped in, she came sixth in the European Championship at Horsens, Denmark – on a course some described as 'impossible'. The team won the title her first medal, and she was on her way. Her background support was paramount: her mother's ferrying of horse meal and stable necessities of hay at £130 a tonne; dressage coaching from Pat Manning and Ferdi Eilberg; jumping by Pat Burgess and Nick Skelton; cross-country from retired competitor Lady Hugh Russell.

By chance I was there almost at the beginning of the climb to eminence, in the wake of Horsens, as she and ten-year-old Nite Cap engaged in 1983 with Badminton, the Frank Weldon-designed 'Cresta Run' of eventing, where reputations are made or broken: an arena of social significance where yeomanry and aristocracy are harmonised in the name of sport in pursuit of the then coveted Whitbread prize. Priceless, fourth the previous year, was recovering from sickness and Mrs Elliott recalls that she and Nite Cap 'were just beginning to know each other, I don't recall where we finished after being second on dressage'. Prominent riders Richard Meade and Princess Anne were absent that year with lame horses.

To get perspective of a tumultuous 12-year cavalcade of success, this is the sequence of medals in the wake of Badminton in 1983:

- Olympic Games – Los Angeles 1984: individual silver (Priceless), team silver; Seoul 1988: individual silver (Master Craftsman), team silver; Barcelona 1992: Last-minute withdrawal
- World Championships – Luhmuhlen 1982: team gold; Adelaide 1986: individual gold (Priceless), team gold; Stockholm 1990: individual unplaced (Griffin), team silver
- European Championships – Horsens 1981: team gold; Burghley 1985: individual gold (Priceless), team gold; Luhmuhlen 1987: individual gold (Nite Cap), team gold; Burghley 1989: individual gold (Master Craftsman), team gold
- Badminton – 1983: Nite Cap, unplaced; 1985: Priceless, gold; 1989: Master Craftsman, gold; 1993: Welton Houdini, gold

Attending the World Championships at Stockholm in 1990, where Griffin, a new mount, was still learning and had come to grief at the 24th obstacle in cross-country, I discussed with the then Mrs Leng the possibility of retirement. Her attitude was rational, as ever, 'I felt I rode as well as ever in the cross-country, and I don't know what happened with Griffin. Perhaps it was because he lost both front shoes at a water jump. For me, it would be a mistake to continue if you are not as good as you should be, but my sponsors are keen for me to continue. I'm grateful for the success I've had, but you can't go on winning.'

Her intent was now more on establishing her training credentials – she was to become Ireland's team manager – at the highest level. 'That thrill is still the same,' she said.

Griffin's elevation had arisen with Master Craftsman, the previous year's Badminton winner, unsound. Ever the defender of her 'partners', Leng had insisted the error with Griffin was no slight on the horse. 'We're still educating him, we've had 18 months, and you need three years to reach a mutual peak. Griffin gave it everything he'd got. It was my brain that was at fault. When I walked the course beforehand, I knew it was going to be rough on the horses.' In the event she was to miss Barcelona, Master Craftsman falling unfit shortly beforehand.

Recently discussing memories, Mrs Elliott considers the first Burghley individual victory with Priceless the best, 'Simply because it was the first, and there might never have been another! The same with the Olympic silver with Priceless in '84.' She considers what distinguishes eventing from other disciplines is the ever-present element of danger, together with 'the comradeship of riders which is what keeps us going, the unchanging team spirit among all nationalities'. Of all her mounts, Priceless was probably the most appreciated, 'I bought him as a five-year-old. He was like an army sergeant – forthright, well built, bossy, a real soldier. He put up with me and my mistakes, and he never had a fault across country. He was genuine, and incredibly intelligent. I adored him!' For many reasons, we inescapably share this life with the animal kingdom, often with affection.

SEBASTIAN COE
Confounding Myriad Critics – Twice

'A celebration of our
identity as a nation'

There cannot be a more convincing advocate for why sport matters than the once secondary school boy from Sheffield who failed the 11-Plus, yet in partnership with an exceptional self-developed coach – his father – became an Olympic and world record-breaker; subsequently transformed a creaking British Olympic host city bidding committee; achieved London's election against all odds, then to stage an event in 2012 acclaimed worldwide; and now strives as president of World Athletics to re-establish equilibrium in a global sport torn asunder, notably among others, by Russia and doping.

You might say a busy man. The UK is fortunate to have been able to celebrate Sebastian Coe's triumphs on the track and his leadership for 2012 on account of genes from an intellectual, escaped prisoner of war, engineer father Peter, at times as autocratic as Montgomery; an intuitive paternal grandmother Vera, East End Cockney char with the conviction that would have seen off Rommel with an umbrella; and, emotionally, mother Angela, demure actor-dancer of benign Indian heritage from whom he inherits his Asian contemplative assurance.

Sebastian and I know each other moderately well, having collaborated on three books over 15 years from 1977, recounting his remarkable athletic career during which four elite middle-distance runners – Steve Ovett, Steve Cram, Peter Elliott and Coe – for much of the calendar commanded international middle-distance tracks. It was my happy coincidental chance to be relating many of his epic deeds; intimate familiarity with some of his hundreds of hours of unobserved ceaseless preparatory training which inspired a few minutes of ecstatic fulfilment, and within which Peter was fundamental to the equation. I came to respect Peter Coe deeply. His first words at our initial discussion – embarking on the first projected book when his 'boy' was a 21-year-old aspirant possessing the European indoor 800m title – were direct, 'Do you know what you're doing?' No messing with Peter.

The story of Coe's track supremacy is difficult to condense within a few pages. I will try. Following the indoor success in San Sebastian, the objective in 1978 was the European Championship in Prague. Third place, with an experimentally too sharp first lap behind an East German winner with suspect 'additive' credentials, was disappointing, but in 1979 there arrived unprecedented three world records in 41 days – 800m and mile, each in Oslo, then the 1,500m in Zurich – creating global attention. A fourth, for 1,000m, was clocked in Oslo three weeks prior to Moscow's boycotted Olympic Games, Britain wilfully present despite Prime Minister Margaret Thatcher's opposition. Prior to the heats, Coe confronted the largest individual Olympic press conference of all time with some 400 journalists representing almost every nation. The horror story to outstrip any was about to happen. Mentally padlocked by expectation – his own, Peter's and that of a few million others – Coe was tactically blind, his mind frozen, and ran as his father would assess 'like an idiot', and came second to totemic rival Steve Ovett in a time three-and-a-half seconds outside his own world record of 1:42.33.

It is worth quoting from some of Coe's recollections of his school days. 'Failing the 11-Plus was one of the best things that happened to me. Going to Tapton, a big-city school in Sheffield, I found a large social mix, a sort of "people's Eton" – tough and more character-building. We were a form of failed 11-Plus, yet many came through with university educations. Peter always had an unbending attitude to my academic side as to my running, if athletics hadn't been able to become an academic thing with him, almost intellectual, he wouldn't have been so interested … When people said to him he had let it become an intellectual exercise, his answer was "you're dead right". I couldn't have asked more from him.'

The defeat in Moscow was incomprehensible to all observers. Father and son each knew how badly he had failed. They battled their way through the crush of reporters after a press conference, searching for their car back to the village. Father put his arm round his son. I was with them, and muttered to Peter there was a camera unit trailing them, trying to get in front of them, with Seb shaking and close to tears, yet they were tears of anger rather than disappointment. As we found the car, Seb asked bitterly, 'How much did I make up?' I said ten metres. 'Oh, Christ,' he said as the magnitude of tactical error sank deeper into his at last conscious brain. An impassive Russian chauffeur drove off, and in the driving mirror I could see Peter on the back seat with his arm around Seb, the way you comfort your infant child when it comes to your bed in the middle of the night troubled by a nightmare. There was no recrimination, only mutual love and shared grief. Back at the village, waiting for dinner, Seb said, 'Thanks for caring,' and I said, 'It's disproved nothing, winning the 1,500 can now only be sweeter.' As we had filed out of the interview room, Neil Amdur, a droll New Yorker familiar with athletics, had observed, 'This was a race without history.'

Reaction to the race was devastating. Coe was utterly condemned, the verdict being that he might break world records but that he had no concept of championship racing; that he had been tactically dumb and that if he now lost to Ovett again in the 1,500m, his career was finished. The most knowledgeable minds in track and field, whether coaches, athletes or media, were uniform in their dismissal of this broken man from Sheffield. With determination, Coe set about re-assembling himself, provoked by the opinion of many whose judgement he respected. Dave Bedford, himself an Olympic failure against all expectation in 1972, believed Ovett was now close to immortality. 'Before Moscow, Steve will have woken in the middle of the night wondering if he had the ability to beat Coe. Move on a few weeks, and his hand is now so close to touching the golden apple. I wonder whether he has the bottle to pick it up, whether he has the visualisation of thinking through the two events beforehand, "What if I win the first one?" I don't think Steve has seen it as an entirety, whereas I think Seb has.' Derek Ibbotson, himself the UK's foremost middle-distance icon 20-odd years earlier, recalled that he thought Coe would be mentally crushed in circumstances when you find out if you are a man or a mouse. 'He'd been found lacking, how's he now going to beat the unbeatable Ovett?'

On the day of the 1,500m final, Coe having qualified with some ease, I encountered Kenny Moore, a US marathon runner and commentator for *Sports Illustrated*, anxious to make contact with Coe, his magazine intent that the world record holder was about to lose again. I was personally less anxious. I had met Coe after an early lunch and wandered down to the almost deserted training track on the fringe of the village. His colleague Brendan Foster, a former frontline runner and now adviser on the British team, had delivered his last pep talk, 'Win this, and the future's yours. The other guy can win it, of course, but you can go out there and rinse it. There's no way he can do that.' We were sitting under a sunshade, Coe so at ease we could have been back home in the garden. In answer to some conversational questions, I asked if there was any single aspect of the race he feared. The answers were unhesitating. I knew he was ready for probably the most important race he would ever run. He was now at one with himself. He was convinced he could do to his great rival what Ovett had so unerringly done to others for the last three years: stay close to the pacemaker and strike on the final bend. I suggested to him that a few minutes of physical and mental pain would be worth the glory. He simply said, 'Why not?' Peter arrived, emphasising that if Seb stayed with the pace at the front, the only way he could lose was by being boxed. His last, pragmatic instruction was, 'If necessary, punch!'

I knew from our conversation that the real runner was now alive, anxious to get out there and get on with it. Coe himself knew that the aggression which was absent in the 800m was now back in harness; that he had recovered himself internally, that he was ready, and so it proved. The final was to be an epic. I had forecast in the *Daily Express* that if Coe was in striking distance of Ovett 200 metres from the line, being the faster man he would win – never mind that when coasting his semi-final, Ovett, for long unbeaten, had cheerily waved to his mother in the crowd. There would now be 20 million back home watching on television. The drama was a while developing: a first 800 metres at a relative saunter, an unbroken pack led by Jurgen Straub of GDR – a formidable challenger – and Coe, with Ovett in close attendance in a relatively pedestrian 2:49. It was now that Straub made the surge which converted a stroll into a burn – which emptied the sting from Ovett's renowned final burst. This was precisely what Coe needed: a final 700 metres of severity in which he alone could still retain a finishing burst. This he did 170 metres out, carrying him past Straub, just as Ovett simultaneously bid to challenge Coe. Split timing revealed Coe was still accelerating from 170 metres to 50 metres out. He won gold, and eternal recognition, with a last 800 in 1:48.5, the then fastest ever in a mile or 1,500m: a career recovery to confound myriad knowledgeable critics. There was more criticism, and confounding, yet to come.

The 1981 season would witness both Coe and Ovett repeatedly breaking each other's world records at Grand Prix events, while avoiding direct head-to-head rivalry: an inevitable commercial strategy now that the international federation had permitted Trust Funds – a contrived shift from long-abused amateurism to a professional reality, payments accepted for 'suspended' accounts with a percentage 'taxation' to national federations' coffers. Coe lowered the 800m to 1:41.72, which would survive for 12 years, and twice improved the mile record, down to 3:47.33, also winning the World Cup 800m in Rome. Two seasons of wretched ill health were to follow with a below-par defeat in the European Championship in Athens; then he was too sick to participate in Helsinki's inaugural World Championships of 1983, by now with Steve Cram, novice from 1980, riding high. In the winter of 1983–84, Coe was wondering whether he could ever return to the track.

Tentative re-engagement in the spring, and second place in the AAA Championships in June, revived prospects for selection for the, again boycotted, Olympic Games at Los Angeles; many critics were sceptical about his condition. Coe routed the doomsayers: now 27, he again took silver in the 800m, short on his world record form in the wake of new Brazil sensation Joachim Cruz. Cram, as now reigning world and European champion, was the poster boy for the 1,500m. The outcome would demonstrate that Coe was still very much an item, feeling ever stronger throughout four successive rounds of the 800m then qualifying with ease for the 1,500m final, though giving his father nerves when 'only' third in his semi-final.

Prior to the race, Cram, a generous-minded rival from England's north-east, had observed, 'Seb always liked to keep away from other athletes, some thinking he was a snob, not wanting to be with the rest of the team, but since I started winning medals I came to appreciate the need for avoiding all the hassle, and now I find Seb's attitude acceptable. When I beat him at Gateshead last year, a make-or-break race for him, he grabbed me to shake hands, and knowing how he must have been feeling, that was a gesture I won't forget.'

Was there now a reversal of roles? Winning or losing would be perhaps on Cram's mind, maybe sensing he had over-raced prior to the Games. It may seem facile to say that Coe was thinking *only* of winning: if so, that could be at least part of why he did. He was confident about the re-arrangement of his 'management' with Peter, that they were sharing problems rather than doubling them. Remembering that the night before the final in Moscow, I had mentioned to him that Peter had said he would 'give an arm and a leg' for his son to win, and Coe reflecting that is the last thing an athlete needs to hear.

Now he was poised: no nerves and more concentration, Peter having been billeted out of town, their relationship confined to training meetings. If Moscow had been do-or-die, in Coe's mind LA was more simple and clear-cut. As he said, 'I wanted something more than I'd ever wanted anything – I wanted to be remembered as the athlete who came back.'

Following his semi-final, I had driven back with him in the dark to the athletes' village in the University College of Los Angeles. He was calmer than I had ever seen him before, prior to a major race. It was almost as though he was going on holiday rather than running an Olympic final, which was the climax of a year of super-human effort to rescue his reputation. On arrival, he jogged up the steps into the village and I could sense it was the gait of a man who would sleep untroubled.

The nature of the final was partially determined by Steve Scott of America attempting to create a hard, fast race, a hard run diminishing a sprint finish which he lacked. This suited Coe *vis a vis* Cram. Yet after two laps, Abascal of Spain took over the pace from Scott; an ailing Ovett – who had crumbled in the 800m event on account of a virus infection – running off the track on the last bend, as Coe and Cram surged past Abascal. As Cram threw a final burst at Coe, the title defender likewise kicked and was away. Into the home straight he led by two metres so kicked a third time, balanced and poised. Again he was a champion, winning by six metres in an Olympic record of 3:32.53. Within seconds of victory his mood transformed from pleasure to anger. Turning towards the press and television ranks, where his prospects had been roundly questioned throughout the preceding months, he gazed with a scowl and shouted, 'Who says I'm finished!' It was a long, lingering gesture, for here had been a triumph as much over criticism as over physical adversity: the inner reaction of the school boy who long ago could not accept it when he was bowled out at cricket, who got nervous eczema in the tension of 11-Plus, who had now proved to the world that he was not the failure predicted. Yet within moments he had relaxed and was off to see if Ovett, recovering on the in-field, needed assistance.

It was a relatively quiet 1985, with an unfamiliar second place in four Grand Prix events, but the following year brought a precious realisation: a European Championship 800m title. The background is an insight into the complexity of an elite runner's physiology, as David Martin, an expert consultant from Atlanta, explains, 'Seb had unusual abilities to tolerate lactic acidosis. This showed us that his enormous performance capacity was explained by not only world-class maximum oxygen uptake, but also by an above-average tolerance to anaerobic work. While his anaerobic fitness was good, even when he was not training anaerobically, and his aerobic qualities were the same as those of the best, anaerobically he was very gifted.

'What I saw was that while he had an excellent running and weight training programme, he may have been stopping the weight training too early, Peter and he tapering off before the start of the serious track season, so that he would be fresher for speed work. Yet big races are at the end of the season, the 800 is almost a sprint, strength-orientated, and by then his strength was disappearing. If he maintained his weight training well into the summer, that strength would synthesise with speed work: if he would back off on his volume of aerobic training, and substitute instead extended weight training, this would give a mix of volume quality running and conditioning to maintain a high aerobic base, quicken his reflexes and refine his fast-running abilities – the objective that in the last hundred metres in Stuttgart, he would be so strong that no one could go past him.'

Tom McKean, a stylish Scot with easy rhythm and undoubted pace, tended to lack the temperament for the big occasion, a flaw not conquered until 1990, though his finishing kick could stun anyone. Yet the principle that Martin explains would pay dividends. Coe knew that to beat him, the pace of any 800m had to be between 1:45 and 1:47, draining some of McKean's finish. With a fast pace set by the German Braun over the first lap, Coe was there at the shoulder of Cram, with McKean leading. As conceived by Martin, the combination of Coe's speed *and* strength told in the final 20 metres to win by a stride. He could now be content with his career profile.

Finishing runner-up to Cram in the subsequent 1,500m – motivation expended? – the track pinnacles for Coe were effectively at an end. Bidding for selection for a third Olympic Games at Seoul in 1988, still legitimately a competitive contender at 31, Coe was mischievously treated by a sclerotic selection committee, riddled with financial envy of his earnings, and immune to his championship racing record. The treasurer of the Wales Women's AAA – yes, she had a vote! – who had growled, 'Have you seen the size of his house?' (beside the Thames) should still be hanging her head in shame. Selected and then de-selected, after under-performing with flu in selection trials – the chairman of the British board failing to support the coaching selection committee – Coe nonetheless had the second-fastest 1,500m UK time for the year, but instead went on holiday. His last gesture of flamboyance was as the runner-up in the 1989 World Cup in Barcelona – then onward to a political life as Member of Parliament, personal aide to Opposition leader William Hague, and a life peerage in 2000.

However, sport still mattered. Immensely. We mostly tend to be the sons of our fathers. Coe's ultimate championship, the hosting by London of a spectacular Olympic Games, acclaimed across the globe – *even* by Americans – was a gift to the UK's foreign prestige, and even to an extent to our own self-appreciation, when up to the eve of the opening ceremony much of our own media, led by *The Guardian*, was speculating on all that could go wrong. In Coe's organisational leadership, I could identify so much of Peter's attitude: let's do it just because people say it isn't possible.

What his son did across nine years, from rescuing a dysfunctional bid committee then transforming the aura of eligibility, with the aid and enthusiasm of such as Labour MP Tessa Jowell, director Paul Deighton and inspirational businessman Keith Mills, convincing the IOC electorate in 2005 in Singapore with crucial input from Prime Minister Tony Blair, was a prolonged exercise in planning and imagination. Above all, there was a conviction on what we in Britain are collectively capable of doing if we are united behind a cause. And this cause was as much about sport as belief in the British. Coe's motivation was the same as that he possessed on the track, confidence in himself as well as Britain. Peter would have been as thrilled by London's 'gold' as by that won by his boy.

Thus was Coe able to say in his opening ceremony address, 'To everyone in this stadium, to every athlete waiting, ready, prepared to take part in these Games, to everyone in every city and village in the world watching as we begin, welcome to London … I've never been so proud to be British or part of the Olympic Movement as I am at this moment.' As he would relate in a later biography, 'What we wanted was a celebration of what we can achieve together, of our confidence in ourselves and our history, our tolerance, our passion, our cultural diversity, but above all a sense of people coming together. A celebration of our identity as a nation ... The following morning, we woke to superlatives across the spectrum, from *The Guardian* to the *Daily Mail*, proof that we had got the balance right. The international response was even more of a surprise. Quirky and eccentrically British as it was, they got it ... It's too soon to know whether my ultimate goal, that London 2012 can inspire and excite our young people into sport and into healthier and happier lives, will be fulfilled. But I am optimistic.' That sport matters. Depressingly, successive governments, national and provincial, have failed to recognise that Olympic success arises not only from sponsored squads, but social grassroots and leisure facilities. Post-COVID, the health of the nation will crucially be dependent upon youth's access to sporting facilities.

SEVE BALLESTEROS
Buoyant idol

'To be a champion, it has to come from inside'

Golf is a strangely fascinating sport: attempting to strike a tiny stationary ball using a thin three-foot stick with a nob on the end, a consequence being that even the accomplished can be majestic and dismal on consecutive strokes. Many of us, of course, can be dismal for all 18 holes but still enjoy the walk.

What distinguished Severiano Ballesteros, said by some to be the best European player of all time, was that his personal appeal was as majestic for an audience, as much when he was erratic as when he was buoyant. Both modes could be frequent: his devoted supporters were as enchanted when his drive was unplayable in a gorse bush as when he hit a par-five green in two, a yard from the pin.

I saw a range of his moods. Of the many sports it was my responsibility to attend, he was one of those who, by his characterful response to his own fortune – or misfortune – would often make one smile. Even laugh. Such a round occurred on the dunes of Royal Birkdale during the Open Championship of 1991.

It was a wet and blustery day, cold enough to be wearing two suits – which is what Ballesteros did, including two hats, one to keep on the other. With charm you can get away with that, publicly. Ballesteros pursued his ball to parts of the course never previously visited, and still approached the 18th to a hero's welcome. The first nine had witnessed double bogeys by many, so single dropped shots at the first, second and sixth for Seve were hardly a disgrace. At this round's conclusion, for a 139 total, he confided his position 'was where I want to be, I don't like to be leading early'. There's psychoanalysis-by-convenience for you.

The 16th had been carnival time: his first drive was abandoned, the second went into a rose bush, this now surrounded by 100 rubberneckers, two policemen and a rules marshal unsure of the rules. With a politician's presence, Ballesteros offered the marshal three options, 'I try the unplayable ball; I free drop two club lengths away; I go back to the tee.' The crowd was cleared, and a four-iron to the fringe of the green meant one stroke was dropped rather than three. Better than the Palladium. Sociability, alongside that precious principle of abiding by the regulations, make golf an admirable paradigm. In the event this time, Ballesteros's fortune would badly fray the next day.

Yet the quality which particularly endeared this emotional, big-hearted Spaniard to an international public was his commitment and team spirit in the Ryder Cup conflict with the US; a duel from 1927, originally against the British Isles and the result almost as inevitable as had been sailing's America's Cup, until the odds were shorted by the eastern team becoming 'Europe'. Sport can take unexpected turns by the coincidental simultaneous arrival of elite performers. Firstly, Ballesteros burst on to the scene with five major victories in ten years between 1978 and '88: three Open Championships, two Masters. Bernhard Langer of Germany, Nick Faldo from England, Sandy Lyle from Scotland and Ian Woosnam from Wales similarly graced the front rank during this time. Here suddenly was Europe putting the US on the back foot, with Ballesteros the emotional inspiration.

Long before, I had heard Tony Jacklin, an aspiring young assistant at Potters Bar, admitting that among, say, the top 20 professionals, the decisive difference under pressure was mental more than technical. Ballesteros was to demonstrate this conspicuously as team member in the Ryder Cup. It was evident, for instance, in the 'home' match at The Belfry in 1985, where in his singles against Tom Kite a wilful Ballesteros found himself three holes down with five to play. His resolute attitude in adversity was a lesson to anyone in sport: a transparent exhibition of 'focus'. At the short 14th came a true drive and single putt to win a hole back. The 550-yard 15th saw two straight drives, a putt from 15 feet, a birdie four, and another one back. Another holed from ten feet meant the encounter was all square. A vital match halved against an opponent who, with his spectacles and eye shade, gave the illusion of being an unchallengeable mathematician, in what ultimately would be a team defeat.

Two years later, at Columbus, Ohio, there would occur a stupendous encounter: America's first home defeat in a match which fluctuated back and forth for three days' continuous tension. It was a drama I have seldom seen surpassed in any ball game, with Ballesteros continuously at the heart of it, either in singles, or foursomes with young compatriot José María Olazábal, all the while Ballesteros exhorting his colleagues from dressing room to dining room, 'We *can* win, we *will* win.'

Jack Nicklaus, the imperious but losing captain, would graciously declare it had been one of the best occasions he ever knew. Amid this had been Ballesteros in his prime, at the climax on the third day, a tenacious singles duel with Curtis Strange: the Spaniard intent on exhibiting to a gung-ho American audience the worth of his acclaimed reputation in Europe, a matinee idol playing like Apollo. With Ballesteros bunkered at the 13th, there were gently mocking cries of 'Yeaahh' from the audience. Ballesteros merely smiled back at them and holed with his wedge. Taking the 17th for two up and one to play, his victory all but sealed a moment in sporting history.

Not merely because of a European triumph over the supposed 'world's greatest nation' – in Donald Trump's overworked claim – this exceptional event at Columbus was yet more evidence of the social value of sport. An audience of over 20,000, while noisily patriotic, responded to each individual European success with knowledgeable goodwill, an acceptance that sport can embrace rather than alienate rival camps, that the sting of defeat is no more than a lesson in life. The memory of famous players from either team, having concluded their contribution, mingling with their family among the crowd to exhort their colleagues in subsequent matches, stands strong. There was honour for both teams, valuably apparent to younger children present.

Ballesteros was born in April 1957 into a golfing family, learning early aged eight on the beaches near his Basque home, with a three-iron from his older brother Manuel, a regular finisher in the top hundred European Order of Merit (EOM). His uncle, Ramon Sota, was Spain's professional champion and had finished sixth in the Masters in 1965. Seve turned professional at 16, and two years later prodigiously was second in the Open at Royal Birkdale, having led after three rounds, then with a 74 tying with Nicklaus behind winner Johnny Miller. Exceptionally, he was to win the (financial) EOM for that and the next two years in a row, ultimately doing so a record six times. His first major title came with the Open in 1979, followed by the Masters in 1980 and 1983, the Open again in 1984 and 1988. It can justifiably be claimed that his pre-eminence created the reputation of the European Tour, and thereby in particular the Ryder Cup achievements, with five victories as player and then captain, this sometimes overlooked in the cascade of acclaim elsewhere. The partnership with Olazabal was epic: 11 wins and two matches halved out of 15. In his reign, the Ryder Cup was won in 1985, retained in 1987 and '89, regained in 1995, and under his captaincy retained in 1997 at Valderrama, the first time it was staged in continental Europe.

Ballesteros was to win 90 international tournaments, including a record 50 European titles, winning at least one for 17 consecutive years from 1976 to '92. His last was the Spanish Open in 1995. Retrospectively, he regarded the final round of his last victorious major, the Open of 1988 at Royal Lytham – on a Monday following abandonment in torrential rain – 'the best round of my entire career'.

His dominance dwindled in the late 1990s, plagued by injury, ultimately retiring in 2007. The following year he was diagnosed with a brain tumour, cancer-orientated. Fighting a losing battle under chemotherapy, his health progressively declined. In 2009 he bravely personally announced the launch of the Seve Ballesteros Foundation in aid of research and the general welfare of young golfers. He died in May 2011.

Here had been a life not just of exhilarating sporting achievement, but so often fun and laughter, of benevolence towards the watching world which made the public glad to share in his excellence. From such people as Seve the rest of us can gain a tonic for life. As the *Irish Independent* wrote, 'He spoke many languages: the dialects of honour, dignity, sportsmanship and fair play.'

It is almost by the way that Santander Airport should have been re-named after him: someone who enjoyed, and prompted, fun and entertainment.

DIEGO MARADONA
Omnipotent Bravado

'A fiesta of abstract joy'

If the tango is the temperamental representation of the national soul, then it breeds an inevitable sense of rejection for Argentina, perched at the bottom end of South America, if the rest of the world, politically, takes little account of the rest of your affairs. In Diego Maradona, an extraordinary and spontaneously gifted footballer born in 1960, Argentina suddenly found a symbol of omnipotent bravado. Via television, Maradona became their international ensign.

Anyone, more tragically everyone, wanted a piece of him: ambitious clubs, the national team, state politicians, the mafia, the media. Maradona's truest admirers were those boasting little or nothing – those from the same background of poverty from where he rose, firstly in Buenos Aires shanty towns, or later Barcelona and Naples, whither he was transferred on million-dollar tickets, and for whom he represented transient glory. A fiesta of abstract joy. Football had long been Argentina's emotional release, which many had experienced in their hosted World Cup of 1978, thanks in part to an incompetent referee repeatedly failing in the final to penalise handball in favour of Holland, the celebrations in the avenidas

308

of Buenos Aires so dense that I was pinned for half an hour in an office doorway.

Yet football is an ephemeral commodity. While Maradona was a mesmeric genius from the age of eight, an irresistibly desirable professional by 17, and imminently a world beater, a brutal truth is that sporting genius is disposable. Soaring with stratospheric fame, the impulsive Maradona could always handle the game, but privately not himself. This was even more evident when the game imposed upon his exotic skill a wanton, physical brutality uninhibited by a governing body, FIFA, which did little or nothing to uphold existing rule protection through efficient referees. Maradona is condemned by some for self-destructive disintegration of his career: the truth is that he was partially sucked into this downward spiral by the sheer greed of those who sought to exploit his genius.

I saw enough of him, not just on the field, but at close quarters, to testify on his sense of honour, fair play and generosity, to bemoan his fall from grace. His boyhood emergence was itself astonishing. In trials for Argentinos Juniors, the coaches could not believe he was only eight; he possessed the physique of a child but the touch of an adult. They checked. He *was* eight. Go forward 18 years to the 1986 World Cup in Mexico, by when he was regarded by eight-man defences as unplayable: in six matches he was fouled 53 times, winning twice as many free kicks as any other player, and scoring or assisting in ten of the team's 14 goals. An appalling foul in the Spanish league three years earlier when playing for Barcelona had all but ended his career. The belated tightening of referees' authority would only be semi-enacted by FIFA at the 1990 World Cup, yet by then the magic was already in decline from the impact of shamefully inflicted injury, alongside the self-abuse of drugs, available in the fawning, surrounding sycophancy that had helped scavenge George Best's life and now throttled Maradona's spontaneity.

It is bizarre the way society tolerates and accepts the eccentricities and tortured genius of Van Gogh, Mendel, Tchaikovsky and Ibsen, in art, science, music and literature, yet hastens to condemn the frailties of sports stars. By the 1994 World Cup in the USA, Maradona was beyond rescue, having already been banned for drug abuse in 1991 and again during those finals. In November 2001, at his final testimonial match in Buenos Aires, aged 41 and graced by the company of such luminaries as Eric Cantona, Maradona courageously took the microphone and told an admiring audience, 'Nothing I've done should be held against the game. I made mistakes and I paid for them ... but the ball itself is never stained.' One of only two players, together with Lionel Messi, to have been awarded FIFA's Golden Boot at both under-20 finals and the World Cup, in 91 internationals, Maradona scored 34 goals. He had touched millions of hearts.

Born in poor surroundings on the fringe of the capital, the middle son between four sisters and two brothers, he was spotted at eight by a coach of Los Cebollitas (Little Onions), the junior team of Argentinos Juniors. By the age of 12 he was giving half-time juggling demonstrations at senior league matches. Ten days before his 16th birthday he made his professional debut, the youngest ever in the first division, promptly 'nutmegging' a prominent opponent. In five years from 1976 he scored 115 goals in 167 appearances before a $4m transfer to Boca Juniors – who immediately won the league, for his only domestic title in Argentina. He was the first player to have a full-time agent, and threatened the chairman he would strike when colleagues were not receiving scheduled victory bonuses. National team manager Cesar Menotti shrewdly omitted the teenager from the home World Cup of 1978 on calculation that he was too young at 17.

Following the 1982 World Cup – more of that in a moment – he transferred for $7.6m to Barcelona, the Spaniards now coached by Menotti. In the final of the Copa de Rey in June 1983 against arch rivals Real Madrid, an El Clasico encounter, Maradona became the first Barcelona player to be given an ovation by rabid Real supporters: dribbling through the defence and past the goalkeeper, then braking to sidestep a desperate lunging tackle before tapping into an empty net. Olé! 'He had complete mastery,' recollects Barca club colleague Carrasco, recalling that the squad would stand watching him in awe during training. Exasperatingly, brutal opposing clubs were bent on grounding him. In September 1983, Andoni Goikoetxea, the renowned Bilbao axeman, broke Maradona's ankle. Recovery took three months. In the Copa del Rey Final of 1984, also against Bilbao, a brawl arose following another brutal challenge by Goikoetxea on Maradona, emotions boiling with racist taunts about Maradona's father's 'native' origin: all this in front of King Juan Carlos. With missiles raining, 60 were injured in the 100,000 crowd. Club president Nunez decided Maradona must leave so a world record $10.5m transfer to Napoli was completed, following 38 goals in 58 injury-hit appearances, with damaging painkillers.

Under camouflage surrounding Maradona's arrival in Italy's poorest and most violent city – the class distinction between the wealthier north of Milan and Turin more emphatic than that of England's reverse cultural gap between London and the working-class north – lay the unanswered question of whether mafia money, the hand of the notorious Camorra gang, had provided the springboard to tempt the world's most alluring performer. A local journalist pointedly asked how it was possible, when the city 'lacked houses, schools, transport, employment and sanitation', to indulge in football fantasy. Whatever: it worked. A crowd of 75,000 greeted him at Stadio San Paolo and improved league performances in two seasons, eighth and then third, culminated with Napoli winning the national championship for the first time in 1987. They were then runners-up in 1988 and '89, and won a second title in 1990. They also won the Coppa Italia in 1987 and were runners-up two years later. An unparalleled triumph, mocked and derided by northern rivals.

Yet the cruel irony of this galaxy of celebrations was that while Maradona magnified the city, the city itself was progressively destroying him: shackled by fame, associating with mafia acolytes, a mounting cocaine addiction, a ceaseless cavalcade of opportunist women sharing his limelight, $70,000 in fines for missing training. 'Disposable genius' was the epitaph awaiting his tombstone. It became increasingly doubtful whether he performed better on the pitch or at parties; whether he would recover from the latter, next in time for the former. Suspended for failing a drug test, Maradona would leave Napoli in 1992, signing for Sevilla for one year, then spending two years back home with Newell's Old Boys, followed by two years back at Boca Juniors.

Amid the rollercoaster club journey, there were the footlights extravagance of three successive World Cup exposures, where the focus on Maradona dominated media and public attention. In Spain in 1982 it was an anti-climax. His reputation was so exulted that every opposition detailed two, three or four defenders to neutralise the uncontrollable – sometimes six arraigned sandbags assembled to halt him by fair means or foul. Belgium did so in Argentina's opening match, then Italy, prominent hit-man Claudio Gentile the executioner with Maradona ultimately losing his temper and later being sent off in a defeat by three goals to Brazil.

Mexico 1986 witnessed a quarter-final between Argentina and England overloaded with post-Falklands animosity regarding Britain's repossession, and intended perceived reprisal for the sinking of Argentina's war ship *Belgrano* with loss of many young lives. English furore surrounded Maradona's opening goal shortly after half-time, which had been a travesty. Maradona handled the ball in a mid-air leap to outwit a belated challenge by Peter Shilton, an otherwise outstanding goalkeeper who was over half a foot taller. So what? Countless strikers have handled the ball, intentionally or otherwise. The fault lay primarily with a Tunisian referee, Ali Ben Hasan, no more than ten metres away who, if unsighted, neglected to consult his linesman, who had a clearer view. Equally at fault was FIFA, nominating referees on a continental egalitarian principle rather than selecting the known best. Maradona was labelled a 'cheat' when artfully claiming it had been the 'hand of God'. Fair play?

Protesting England conveniently overlooked that in the first 45 minutes they had never strategically escaped from their own half, or that central defender Terry Fenwick had elbowed Maradona in the face shortly after having already received a first yellow card. In a concerted attempt to stifle Maradona, England's midfield had stuttered. No serious cheat commands the efforts of three or four men to try to halt him. England's back four awaited Maradona's sorties like an India rural village not knowing when the tiger would next strike.

Maradona's second goal, four minutes later, was proverbially out of this world: receiving the ball in his own half, then weaving past five players like mist – Beardsley, Hodge, Reid, Butcher and Fenwick – and finally feinting to send Shilton the wrong way and gliding the ball into an empty net. In such moments is history made. He then scored twice in the semi-final against Belgium and gave the carved pass to Burruchaga for the decisive goal in a 3-2 final victory over West Germany.

The 1990 World Cup in Italy saw Argentina and Maradona reviled by home fans on account of achievements by disregarded Napoli. Abusive chants were directed at Maradona, though coincidentally FIFA had at last awoken and referees were instructed actively to protect entertainers from executioners. Defending champions Argentina lost their opening game to Cameroon, who had two sent off and three booked by French referee Michel Vautrot. It was 20 years overdue; he was simply applying existing laws. Maradona, who finished with stud marks on one shoulder, was hooted throughout by Italian fans. He was to have his reply in Argentina's victory over Italy on penalties in the semi-final, similar to their defeat of Yugoslavia in the quarter-final. He had scared the host nation witless with his vision and timing, eminently outperforming Italy's supposed match-winner Salvatore Schillaci. We had seen a glimpse of the old Maradona in the quarter-final: awaiting the shoot-out against Yugoslavia, lying on the turf, he had juggled ice cubes on his shins before flicking them away. Sadly, the final against West Germany was to prove a non-event, Germany winning with Andreas Brehme's 85th-minute penalty. In the autumn, Maradona received a year's drugs ban and returned home.

The descent was to continue and another drugs suspension and humiliation came midway through the 1994 World Cup in America. It was the final disposal of genius, which the world's most cherished game could but lament, the remainder of his time professionally anonymous, buoyed by incomparable memories prior to his death at 60 having been a gift to a global audience within which exploitative manipulators had steered corrupt practices.

A coincidental significant contribution to the game, certainly in Europe, was Maradona's inspirational capacity with Naples to break the effective monopoly of Serie A by Italy's northern four: Milan, Inter, Juventus and Torino. The potential for supposedly 'lesser' clubs to gain an upper hand, that financial power should not dominate league tables, was dramatically threatened in 2021 by the attempt of a dozen clubs, three each from Spain and Italy and six from England, to create a breakaway European super league.

This affront to democratic sport, to the principle of promotion and relegation, fortunately collapsed almost instantly, vehemently condemned by those clubs excluded but especially by the majority of supporters of elite clubs of England's Premier League, which played truant: Chelsea, Arsenal, Spurs, Manchester United, Manchester City and Liverpool. The relevance of the scope for fluctuating fortunates was swiftly emphasised in England by modest Leicester winning the FA Cup, at their fifth attempt in a final – to add to their League title five seasons earlier – and then by Manchester City, hitherto only intermittently in the front rank, reaching the Champions League final in a season of spectacular dominance, then sadly to fail against previous winners Chelsea.

CHAPTER EIGHT

CENTURY'S CLIMAX

FRED COUPLES
More Grace Than Glory

*'I'm not into shaking my fist
after some great shot'*

As an itinerant commentator on several sports, one can be unlucky. I missed Real Madrid's historic 7-3 thrashing of Eintracht Frankfurt in their fifth consecutive European Cup Final, in 1960, because the *Daily Telegraph* needed me on an England under-23 tour of GDR, Poland and Israel. I missed David Hemery's world record hurdles in 1968, a rare British success at the time, because I was Olympic night news editor – eight hours' time difference – for then inaugural independent television in London. Yet I was there, at golf's most picturesque course, when Fred Couples won his sole 'big four' title, Augusta's Masters in 1992. It was the best day of his life: certainly one of mine. Golf is unique in the sense that it is four competitions in one. Firstly, you are exclusively controlling your own ball and your technical physical capabilities. Secondly there is a temperamental response to what your immediate rival, and the others on the course, are simultaneously achieving. Then there is the challenge of the geometric complexity of the course design. Last, often crucially, variations of the weather. To experience this recipe for drama at elegiac Augusta, as player or even viewer, is indeed a rare privilege.

What made Couples such a joy to behold, for his intoxicated followers and indeed anyone else, was that his amiable, relaxed yet supreme style made his victories seem like a stroll on the beach. Herein lay his ultimate limitation. Perplexingly for others, he himself did not appear to mind.

Not attempting golf until my 30s, I was a scatter-ball novice but was absorbed as a spectator by the theatricality of the game's demands, the personalities of great players I was able to witness, from Palmer, Nicklaus and Watson, through Faldo and Ballesteros, to Tiger Woods, but if I had been a proper player I would have wished to have been vaguely like Couples. There was something so gracious about his carefree manner, the languor of those hazel eyes, the smile of David Niven (for those old enough to remember). Couples once engagingly said, 'Someday I might look back and think I should have worked harder, but now it's the furthest thing on my mind to be the best player in the world ... maybe *fifth* best.' At the time of that comment, he had recently defeated Watson and Ballesteros in the Tournament Players Championship, aged 25, and had finished in the top ten of the Masters, US Open and the Open Championship in the UK.

Couples had never in his life had a coaching lesson. Self-effacing to a degree, he reflected prior to his 1992 triumph, 'I'm going to learn a lot this week, maybe hit some smart shots, but I'm not into shaking my fist after some great shot ... if I can eliminate my mistakes, I could play well here.' And some. For the last year, he had played like a new Nicklaus with five victories out of 19 top-six finishes in 24 tournaments. Of 36 rounds, 32 had been par or better. What was as yet missing was a major. Only once had he led the final day of a major, the 1990 PGA Championship, and blown it on the greens. Never mind the rhythm of a great jazz player, perfectly balanced hips, upper body seemingly jointless, with the sweet slow swing of an elephant's trunk which could belt the ball all but 400 yards. Now at Augusta, the audience longed for him to join the litany of past illustrious names in the wake of eminent, amateur Masters founder Robert Jones. Moreover, an American victory was overdue, with seven European winners, including four Brits, during the past 12 years. Was his mood right? None but he, in Monday's practice round, could have indulged a huge gallery with random additional mighty drives, just for the hell of it.

To bypass the opening three rounds, rain and darkness having prevented the last three pairs concluding on the third day, obliged them to finish the last three or four holes on the Sunday morning; the leaders being Australian Craig Parry on 11 under par, Couples and his sage and mentor Raymond Floyd on nine under, with defending champion Ian Woosnam behind on six under. By the afternoon's third hole of the final round, Parry, with a three-putt bogey, and Couples were tied. Both bogeyed the fifth; Parry's putting then deserted him, and by the sixth, with a birdie by Floyd, there was a three-way tie. Could nerveless Couples survive notorious Amen Corner, the treacherous sequence of holes 11, 12 and 13? As a rival once observed, 'You cannot not admire Freddy, there's no one like him. Other guys are just happy he hasn't realised how good he is.'

That might have remained so – until the beguiling, nightmare 12th, that pretty bookshelf green perched on the lip of a bank falling into the quiet Rae's Creek trout stream: a golfer's poisoned meringue, and aptly labelled 'Amen Corner' by *New Yorker* writer Herbert Warren Wind. Couples would later admit, having had a precipitous tournament-deciding escape, that he had never been as nervous. With a sliced eight-iron off the tee, his ball bounced backwards from the bank, teetering downwards to within a foot of the water, and perched on a few blades of grass in a perfect lie. At this moment in time a career was being almost lost, but was instead saved with gravity defied. On the mini grandstand 100 yards away, we could hardly breathe. A chip, and Couples still had his par three.

Meanwhile, ahead, Floyd had closed to within two shots with birdies at the 14th and 15th. The heat is still on Couples and his drive at the left-hand dog-leg 13th leaves him obstructed behind a pine. He plays out safe to 130 yards, then pitches perfectly to 14 feet. As he shapes for the birdie putt, the bank of azaleas curls round the green behind him like the backcloth of some princely mediaeval court. In the hush, he rolls six inches past for par. A glorious pitch to the 14th, the ball checking and rolling left downhill to within three feet, releases a throaty roar. Putt holed, two-stroke lead restored, followed by a clever short chip at the 15th and a two-putt for par. The non-champion is looking good with another par at the 15th. 'He's so attractive to women, they just can't stop trying to catch his eye,' murmurs Herb Wind, sitting beside me at the 16th, as Couples requests a blonde girl pressing against the ropes at the tee to keep still. Now comes a safe shot to the centre of an awkwardly sloping green. 'He's not trying to be too clever,' Wind reflects, as the two-shot lead over Floyd is retained.

The table-flat green of the 400-yard 17th is one of the few holes at Augusta where the ball does not wilfully glide around like a marble on ice. Couples, who is as agreeably American as James Stewart, and has the huge gallery aching for his success as it swells behind him over the few final holes, makes his short-iron approach safely to 40 feet from the pin. A buttermilk sun bathes the fairway, and the tall firs behind the green take on an almost luminous velvet shade; the mood of stillness can be illusory. As Couples addresses the ball, Floyd having already left the 18th green, Couples's bloated shadow stretches ten yards or more almost to the hole. He marginally misreads the line. The first putt rolls five feet past. The gallery is motionless. Four thousand breaths surrounding the green are held while he contemplates the short one back. Thirty thousand more out of view are suspended in anxiety. This is the man many have said is a choker. He crouches, shades his eyes as he studies the line, stands, pauses, adjusts the feet, lets go the brief pendulum swing. The ball drops. Couples straightens with an inaudible sigh, and the small gesture with his right hand says it all, 'I didn't fluff.' One to play, and five shots in hand for the Green Jacket. Here is not carnival, but a microcosm of life itself.

For six holes, this gentle man has lived on the brink of triumph, yet there is not an ounce of tension visible in his body. He has the supple movement of Gene Kelly, his constant swing as beautiful as a reed bending in the wind. He makes a profound game look so easy. Now there is an uphill drive to the 18th, the final test of nerve. He is bunkered to the left the way Sandy Lyle was four years ago. His wedge climbs high, the sound as it drops pin-high 30 feet to the right is simultaneously the audience's cry of acclaim and relief. Fred Couples has a 150-yard walk to fame; he can three-putt and win the Masters. And the only probable thought drumming in his brain as he slowly ascends the fairway between the ranks of jubilant

*Tanzania's first gold denied,
Filbert Bayi, world record
1,500m breaker in '74, settles
for Moscow's steeplechase silver.
(Image IOC)*

Johan Cruyff, Total Football's ringleader, confounds Argentina's keeper Daniel Carnevali to score as Holland gallop through 1974 World Cup quarter-final.

Cassius Clay (later Mohammad Ali) reportedly threw his light-heavyweight Olympic gold from Rome into a river in segregation dismay. (Image IOC)

Arthur Ashe strove to
mitigate four centuries'
history of segregation.
(AELTC)

*Billie Jean King,
precocious teenager,
veteran champion of
gender emancipation.*
(AELTC)

Sub-four-minute 1954 trio: Roger Bannister (L), Chris Chataway and London Marathon founder Chris Brasher (R)

The ultimate: Jahangir Khan of Pakistan commands British Open 1983.

Torvill and Dean enchanted
Lillehammer audiences but not
shamelessly biased Olympic judges
in 1994. (Image IOC)

John Bertrand,
historic
Americas
Cup winner
for Australia,
who all but
squandered
innovative boat
design.

Synchronised
discipline for
Virginia Leng
and Priceless.

Sebastian Coe, only Olympic 1,500m champion to defend the title, signals to sceptical media 'still number one', LA '84. (Image IOC)

Seve Ballesteros: an entertaining, wilful flamboyance.

Sorcerer Maradona leaves England dizzy, World Cup quarter-final '86

Serene Fred Couples evades trouble — the world's fifth best?

Style the prerogative: David Gower, Leicestershire and England.

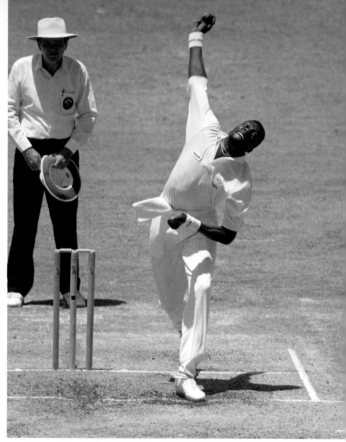

West Indies terror: Curtly Ambrose delivers.

Oksana Baiul, angelic, abandoned Ukrainian child with steel nerve for figures Olympic gold, Lillehammer '94. (Image IOC)

Ayrton Senna: celestial optimism and commitment.

A Kiwi power beyond experience, Jonah Lomu made opponents tremble.

Passport to a future education, labourer Josiah Thugwane's centenary marathon title gains South Africa's first democratic gold medal. (Image IOC)

Ethnic ideology: Cathy Freeman, supreme Aboriginal, determines 400m victory at Sydney 2000. (Image IOC)

Steve Redgrave's totemic fifth Olympic Gold, coxless fours 2000.

Accomplished technician, Jonny Wilkinson was consumed by self-analysis.

Jamaican Usain Bolt's personality buoyed track and field's ruptured honour at his three successive Olympics. (Image IOC)

Roger Federer, ultimate elegance, retrieved immutable Swiss temperament. (AELTC)

England team unity.

Americans is, 'It's over.' He putts – after an interminable delay for crowd clearance – to within three inches. Was he not already a great player without this, someone later asked. 'I couldn't care less,' Couples replies, with an unaffected smile.

But what of the future? Could Couples replace Watson as America's foremost player? He had accepted, after winning the Players Championship in 1984, that he had squandered his skills, dropping from then seventh in the tournament money-winning list to 76th by 1986. Pressure had overtaken him in a losing Ryder Cup in 1989. Affiliation with the US captain, Floyd, began then, blossoming in Ryder Cup success in 1991, in which together they were unbeaten. In the generosity that can, and should, infuse golf, it was to the satisfaction of both men that the Augusta outcome of 1992 went the way it did, Floyd thereby becoming runner-up twice in three years. There is a much-quoted anecdote from three-time British Open champion Henry Cotton, who, on the first occasion, remarked that, like a medical student passing an exam, he had been as knowledgeable beforehand as afterwards, 'But now I am qualified.' In 1992, Couples became qualified.

He was born in October 1959 in Seattle. His paternal grandparents were Italian immigrants who changed their name from Coppola to Couples, his father a groundsman with Seattle Parks, their home adjacent to the Jefferson Park golf course where young Fred developed spontaneously. He had a swing that might make purists frown, but with its supple timing delivered such unusual power. Graduating from high school in 1977, he gained a scholarship to the University of Houston, and at 19 won a play-off in the Worcester Open of 1978. An opening professional victory came at the Kemper Open in 1983 after a protracted five-way tie which Couples won with a birdied second-hole play-off. In the following ten years, 14 tournament titles were accumulated. There were tales of his driving the green on a par-four 410-yard hole at Tyler, Texas.

Yet another major was not forthcoming. He boasted nine top-ten finishes in the Open, including third in 1991 at Royal Birkdale with a final round of 64; third again in 2005 at St Andrews, plus back-to-back European titles in 1995, the Dubai Desert and John Walker classics. In 2006 a second Green Jacket loomed at Augusta, conceding to Phil Mickelson in the final round, aged 46: the same age as Nicklaus, the oldest winner. Couples made the Masters cut in 2007 for the 23rd consecutive time and was then absent through injury for a couple of years. With Jason Dufner he was the midway Masters leader in 2012, aged 52, but a third day's 75 saw him finish 12th. On the Champions (Seniors) Tour for 2010, he was runner-up to Watson at his first outing in Hawaii, then won the Seniors Open Championship two years later, but a back injury forced retirement from the Masters in 2016. What Couples had given to his sport was more grace than glory; a gentlemanly ambience enviably short on greed.

DAVID GOWER
Spontaneous Entertainment

'Commanding anyone's acclaim'

Just imagine. The UK Prime Minister has to govern not from 10 Downing Street but from the large pub on the corner, the Red Dragon, with its regular mob of some hundreds all telling him, mostly with good humour, who should be in the Cabinet, when to declare a public holiday, what should be the target GDP, whether there should be prison sentences for speeding, is he too generous towards the Opposition, should he sack his chief policy advisor. There in a nutshell you have effectively the platform of England's captain of Test cricket.

Alternatively, reverse the image. Do you want as captain, say, a Gordon Brown, fiercely obsessed with numbers, returns, projections, statistics, social conventions, or instead perhaps a kind of cross between Nigel Farage, Eric Morecambe and upper crust Hugh Grant, who would be relaxed on protocol, sense the appeal of freedom of expression and the occasional risk of impulsive entertainment? There you have what was, too briefly, the chequered captaincy of gifted shot-maker David Gower in the late 20th century: a modern equivalent, say, of C.B. Fry, or in football Jimmy Greaves, carefree souls who identified with the physical, and visual, joy of adventurous sport for both

323

performer and viewer. In an industrial, professional, economy-driven world, entertainment needs this, yet as a public figure – prior to his premature retirement in 1993 and conversion to Sky pundit – Gower, born in April 1957, remained something of an enigma. Public school education's classless contemporary mannerisms were a camouflage, Gower seemingly wanting to be Mr Everyman yet simultaneously gregarious and private, a spontaneous accomplished winner while lacking the professional's exclusive killer instinct which monochrome diehards demanded. He was so laid back, someone said, 'He was almost comatose.' This was, however, never a reflection of the old, socially disagreeable chasm between 'gentlemen and players' and separate gate entry on to the field at Lord's, through to the mid-20th century. Gower's mother, conditioned to his father's stereotypic Colonial Office role in Tanganika prior to returning to Kent, identified her son's aptitude for adjusted accent, between home and classless 'work'.

Hindsight would suggest that the courtly Anthony Hopkins of the crease was never emotionally equipped for the most complex responsibility existing in the entire world of sport, as Test captain. In the field, making perhaps 100 judgements a day, in a contest lasting four or five days, instructing ten fielders and maybe six bowlers on their strategic placing or intended delivery of a new or worn ball; as batsman, of setting an individual example, ball-by-ball, if possible for several hours, in a leadership brand that admits no flaw while exposed to the judgement of not merely enthusiasts but many of a bevy of MCC members educated to believe their opinion is gospel. What imaginative mind would not want to buzz their colleagues like a seagull, in a handy Tiger Moth, just for the hell of it during a practice match in free-speaking Australia, as Gower once joyfully did with inevitable reprimand.

The maddening aspect for Gower's league of admirers was that while – appointed perhaps prematurely – he might have lacked the pragmatic captaincy of his forbear Mike Brearley, who was no more than a moderate run bank, Gower possessed an elegant array of presumptuous shots that were the envy of any opposition. Never someone with a calculator in his pocket, like a Boycott or a Gooch, Gower's statistics at the time of his early retirement aged 36 ranked among all-time exemplars, commanding anyone's acclaim:

- Fourth behind Bradman, Hutton and Hammond for his percentage of century innings climbing above 150 (eight out of 18)
- Fourth in percentage of two-innings top aggregate score per Test (32 in 117) behind Hobbs, Hutton and Botham
- Sixth among those scoring 8,000 runs in over 100 Tests (117) behind Border, Gavaskar, Gooch, Miandad and Viv Richards
- Tenth as top scorer, 46 times in 204 innings, ahead of Cowdrey and Botham
- Youngest Englishman since Peter May in 1951 to score a Test century
- His 187 in eight hours against West Indies in 1981, evidence for disbelievers of his concentration

Yet reservation among those in the upper echelons of cricket society, who considered cricket and all its ethos to be the gospel of Britishness, clung to his suspect reputation. If he was at ease *with* dyed professionals, he was not *of* them. Maybe he was simply debonair like Compton, yet there was the perception that he played daredevil shots simply to prove he *could* play them. His nature was showmanship – not boastfully, but for the simple personal pleasure. While recognising that the county game was the working cricketer's weekly wage, Test cricket was his motivation. His Icelandic wife Thorunn acknowledged his bias, 'If he could have played *just* Test matches, he would have continued longer.' With Leicestershire, for whom he played prior to switching to Hampshire, the general secretary Mike Turner reflected that Gower, like Ray Illingworth before him, needed time mentally to 'downgrade' to the county concept in the wake of a Test summit. Many had cause to suspect that for Gower, life extended beyond cricket. At many moments in his career as captain, watching him fielding at mid-off, he appeared to be observing the conflict rather than directing it.

The occasions when I had opportunity, amid my itinerant schedule, to discuss the game with Gower, were usually upbeat rather than when he was reeling, say, from a chasing inflicted by West Indies. We once chatted in Sydney when, after his exit as captain, he was contemplating the search for re-motivation, to dispel disillusionment. 'The hardest part, having stepped down,' he admitted, 'is not to let the mind wander, where's the stimulus? Being captain adds to the responsibility you have to *yourself* as a player. Freed from the responsibility as captain, you're not calculating the tactics moment by moment with a captain's eye view. You can switch off. You want to be either involved, or not at all. Being on the selection committee, you can be as authoritarian as you like, but the captain has the final say, his strategy, his show, his responsibility.'

Born an individualist, Gower had been shaken when overhearing conversation which questioned his future as a 'discarded captain'. He reflected, 'To keep playing Test cricket, I have to be playing well. If I can maintain concentration, I think I can still be good for some time to come. I'm eternally grateful to the game, realising what I have to lose and how much people appreciate what I can do. Way back, without being arrogant, I wasn't bothered whether I did well, I thought it was fun, and runs were a bonus. I was happier when I wasn't soul-searching. If some say, "If he'd had a few less bottles of fizz and a few more nets, he'd have been better," they might be right, but it hasn't been a fluke, keeping an international career going for nine years.'

The next time we met, the captaincy had been restored on evidence of Gower's apparent maturity at 32, sitting in partnership with Ted Dexter as chairman and team manager Micky Stewart. This is, coincidentally in my opinion, the formula of triangular responsibility that was so often to puncture the integration of an England team, with its inevitable division of opinion between three. The imbalance was once again a situation which Gower, so accessibly convention's outcast, would not survive. There was now, initially, the mood that Dexter and Gower, fellow ex-public school products, would liaise. 'I hope the chairman's broadmindedness can work, being the same as mine,' Gower said. 'I hope I'll be a better captain.'

Was this optimistic? There was a prevalent view at county level that team discipline fluctuated because the professional game was now finance-orientated, and captains were reluctant to take decisions with financial loss consequences. Gower denied this was likely with him, 'You're working with bowlers to win, and if they can't do it, you change them. As captain, you have to take responsibility. You shouldn't be seen to be implementing someone else's policy. To win, you need good players, you have to back them, give them the right atmosphere, which means relaxation and not too many orders. The mistake I made before was not cricket judgement, but PR. It's naïve to think you can get by without recognition of problems off the field. You're under pressure if things don't go well, but it's not the *rational* press you have to worry about. If we lose the summer series, some newspapers will club us.'

Fortune was not to smile upon this rare talent, a seeming iconoclast of convention, whose personal career blossomed with over 26,000 runs at an average over 40, yet was ultimately abandoned by the 'in-house club'. There was the mockery of a style which so much of the public welcomed. Alienation of certain principles alongside fixated contemporary Graham Gooch, whose attitudes conflicted with Gower's easy nature.

In Rob Steen's perceptive and sensitive biography, *A Man Out of Time*, he poses the inevitable question: what about the joy that statistics condense, the way Gower did the things he did, the very qualities that lifted him above the merely competent into a class of, if not one, then certainly very few? Does being the embodiment of an ideal not compensate for an imposed sense of underachievement? Gower's response was typically truthful, 'Yes, it does. That's actually quite important to me, flattering. You feel as though there's something extra you've achieved, because it's so easy to hide behind statistics. I'm very happy to accept things on a different level. If, for some extraordinary reason, it has made a difference to the quality of life, in terms of going to Lord's and watching a fun game, then fine. In a way, that's how I prefer it.'

Steen aptly concludes that in the case of David Gower, cricketer, means were always more important than ends. At the crease, Gower echoed Couples on the tee: a mind in which style, in manner as much as in technology, was of equivalent value.

CURTLY AMBROSE
Harpoonist Destroyer

'A debilitating psychological influence'

I was too young to have seen Harold Larwood – the innocent instrument of England captain Douglas Jardine's 'bodyline', anti-Bradman Australian tour of 1932 – who retired the year after I was born. Bowlers, whether harpoonists or spinners, always seemed to me more the fascination of cricket, ever since I first started reading about Don Bradman or the renowned Jack Hobbs when I was aged eight. Bowlers, with the complexity of attempting to topple three stumps with a bouncing ball, essentially play mind games with the batsmen. My father bought me a mini net for our mini lawn, and I spent hours experimenting, without a batsman, as a would-be 'away' swinger: tempting that late cut and slip catch, the former my forte with a too-heavy, only wartime available adult bat as a schoolboy.

A couple of senior school 90s with the bat – there was no scoreboard so I was unaware, when out, of proximity of the magic three digits – were fun, but bowling was the *science*. As an itinerant, ubiquitous journalist, I was only intermittently on cricket's footplate, but the opportunity in 1994 to witness one of the game's all-time harpoonists, Curtly Ambrose of the

West Indies, coincidentally happened to give the experience of a lifetime. John Woodcock, an eminent critic for half a century, in his '100 Greatest Cricketers of All Time' for *The Times*, wrote, 'For some years West Indies would have been lost without Ambrose.'

Fast bowling embodies the bravado of the game by batsmen. Cricket is not for sissies. The guile of a spinner, such as Australia's Shane Warne, can inflict a brand of mental torture, but the onslaught of pace brings occasional broken bones. In my younger days, West Indies had been conspicuous for the three Ws – Worrell, Weekes and Walcott, all with five-figure run aggregates – subsequently all-rounder Sobers, then run-harvester Richards. Then, for two decades, West Indies had fluctuatingly dominated the fielding game, with exclusive, four-pronged speedsters: a negative mental attitude which was more about preventing the opposition from winning, with marksmen such as Michael Holding and Joel Garner. Ambrose, born in September 1963 in Antigua, was successor to this policy yet notable, notwithstanding his height of 6ft 7in, for constantly bowling *at the stumps* rather than bouncing the ball shoulder high. He was a lethal, honourable attacker, of whom Viv Richards said he possessed 'the biggest heart of any bowler I knew'. England, and other Test opposition, were to discover the cost of resisting that force.

Ambrose's menace seldom had swing, but had an unpredictable lift on the bounce, given his height, his ruthless focus on the off-stump bullseye, and uncanny pitching – until his power later faded – of lightning yorkers. In what might be said to have been his prime three years, 1992–94, Ambrose's claim of wickets was all but reaching ten-pin bowling figures: at times an average approaching one per over. What I was to see in Port of Spain was one in a chapter of destructions.

Having toyed as a teenager with the notion of emigrating to the US, being fond of baseball, encouraged by his mother he switched to cricket and in 1983, in a Leeward Islands competition, he took seven wickets for six runs for Antigua against St Kitts. The following year he made his first-class debut for an Island XI. A Viv Richards scholarship opened a path to England and a place with Heywood in the Central Lancashire League, where he took 115 wickets in the season, then returned to represent Leeward Islands – claiming 12 wickets, nine bowled, against Guyana. He was taking time to mature but by 1988, and Pakistan's tour of West Indies, Ambrose was ready to step into the shoes of matador Garner. In a one-day international at Kingston, Jamaica, he took wickets with his third and ninth deliveries, and recorded 4-39 in ten overs, followed by 4-35 in the second match. This level was unsustained in the immediate Test series. Selected then to tour England, he played all five Tests, with 22 wickets for a run average of 20.22.

Touring Australia in 1988/89 and winning the series 3-1, Ambrose's aggregate was 26 wickets at an average 21.46. By now he was established as the prime force of any West Indies team. That summer, he made his County Championship debut in England with Northamptonshire – having signed the previous year but ultimately being unavailable – a moderate launch conceding nearly 30 runs per wicket with 28 claimed in total. Early in 1990, England toured West Indies and had their first experience of Antigua's volcano, conceding the series 2-1. In the fourth Test, with England needing 356 to win and only an hour remaining, they were five wickets down with a draw likely. Ambrose took the new ball and rattled through the tail with 5-18 in 46 balls, four lbws being testimony to relentless accuracy. A following Test series in England was drawn 2-2, *Wisden* commenting that Ambrose's accuracy had risen to the point 'where a batsman had to play every ball and not necessarily with a scoring stroke – an ability to exert a debilitating psychological influence'.

South Africa toured West Indies for the first time in 1992 – the country's first Test match for 22 years – with a new international regulation limiting bowlers to one bouncer per over. Ambrose and partner Courtney Walsh seemed unimpeded, Ambrose claiming 6-34 in the second innings. The whirlwind that was Ambrose remained unabated. In January 1993, an Australian Test series resounded to the splintering of home stumps – Ambrose recording 3-56 in the first Test and 19 wickets in the final two encounters, including 6-74 in the first innings of the fourth with three wickets in 19 deliveries in the second, West Indies winning the match by one run. On the first day of the decisive fifth Test, Ambrose excelled even by his standards with 7-1 in 30 deliveries, concluding at 7-25. Flawless.

Returning home and representing Leeward Islands once more, and seemingly weary, his ten wickets cost a moderate 120 runs. England arrived, under the severest preparation from experimental team manager Keith Fletcher. Less than usually alarming, Ambrose claimed ten wickets in the first two Tests. In the third he took 5-60 in the first innings, but with England nonetheless gaining a substantial advantage and then dismissing West Indies relatively cheaply in their second innings, they were left needing 194 for a winning lead in the series and an hour to bat on the fourth evening. On my first visit to Port of Spain, I was looking forward to an intriguing final day and possible victory, especially if captain and opener Michael Atherton could carve early authority.

Yet what now struck was awesome. Electric. Unforgivingly aligned on the off stump, Ambrose's first ball demanded

Atherton's precise defence: fractionally late, he was struck just below the knee, lbw and gone before the scoreboard had moved. What was about to follow was a collapse of historic despair against Ambrose's tornado of seven overs with barely one delivery not rifled at the stumps, and the series all but surrendered in the hour. As an involuntarily biased spectator, I also felt limp as Ambrose's slaughter of 6-22 left England on 40 runs with only two wickets remaining overnight.

To a degree, England had not helped themselves. In that same first over, Mark Ramprakash contrived to run himself out – chasing, in the first over, in confusion with partner Alec Stewart? – then with Robin Smith, Graeme Hick, Stewart himself, and Jack Russell and Graham Thorpe following in a trail of sleepwalkers as Ambrose buried their dreams. How the baying, chanting audience celebrated the laying low of once colonial masters. The West Indies had long been distinguished as the best in the game by their ability to rise from casual concentration to deliver knockout attack against opposition unjustifiably confident. This we had just witnessed on both counts as the rout was completed in the morning with England all out for 46, by two runs avoiding their lowest score since 1887.

That quoted figure for me symptomises the downside of one of sport's most elegant and dramatic occupations: the obsession with statistics rather than style. What we had just witnessed was not an assortment of mathematical averages – contained in the indispensable *Wisden* – but an exhilarating exhibition of unparalleled physical synchronisation, occasionally witnessed in this most unique of all team sports, which is in fact dominated by wholly independent individuals governed as much by their character as technique.

OKSANA BAIUL
Symphony of Springtime

'More important than Olympic gold'

Sport can quite often be a pathway to redemption for those whose life is in disarray. Oksana Baiul is the epitome of such forlorn circumstance. She is born in November 1977, in Dnipropetrovsk, a Ukrainian Soviet satellite city and missile manufacturing centre. From the outset her existence is emotionally bleak. Her parents divorce when she is two, her father deserts her, she is raised by her mother Marina, a French teacher, who dies of cancer in 1991 when she is 13, her grandparents having also recently died. Her grandfather has nurtured her precocious skating since she was three, her talents technically directed by Stanislav Koritek, an experienced coach. She scorns her father's attempted reconciliation at her mother's funeral. Her early instinctive feel for ballet is apparent in her delicate, rapid progress on the ice rink.

With the disintegration of the USSR, and shrinking Ukraine economy, Koritek leaves for relative prosperity in Toronto. His father Alfred, the secretary of the national skating federation, organises for Galina Zmievskaya as alternative coach. Galina graciously accommodates Baiul as a student at her small home in Odessa. Baiul's expectation is supported by state subsidy, moving into a dormitory in 1993 aged 15; by now so accomplished that she wins a silver medal at the European Championships in Helsinki, and then exceptionally gold at the World Championships in Prague. She is as slender as a daffodil yet with balletic syncopation.

In 1994 she repeats her European second place at Copenhagen, while across the Atlantic scandal grips America's media. Nancy Kerrigan, Baiul's prime rival for the Olympic title, is subversively mugged and injured by accomplices of Tonya Harding, another prominent contender. Hundreds of media vultures descend upon Lillehammer, the Norwegian Olympic host city. Kerrigan recovers, Harding evades prosecution, her Olympic eligibility upheld by the US Olympic Committee. Attention on young Baiul's unprecedented ambition, that of emulating Norway's child prodigy Sonja Henie between the wars, is submersed within America's news frenzy. On Baiul's socially fractured journey, she is given succour, financial and moral, by compatriot Viktor Petrenko, men's figure skating champion at Albertville in 1992, while Zmievskaya is the attendant for technical supervision. As an intended impartial commentator, my private emotions are unequivocally behind this tender girl-princess. Her prospects are possibly compromised when, during practice between the compulsory short programme and the free skate, she collides with Tanja Szewczenko of Germany, straining her back, her shin needing stitches and the pain requiring drug-acceptable painkillers.

Yet this lonely, all but isolated Ukrainian maintains the will of would-be champions. The Harding–Kerrigan controversy bypasses her even when, as the last six leading contenders prepare for the free-dance, tearful Harding on the ice requests and is granted a restart when a skate lace snaps in her first minute. 'I don't pay much attention to the Harding–Kerrigan affair,' Baiul says. 'You cannot let outside issues influence your thoughts. I am calm even when I have to wait for the rink to be cleared of flowers thrown after Kerrigan has finished.'

As Baiul takes to the ice, the margins confronting the nine judges are fractional. From the short programme, Kerrigan is leading Baiul, with Surya Bonali of France and China's Chen Lu hard on Baiul's heels. Gazing at her, in her shimmering pale lavender attire, seeming innocent eyes beneath pale bronze bouffant hair, she could be my own daughter aged about ten in junior ballet school. Kerrigan's supporters believe she is effectively already victor, with a succession of 5.8 and 5.9 approval from the judges. Baiul is now under way to a medley of Broadway ballads.

This doe-eyed girl, who has metaphorically come from nowhere, who is reaching out to fortune, is simultaneously so elegant and yet so slim you suppose that her legs cannot have the power for triple jumps, her narrow, elegant shoulders not the rhythm for sustained spins, yet it is all there, a symphony of springtime. She concludes, possibly the definitive final element in decimalised adjudication on the bench, a triple toe-loop. With eight judges divided 4-4 on presentation between Baiul and Kerrigan, and a tie by the ninth, Baiul is Ukraine's first gold medal champion and equivalent of Henie. She crumbles, sobbing, in the arms of Zmievskaya. On the podium, as Ukraine's sky-blue-and-yellow emblem rises, Baiul has all the trembling appearance of a young, rescued hostage. Of such unforgettable moments are the Olympics made. While Kerrigan is a gracious presence, executing an elaborate routine, Baiul is a theatrical whole, something of subtlety, complete yet somehow uncertain. Kerrigan can expect domestic fame and riches, Harding a three-year probation, 500 hours of community service and a $100,000 fine, but what next for child-adult Baiul, about to leap as financial migrant into America's consuming commercial fish-net?

Arriving in Simsbury, Connecticut, home of that state's international skating centre, Zmievskaya negotiates for Baiul a contract with William Morris Agency. A professional tour commences, yet teenager Baiul is temperamentally adrift, exposed and vulnerable to the off-duty alcohol relaxation of professionals' routine. Within three years she is fortunate to survive a drunken car crash, sidestepping prosecution with an alcohol rehabilitation programme, which she comes to regard 'as more important than Olympic gold'. She follows her current coach, Valentyn Nikolayev, to Richmond, Virginia, and thence to Cliffside Park, New Jersey, romantically encountering Gene Sunik, a fellow Ukrainian migrant.

In a continuing search, aged 25, for her own true personality, she is assisted by Sunik in tracing back home, her father and a Jewish ancestry on her Romanian Jewish maternal grandmother's side, in contrast to Russian Orthodoxy under which she was raised. Elusive search via Odessa's ice rink bears success. Reunited with her father in 2003, by 2005 she adopts the Semitic faith. 'Being Jewish feels natural, like a second skin,' Baiul confides with the *New Jersey Jewish News*. Baiul accepts an invitation to become fundraiser for the children's charity TIVKA, alongside Lenny Krayzelberg, the Jewish Olympic swimming champion originating from Odessa. As Baiul would recall, 'I was interested because it was an orphanage, and because it was Ukrainian ... It was going to touch my soul. I had been an orphan, we could work together, it was perfect. It made me feel so good about myself.' At last.

In December 2006, Baiul skates in an exhibition at Moscow's Red Square together with multiple champions; the following year collaborates with ballet choreographer Saule Rachmedova and the Ice Theatre of New York. Carlo Farina, her manager and future husband, co-ordinates her fashion companies, and lawsuits for embezzlement by employees within her multiple estate. Still skating, Baiul temperamentally re-enters that past representation of Tchaikovsky's white swan that is the real expression of herself. Sport which collaborates with music can extend the sensitivity of both performers and audience.

AYRTON SENNA
Messianic Belief

*'Our body is on the limit
before the car is'*

Our individual existence, part fashioned by nurture, is as much governed by the coincidence of our genes as by chance. I am what I am, accidentally as it were, because my mother's initial fiancé happened to ski, off-piste, fatally into a pine. Ayrton Senna, deified by millions across the world, calculatedly lived his adult life on the shoulder of death, yet an horrendous end at San Marino's Grand Prix on 1 May 1994, was triggered by a mechanical design flaw. That morning he had been planning, with the Formula One drivers' union, for improved safety regulations.

Yet Senna himself, with a messianic belief in his destiny as champion, was temperamentally wedded to the necessity of danger as the alchemy of triumph. There was no doubting his sincerity. He had said to me and many others, 'To survive in Grand Prix racing, you need to be afraid. Fear drives both your concentration and ambition.' This concept carried him to the hem of perfection and was met by equal admiration and at times accusation of arrogance by rivals, mostly in awe at the refinement of margins he fractionally skirted at the wheel. Was this genius or ruthlessness? The majority of those who knew him best, either on the track or fascinated from the grandstand, believed him technically and temperamentally peerless. Sir Stirling Moss, the legendary British racer of the years after the Second World War, wrote of Senna's death, 'Ayrton was the only one who approached the genius of Juan Manuel Fangio of Argentina, who was five times world champion in eight years before retiring in 1957. Ayrton was quite simply the best.'

Underpinning Senna's confidence was his religious conviction, enhancing his sense of superiority. He had turned to the Bible early on the morning of his death. This seemingly aristocratic detachment riled some rivals, including the foremost Frenchman Alain Prost, who way back had observed, 'Ayrton thinks he can't kill himself [by the margins he risks] because he believes in God, and I think that's dangerous for other drivers.' British rival Nigel Mansell shared Prost's view, considering that Senna's nth degree margins scared other drivers into letting him pass. It would be presumptuous of me to claim a close friendship with Senna: we enjoyed a warm working association, discussing issues during Grand Prix at Monaco, Adelaide, Tokyo or Phoenix, exchanging Christmas cards, my visiting his home in Sao Paulo. Because I had no professional vested interest in Formula One, he felt he could trust me with confidential opinions, wishing to make comparison with administration in other international federations.

Senna's almost remote intellectual analysis of the Fédération Internationale de l'Automobile brought him into constant conflict with a multi-billion-dollar bureaucracy during his 11 years as one of the most illustrious figures in world sport, right up to his final month. By an ironic twist, in the very week that he died, *Esquire* magazine published a prescient analysis by Laura Thompson on what separates a true star from the merely famous: those such as Garbo, Olivier, Nureyev being of loftier magnitude. The star, Thompson wrote, is giving, yet not giving, revealing everything, yet nothing. Racing drivers, she defined, 'live lives that other men dream of – crystallising contemporary image of glamour … driving fantasy cars, sleeping with fantasy women, earning fantasy money, living lives that can only be found in the shadow of death'.

Born in March 1960 into a wealthy Brazilian-Portuguese family, Senna had begun his career as a junior in karting, climbing the trainee rungs. He was the 1983 British Formula Three champion, and made his Formula One debut with the Toleman Hart team in 1984, switching to Lotus-Renault the following year and winning six Grand Prix over the next three seasons. His first pole position came in Portugal in 1985, and a victory in wet conditions he would later claim 'the best in my career'. By 1987, Lotus had a new Honda engine and Senna his first rift: a collision with Mansell, who later assaulted him in the pits. Disenchanted with Lotus, he joined the McLaren team for 1988 following a suspension for a mechanical irregularity in Australia, and he finished third for the season.

The McLaren partnership, which would last for six years, was emotionally torturous, sharing the footlights with prominent Alain Prost, the duo both partners yet intense rivals. An incident at Monaco, where Senna crashed in a mid-cornering manoeuvre alongside Prost at 180mph, provoked antagonism and an apology by Senna. The pair dominated the season with eight wins to Senna and seven to Prost, the Brazilian's first world title. The following season the irritable partnership still commanded the circuit, an early points lead by Senna languishing to give Prost the championship. The decisive race involved a collision between the two on the 46th lap at Suzuka, Japan. The tangle left both stranded on an escape road, Prost retiring, Senna proceeding to victory but being disqualified for irregular re-entry of the circuit. A temporary suspension and a winter's dispute between Senna and Jean-Marie Balestre, autocrat president of FIA, whom Senna accused of improper suspension so as to favour a French compatriot, soon followed.

Arriving in Phoenix, Arizona, for the opening of the 1990 season, I found Senna in a quandary: uncertain about either McLaren's competence, the principles of current racing regulations, or his own commitment. His devotion to the background team, to the engineers back at the Woking base in England and at Honda, the mechanics there in the pits, was what drove his loyalty. 'I hope the [new] car goes the way I want to go,' he reflected over dinner. 'Otherwise there's no way I can maintain involvement. I need again that trembling feeling when I stand beside the car that you have when you see the woman in your life that you are crazy about. When you step into the car, it's like an embrace, your whole mind and body is stimulated, but with an intensity you cannot find with a woman. You are playing with your life, with unknown factors at every corner, lap after lap. When I went for testing the new car in England this winter, that feeling wasn't there.'

Now his mood was that he could not fail Ron Dennis, McLaren's head, or Honda – that they needed him more than he them. All would depend on how an improved Honda engine would fare against Williams-Renault and Ferrari, the latter now boasting Prost alongside Mansell. The concern for Senna was that design was getting ahead of drivers' scope:

cars literally running away from them in cornering capacity, beyond drivers' control. 'We are finding our body is on the limit before the car is.' Prost and Mansell were evidently equally concerned.

In the event, Senna's sublime skills would prevail, with six victories, two seconds and three thirds. With two races remaining, nine points separated him ahead of Prost. In Suzuka's penultimate race, with Senna on pole, there was a dispute with Balestre over the start-grid position preference; Senna was over-ruled. The two drivers consequently collided at the first corner and Senna was champion. In 1991 he retained the title, becoming the youngest yet to be a three-time champion, with seven victories, and raising his pole-start to 60 from 127 races, while continuing to express reservations about another new Honda design for McLaren. Erratic Ferrari design left Prost an outsider. Mansell's challenge evaporated at Suzuka, where Senna courteously allowed team-mate Gerhard Berger to slip in front to win that race in recognition of collaboration over the season, explaining, 'When Mansell spun off, I decided to have some fun with Gerhard.' Meanwhile, Honda's CEO made every effort to dissuade Senna from departing to the Williams team. Three hours after the race, Senna emerged from the pits to be greeted by an army of Japanese fans: his second home, a Japanese appreciation of his flamboyance, absent from their psyche. 'This is the sweetest of my championships,' he said. 'The first in '88 was great, in '89 I was robbed, what happened in '90 was a direct consequence of what happened the year before, this year I won cleanly – a victory for sport.'

McLaren's fortunes sank in 1992 with a semi-automatic gearbox proving ineffectual. During the Belgian Grand Prix, Senna's immediate assistance for a seriously injured French driver, Erik Comas, entrenched his reputation for generosity. In relations with McLaren he was driving without contract, uncertain whether to join Williams' now super-team. Early in 1993, I met him at home in Sao Paulo, when he was more than ever disillusioned at the extent to which computers were usurping the skills of drivers and still unsure if it would be right to join Williams. Renowned for being detached, aloof, exclusive, a perfectionist, he now found his perfection was redundant. Machines, he asserted, had taken his sport away, away from the public who come to see individual duels at reckless speeds. 'I want to be challenged by my own limits up against someone else's limits,' he said, 'where the difference is between brain and experience and adaptation to the course, not challenged by someone else's computer. I don't want a car from Ron Dennis that enables me to win, but a car to allow me to compete. Machines have taken away the character, and it is character that sponsors and public are looking for. If I give a hundred per cent to my driving, which is my hobby as well as my profession, I can compete with anyone, but not with computers ... the difference between computerised cars is huge.'

In the previous season, Williams-Renault were never overtaken between the starting grid and the first bend. More significant, he reflected, was the electronically controlled suspension, regulating the height and inclination of the car at every curve. 'It is no longer the driver who determines the difference between first and second, or second and sixth ... nobody seems to see the hole we are going into, Formula One is not a matter of just six cars, it has to be a proper race with many having a chance. The current problem is that there is no leader among the drivers. At the top, you have a few characters of conflicting personality, while the rest, without good results, don't have any credibility. So Williams, McLaren and Ferrari go their own way for what they can get ... we must change the rules to find a way in which we can all work.'

Senna's dilemma would remain unresolved and Prost was instrumental in freezing his attempt to join Williams; McLaren utilised inferior Ford engines and engaged Senna on a race-by-race agreement, reportedly £1m per race. He won five of 16 races to finish second behind Prost at Williams. With Prost then retiring, Senna was finally able to join Williams in 1994, reportedly on a £20m salary. Yet with engine computer restrictions imposed, Williams were operating on reduced power and Senna expressed grave doubts, notwithstanding three pole positions in his first three races. He warned, 'We'll be fortunate if something really serious doesn't happen.' It was an unintended, macabre forecast. In Saturday's qualifying Roland Ratzenberger of Austria died following a crash, Senna immediately visiting the scene to assess the circumstances and then attending the hospital.

On the morning of 1 May, Senna met the retired Prost to plan re-motivation of the Grand Prix drivers' association for improved safety measures. When San Marino's race began, with Senna in pole position a record 65th time, there was an early crash and it was stalled. The red flag was then lowered and on lap six in full throttle, Senna was leading Michael Schumacher. At the top-speed Tamburello corner on lap seven, Senna lost control at 190mph, rocketed in a straight line into a retaining wall and was killed instantly, with multiple head and brain injuries and a ruptured artery.

In England, I was driving home from a Football League match, listening to radio commentary from Italy. As the detail emerged, I had to stop, weeping: it was the bleakest moment of my professional life, alongside the Manchester United air crash 36 years earlier with the deaths of eight players who were my idolised contemporaries. Even if in reality, distantly, I had regarded Ayrton Senna as the ultimate idealist, he could not be held to account for the insane market-rate, commercially created by television advertising and a fortnightly parade of a dance with death, to which he had just contributed, together with Ratzenberger, the jackpot of conclusions, which he himself had always acknowledged was the hidden catalyst of his profession.

The funeral in Sao Paulo saw an estimated three million people crowding the streets in salute, 200,000 attending the lying in state, and seven Brazilian Air Force jets performing a flypast. Seventeen colleague drivers were there as pallbearers to pay homage, including Prost and past British champion Jackie Stewart. Team managers Ken Tyrrell, Peter Collins, Ron Dennis and Frank Williams were there. The gravestone epitaph reads, 'Nothing Can Separate Me From the Love of God'.

In a criminal trial for responsibility in 1997, the prosecution failed. In 2007, the Italian Supreme Court ruled the accident was caused by 'steering column failure ... badly designed and badly executed modification'. There was no prosecution because judgment had fallen outside the Italian legal time limit. The Williams team concurred with the finding: the emergency alteration, at Senna's direct request, had been inadequately constructed in time for the race.

Polls by both *F1 Racing*, the sport's official magazine, and by Germany's *Bild am Sonntag*, listed Senna as the best F1 driver of all time; echoed in 2009 by a poll of 217 present and former drivers. In 2006, a Japanese survey ranked him the second most favourite person – in history. It is said by historians who collate such statistics that his grave is attended annually by more people in Brazil than Americans in the USA visiting those of JFK, Marilyn Monroe and Elvis Presley collectively. All F1 drivers live with the awareness of the imminent potential companionship of death. In Ayrton Senna, I detected a kind of spiritual sensitivity which shocked some of his rivals.

JONAH LOMU
A Sprinting Tank

'Playing a different game!'

Jonah Lomu, a New Zealander of Tongan origin, swept across rugby union like some Pacific tornado: one of those rare instances when those within a sport can justifiably assert that in one match the face of it was changed. By fortunate professional chance, I was privileged to be there in 1995 at Newlands Stadium, Cape Town, when Lomu, a sprinting tank of a winger with only two previous internationals prior to the tournament, individually massacred England in the World Cup semi-final with an avalanche of four tries. For three reasons, it was a week in history – not just sporting.

Besides the embarrassing 45-29 rout of an otherwise respectable and confident England team, the devastation of one player's solo performance nailed on to the minds of the international rugby federation that professionalism, for years hammering on the door, must swiftly be admitted if outstanding performers were not to cross the road to rugby league or to American football. Secondly, New Zealand's tactics – to be emulated in their unexpected defeat in the final by hosts South Africa – exposed a strategic shift in the game as fundamental as that by Hungary, later Holland, in association football in the 1950s. Lastly, South Africa's final victory would be an ecstatic political and cultural as well as sporting moment for the nation's globally respected segregation terrorist rebel turned saintly, diplomatic president, Nelson Mandela. To have been present was a momentous experience, not to say that South Africa's celebration was to prove prematurely optimistic about social reform.

There are of course pivotal, emergent moments in any sport: Pelé aged 17 in Sweden in 1958, Bjorn Borg in tennis, Tiger Woods aged 19 in golf. Lomu was, simply, physically devastating with the gift of a body so powerful at 19st (120kg) – bigger than many forwards – and simultaneously so swift, with 11 seconds for 100m, that he was, muscularly, all but irresistible. He scored tries against every nation bar South Africa in two World Cup finals competitions, 15 in total, with the sense of balance and 'gear shift' of a gymnast. He had crucially switched from being a forward to the wing. Tony Underwood, his immediate England rival in the semi-final, wiltingly described him as 'unstoppable'. New Zealand's coach Lawrie Mains reflected that Lomu 'brought to the game something the world hasn't seen' as he scored seven tries in five matches in the 1995 tournament. His career aggregate would be 37 tries in 63 internationals.

The impact upon optimistic England was that of instantaneous shell-shock. Beginning with an unorthodox kick-off, towards Lomu rather than packed forwards, within two minutes New Zealand were ahead. A long pass from scrum-half Bachop found Lomu who brusquely handed off Underwood, side-stepped captain and centre Will Carling, then stormed through a tackle by full-back Catt as though he were no more than a bedsheet on a washing line. When New Zealand full-back Glen Osborne sent Lomu through again for his second try, the All Blacks were 25 points ahead in as many minutes. All over. Lomu was to score a further two tries, England ransacked in a worst ever defeat with their own point response coming late, as the opposition took a breather in the last quarter.

Lomu's Armageddon could be compared to that of George Best for Manchester United almost 30 years earlier, against Benfica at Wembley. The adjectives flooded after England's annihilation. 'He's scary,' admitted Nick Farr-Jones, Australia's skipper from four years earlier. 'Amazing athlete, incredible,' murmured Carling. 'We were in shock. It was not until the second half we got even with the pace. Most sides would have folded in the face of such an attack.' England coach Jack Rowell found it difficult to admit his team's incompetence against an opponent who ran through them like a row of flowerpots. 'They are playing a different game!'

So different that there was no begging the question: where was the international federation to go from here to assuage a mass departure to a professional arena? Without capitulation to commercial forces – notably Rupert Murdoch's eagerly attendant television-hungry empire – rugby union was in trouble. There was, too, the matter of how the northern hemisphere would respond to the prospect of the southern's strong-arm imposition. Rob Andrew, the intellectual fly-half from Wasps, reflected, 'Unless we in the north establish some authority of our own, we could end up with two games: power and pace in the south, improvisation in the north, led by England and France, always a step behind. We had believed in our defensive pattern, the way we defended historically being good enough, but it was like a man against boys. New Zealand as good as won the game in the first 15 minutes.'

There was a hidden, alarming downside, ultimately tragic, to Lomu's volcanic exhibition. Already there were symptoms in 1995 of nephrotic syndrome, a kidney malfunction which would overpower his physique in the manner he interred opponents. There was no knowing with hindsight whether this impediment was already influential in the marked, lesser contribution Lomu made in the unexpected but devastating tumultuous victory by South Africa in the final, precipitously winning 15-12 in extra time as a 43 million population – predominantly black – held its breath. As against England, early in the match New Zealand tried to play the ball wide but could not find the gaps. South Africa's winger James Small, a key defensive figure, stayed wide, crowding Lomu and forcing him to play deep, submerged behind additional cover and less committed when needed to engage his power in loose play.

The All Blacks lost a game they should have won. They enjoyed enough possession with their integrated game, yet South Africa contrived an answer: resolute defence alongside a match-winning fly-half, Joel Stransky of Western Province, with a performance almost to rival Lomu as player of the tournament. Stransky's tactical wisdom, keeping the play focused around the power of his forward pack, denied the All Blacks freedom. It was Stransky, with the score level 9-9 after 80 minutes, who touchlit national ecstasy. A penalty kick by Canterbury fly-half Andrew Mehrtens gave New Zealand hope only for Stransky to level. With seven minutes remaining, his dropped goal from 30 metres prompted a national riot of celebration.

Forgive a moment of personal reminiscence. Besides the visual involvement with an epic sporting event, it was emotional to witness the eruption of joy in an entire nation, astonishingly motivated by victory in a sport which had previously been anathema as the personification of a resented apartheid regime. Fleetingly, I had five precious minutes prior to kick-off with President Mandela, transformatively wearing a traditional Springboks team shirt. For any other African head of state to have thus appeared would have seemed opportunistic. For him it was a touch of genius: to don the very colours of your historic enemy, cultural, sporting and political, after decades of imprisonment on Robben Island, and raise them aloft as a symbol of brotherhood was more powerful than a million words.

The wider watching world was entitled to be open-mouthed in admiration for this spontaneous stage management of a figurative moment in the nation's evolutionary crisis: a man blessed with both humility and innate leadership, so that Bantu and white *Bokke* could equally approve. It was challenging what evolution to expect as an invisible emotional lid was lifted. For what did Mandela hope, I tentatively asked? 'It is the occasion that matters,' he responded. Win or lose – and victory would be immeasurable – South Africa was celebrating international identity: it was incidental that all but one of the team was white. Only a year before, Mandela's African National Congress colleagues had been still ardently anti-Springbok, demanding abolition of the Springbok emblem. Mandela had encouraged, in pursuit of 'one team, one nation', the maintenance of the emblem, and two anthems in parallel. The unaccompanied rendition by a black choir, at the closing ceremony preceding the match, of the tribal 'Nkosi Sikelele Afrika' ('God Bless Africa'), followed by 'Die Stem' ('The Voice') was one of the most moving occasions I have ever known.

In sporting terms, it was anti-climactic that the towering Lomu should be regularly pitch-poled by heroic tackling. Afterwards, I was in haste to return home overnight so as to attend my 35th Wimbledon Championships: *The Times* worked one hard for the money. With my taxi to the airport, I was unsure which was the older, driver or cab. For the entire 20 minutes he blew his reedy horn at anybody and anything. He had watched the first half of the match on television and then, back on the road, listened to every kick of the remainder on his rickety radio. It was undoubtedly the greatest day of his entire life.

Lomu was so much more than a one-match wonder, but his illness was to curtail an otherwise lengthy and more glorious career. Born in 1975, his had been a tormented childhood, initially with relatives in Tonga then a downbeat district of Auckland riddled with gang violence, in which he lost relatives including a stabbed grandfather. At Wesley College, he had excelled in all athletic events, then in rugby league, starting rugby union as a forward only at 18. He represented New Zealand at under-19 level in 1993, participated in the Hong Kong Sevens the following year, and made his full international debut against France in 1994.

Immediately prior to the 1995 World Cup, the triple round-robin tournament of South Africa, Australia and New Zealand was launched, Lomu scoring in the inaugural 43-6 victory against Australia; shortly his illness would exclude him from the 1997 triple series. In 1998 he was part of the Commonwealth Games Sevens victory at Kuala Lumpur and in the 1999 World Cup he scored eight tries, including one in the quarter-final against Scotland, then two in the semi-final when losing to France. Part of the winning 2001 Sevens World Cup team, he played his 50th Test against South Africa that year.

By 2002, his illness was prohibitively debilitating, needing a kidney transplant. A limited return to the game was made in 2005, retiring once more in 2007 bar occasional charity matches. Involved in promotional work for World Cup 2015, he died suddenly from a heart attack on returning home in November. A shooting star was forever mourned, at times a force beyond comprehension in a sport designed to accommodate legal brutality.

JOSIA THUGWANE
Closest Ever Marathon Victory

'Winning eliminated the poverty'

Throughout the 1980s I was constantly involved, reporting for *The Times*, with an escalating campaign by the anti-apartheid movement, both global and internal, to restore South Africa to the Olympic movement, having been suspended since the 1968 Games in Mexico. Much of their domestic sport was already integrated but under the Gleneagles Agreement, international participation was excluded from any arena. IOC president Juan Antonio Samaranch had initiated a committee to further South Africa's interest, in collaboration with the fundamentally political South African Non-Racial Olympic Committee. I attended many competitions – boxing tournaments with black, white and Asian contestants, spectators and referees; national athletics championships where white children crowded the infield to seek autographs from black champions; integrated soccer. In 1983, with acclaimed black 800m winner Freddie Williams, we went for dinner to a Cape Town restaurant with an 'international' licence, all races admitted, yet were refused entry. Freddie resignedly smiled. I told the white manager that he was heading for the precipice. We were warmly greeted down the road elsewhere.

In 1990 I accompanied the first IOC official visit in 23 years, a delegation of Samaranch's Apartheid Commission, detailed to negotiate a return to Barcelona's Olympic Games in 1992. The delegation was headed by international lawyer Keba M'Baye (Senegal), together with Kevan Gosper (Australia), Jean-Claude Ganga (Congo), Major General Henry Adefope (Nigeria), Ed Moses (US gold medal winner), Amadou Lamine Ba, secretary general for the Supreme Council for Sport in Africa, and IOC secretary general Francois Carrard. Private meetings were held with South African president F.W. de Klerk, Qwazulu's Chief Mangosutho Buthelezi and newly liberated Nelson Mandela. To cut a protracted, historic story short, the finishing post of a political/sporting revolution was South Africa's first black Olympic gold medallist at the Centenary Games in Atlanta in 1996: the narrowest Olympic marathon victory ever by Josia Thugwane, a once illiterate gardener-come-cleaner: millions could celebrate re-establishment of simple social liberty. With democracy imminent, the delegation's findings had been debated and approved by the IOC session at Birmingham in 1991.

Many drew a parallel between Thugwane's triumph and that of Jesse Owens 60 years earlier, a moment of racial parity, though time would show that total democratic equality remained distant in an economically divided nation. Thugwane, however, gave attribution where due, 'I won the medal for all the people of South Africa, but especially for our president, Nelson Mandela, who has made it possible for us to be part of the international community.'

His climb to fame had been a truly moving tale. Born in April 1971 in Bethal, a tribal community, he was only six when his parents divorced and left him in the care of a penniless grandmother. Unable to go to school, he started work as a farm herd and his early sport, as for so many urchins, was barefoot soccer at the Koornfontein coal mine, 60 miles east of Johannesburg. He could only communicate in the dialect of his Ndebele tribe. 'One afternoon in 1988, a group of runners passed the house where I was working as a gardener. I followed them in my casual clothes and working shoes and soon caught up with them. They were from the athletic team of the local mine, and invited me to join them each day. Soon I entered a few local road races, winning one of two, and because of this I was selected to represent the province at the national championships. Five years later, I won the national marathon in Cape Town, but then had to stop running to attend my tribe's initiation school to obtain manhood, a prerequisite for marriage. In 1995, I started running again, did quite well in the national half marathon, and was selected for the World Championships, where I finished fifth. I won in the humid Honolulu race, and after that the national title in '96, which meant I was selected for Atlanta.'

Road running was one of the few leisure activities open to blacks, there then being only one all-weather running surface in the country, in the township of Soweto. Thugwane's rise, however, was not without incident. When selected for Atlanta, he had bought himself a small Mazda van. A fortnight later, he was hijacked by a gang, one pulling a gun and leaving him with a bullet wound across his chin as he jumped from the moving car, injuring his back. Fortunately, he healed quickly and was able to join colleagues Xolile Yawa, Lawrence Peu and Gert Thys for altitude training in New Mexico. Jacques Malan, his coach and mentor, was essential to the exercise, both in domestic care and psychological preparation for the mammoth experience of an Olympics. Thugwane was not without credible experience, in 1993 having finished third in Israel's marathon in Tiberias, then winning Pretoria's in 2:15:57, and gaining tactical experience in Honolulu's humidity where he returned as winner in 1995. Alongside his advance, under the national unity now prevalent under President Mandela, sport was progressing elsewhere: rugby world champions in 1995, African Nations football champions in '96. Collective pride was mounting.

Yet despite his credentials, Thugwane went to the line in Atlanta ranked only 41st in the world, the shortest in a field of 123 at 5ft 2in (1.58m). In heavy humidity, the leaders were still bunched after half the 26 miles, though Thugwane, Peu and Thys were there among the pacemakers, together with Lee Bong-ju of South Korea. Midway in the race, Luíz dos Santos of Brazil was mounting a challenge, but then found himself overtaken by Thugwane and Lee, with Erick Wainaina of Kenya joining them. 'I had done the right training for the course,' Thugwane recollected. 'I didn't have any problem among those I was running against. I knew that if anyone made a break, I'd stay with them.' Approaching the stadium, Thugwane accelerated, gaining a three-second lead, with Lee and Wainaina holding on. On the final lap, Thugwane was 20 metres in the lead. Confidently he held his ground, with Lee and Wainaina taking silver and bronze, respectively three and five seconds adrift, closest climax ever.

Here was a new world for the previous illiterate: a domestic reward of $11,000 from his National Olympic Committee. 'Winning the Olympics eliminated the poverty I had known all my life, but much more important, Jacques Malan arranged for me to have an English teacher, Welcome Mabuza, who taught me how to read and write in Zulu and starting to speak some English, the education I'd been denied and which I would now be able to give to my children.' Yet fame and wealth now made him a target for begging neighbours and threats from criminal gangs, necessitating repeatedly moving house; on one occasion his wife was greeted at the garden gate by the sight of a severed monkey's head impaled on the garden railings. 'Many people were jealous, and I received death threats, so the mine company where I worked contributed to help me buy a house in Middleburg. This was really something – no longer having to fetch water and light candles at night,' Thugwane explained.

In 1997 he was again hijacked in his car, receiving several injuries, but was able to recover in time for the London Marathon where he proved that Atlanta was no fluke when taking third place in his best time yet, 2:08:06, subsequently lowering that for a South African record of 2:07:28 when winning at Fukuoka, Japan. Seventh in the 2000 London Marathon and sixth in New York confirmed his eminence. So he headed for Sydney's millennial Games of 2000, only the third man ever to seek to defend an Olympic marathon title. With Malan no longer at his side, a victim of cancer, he was a disappointing 20th, though that was not the end of his racing itinerary as he came second in South Korea in 2001, was the winner in Nagano, Japan a year later, second in that race in 2003, and fourth in Poland in 2006.

In November 1997, Thugwane had received the President's Gold Medal for Sport from Mandela. 'I knew that if I was hijacked on the way home from the function, the thieves could steal my medal, but what they could not steal was my new education and all that Welcome, my teacher, had taught me.' There would be further honour in 2011 with the Silver National Order from President Jacob Zuma, Thugwane modestly reflecting, 'I'm happy to have been remembered.'

He would be for all time: five marathon victories, four times in the top three, two in the top six, and many half-marathon winning memories. Up against the five-hour time distance from London, I had seldom filed a rushed story so contentedly as his victory at Atlanta's Games: a nobody utilising the vehicle of sport to ennoble not just himself and his family, but his nation.

CHAPTER NINE
CONTEMPORARY

CATHY FREEMAN
A *Lesser* Australian

''Cos I'm free'

I have long been aware that there is something unique and special about the inner spirit of Aboriginal peoples, the Native American Indians and those of Australia. As a four-year-old with my own wigwam, I fantasised about riding bareback with a bow and arrow, of bonfires and smoke signals, Red Indians smarter than cowboys; later, as an adult, I was distraught at the account of genocide of Sitting Bull and the Sioux tribe at Wounded Knee in 1890; then elevated, more personally, by the spiritual tranquillity of Evonne Goolagong-Cawley in three Wimbledon finals, and the triumphant Cathy Freeman's gem, her 49-second coronation at Sydney's Olympic Games in 2000. Talking to Freeman in a silent hotel lounge, in preparation of my official IOC history, long after an event that momentarily halted Australia's mind, it was apparent that while fame had made her public property, she still privately existed in a secure, serene other world fashioned by her forebears: more a friendly sister than some billboard national icon.

While Freeman had 'officially' claimed her nation's heart, integration in a land born of 60,000-year-old inhabitants does not sit comfortably for the now predominant race of immigrant invaders, initially from Britain but later from across the globe. I have the truest, long-standing friends Down Under, yet an infectiously welcoming humour can have its prickly edge, if recalling the safari game park ironic warning, 'On no account leave your car – Poms on bicycles welcome.' In recent years, there has remained a thread of ingrained hostility, for instance toward Adam Goodes, Australian Rules celebrity with Sydney Swallows, who has played more league matches, over 370, than any Aboriginal. Freeman, so eminently belonging in her own land – where her grandmother as a child was socially 'abducted' in attempted, enforced integration – unaffectedly devotes herself to promotion of her educational foundation, which assists indigenous children in remote communities to achieve equivalent life chances with the rest. 'It started with my mother's voice and my birth-right and my passion ... I think my story and my name represent a possibility that's really powerful.' Freeman echoes the wisdom of Chief Dan George of Canada's Coast Salish Burrard reservation, protector of Indian land during Calgary's Winter Olympics preparation for 1988, who wrote, 'Man's vanity has the power to do away with all life ... Honesty, the kind that carries respect for life, is the only force to prevail over vanity.'

Underprivileged childhood overcome, Freeman's was to be a fairy story. Born in 1973 at Mackay, Queensland, to Cecelia of Kuku Yalanjic heritage, and Norman, of the Birri Gubba people, she attended several schools prior to a boarding scholarship of Fairholme College, Toowoomba, where she was raised in the Baha'i Faith, with its emphasis on equality. Cecelia was born in the Aborigine community on Palm Island; her great-grandfather, being of mixed English-Aboriginal stock, had served in the First World War's 11th Light Horse Infantry.

Cathy began running at five, initially coached by stepfather Bruce Barber, and later moved to Kooralbyn International School, where she was professionally coached by Romanian Mike Danila, a strict disciplinarian with a prime lesson for life, 'You have to turn up.' In her own estimation, Cathy oscillated as a teenager somewhere between, she recalled, 'a wildcat and a child', while always being advised by her mother to 'concentrate on your spirituality'. By 1988, already with an assembly of junior titles aged 15 at Fairholme, she became a candidate for the Commonwealth Games of 1990 in Auckland. A member of the winning 4 x 100m relay team, she became the first Aboriginal Commonwealth Games gold medallist and the youngest at 18. Following that, her then-manager Nic Bideu – and simultaneous romantic thorn bush – transferred her talents to Peter Fortune, coach for the remainder of her career. At Barcelona's Olympics in 1992 she reached the second round of her new event, the 400m, then came second the following year in the 200m World Championship.

Vancouver's Commonwealth Games of 1994 brought international acclaim at 21 with gold in both 200m and 400m, and as a member of the 4 x 400m relay team. To disapproval of the team management, she had celebrated by parading both Australian and Aborigine flags. A blank year, with fourth in Gothenburg's World Championships, was followed by Atlanta's 1996 Olympics and silver behind lofty Marie-José Pérec of France with an Australian record of 48.63s, Pérec posting an Olympic record of 48.25. There followed gold at the Athens World Championship in 1997, an injury interlude in '98, and a retained world title in '99. Thus far, fairly special.

All the while, at the back of her mind, had been a moment in 1993. 'When president Samaranch stood up at the host city election in Monte Carlo and said, "For 2000, Sydney!" I knew instantly I had to be determined about my objective. That was when my goal took shape. My running by now was something I had total control of, and nothing was going to get in my way: I was going to give myself every opportunity of winning in Sydney. I was still on my way up, never mind previous results, my expectations higher.

'Year after year I remained focused, and with a second world title I had built up momentum. My fear was of losing control of my emotions, putting too much significance on the Olympics. In Gothenburg, I was so taken up with the idea of being world champion after being semi-finalist two years earlier, that it was a jolt when I came fourth. In Gothenburg I learned not to focus on the result but on mental control. When I wasn't recognised in the Sportswoman of the Century awards, I thought, never mind, I'll win in Sydney. With speculation about Pérec possibly not competing in Sydney, I didn't calculate what that would mean for me. Either she fronted, or she didn't. I just switched off.'

Intervening upon her life's ambition was the small matter of her selection to light the Olympic cauldron at the opening of the Games: a supreme honour, but an inevitable mental obstruction for an intent athlete. 'People talked a lot about my lighting the flame, but for me the race was always more important. I recognised the honour, but I was so focused on the race that I could have lit the flame even if they'd asked me to do it naked, in pink high heels and a yellow wig. I wouldn't have noticed. I thought initially it was a mistake when they invited me a month beforehand.'

It was no mistake, but involved being up until the early hours for the rehearsal, missing a day's training, and being subjected to the televised gaze of billions while standing beneath a cascade of a falling fountain while doing the deed – all in addition, in the event, of a minor cold for which any medication was barred in the light of drug testing.

A dramatic turn would be the absence from Freeman's race-of-all-time of Pérec, whose temperament was inadequate beneath the glare of Australia's focus on the outcome for their heart-throb heroine. In a fit of nerves, Pérec fled from Sydney because she could not withstand the pressure, offering a parade of lame excuses including claiming she was harassed by media attention, and even alleging she had been threatened by a stranger in her hotel, though there was no video evidence of such an approach, the inference being her own psychological breakdown. She had withdrawn from the World Championships of 1997, was unwell the following year, and raced intermittently in 1999. Introspective and a loner, she had lost sympathy within her own nation, the president of her own athletics association declaring that she had quit Sydney 'like a thief'. I could understand her stress: arriving in Sydney, I discovered that an Olympics of some 28 sports was being regarded as primarily a single race.

The challenge for Freeman was ensuring not to be similarly emotionally fraught. 'I didn't feel any anxiety before the final. During previous months, I'd had occasions of momentary panic, but would quickly get back to normal – I knew I had to do what I had to do, that what was needed was fitness, skill, experience, the support of the crowd. Going out for the start, I was calm, saying to myself, "take it easy", the crowd made me feel strong.' The thunder of sound when she appeared for the start was like a squadron of jets at take-off. Fortunately, she had recovered from laryngitis, and the tactics discussed with Fortune were simple – fast out, relax down the back straight and into the start of the second bend, then attack coming into the home straight. All went to plan, never mind the threat in lanes three and four from Katherine Merry of Britain and Lorraine Graham of Jamaica, while Donna Fraser of Britain in lane two was holding ground. Into the home straight, Graham and Merry were perhaps fractionally ahead: now attack. The strength and the will were there, Freeman pulled clear, the roar ear-splitting. She had done it.

In this moment of explosive achievement, the self-contained composure remained: a moving exhibition of privacy in the face of an audience of billions. Instead of immediately cavorting, as many do in self-acclaim, Freeman sat down on the track in her hooded, enveloping green bodysuit, and for another whole minute or more remained there, contemplating who she was and what she, alone, had just done. She has a tattoo on her arm that reads 'Cos I'm Free'. Now she truly was, and she wished to savour it. She would later reflect, 'Sport is this great arena for drama, it's a reflection of life. Sometimes favourites don't win. My dream came true when I crossed that line. It was just relief, I was overwhelmed, because I could feel the crowd, around me and all over me. I just felt everyone's happiness and joy, so I had to sit down and make myself feel normal and get comfortable.' A vivid response to a unique moment: a symbol of the Aboriginal people who had waited more than a decade for the ultimate opportunity for it to be expressed so gloriously, the identity of an oppressed race. It was beside the point that her winning time of 49.11s was inferior to her Australian record four years earlier.

Freeman herself would admit, 'It was one of my most conservative races, with respect to the others. It would have been easy to have been too emotional, go out too fast and then hit the wall. It was fear that restrained me, I was so aware of the danger of being emotional. I had every incentive to have sensationalised the race in my head, but forced myself to be practical.' She was only the second Australian Aboriginal Olympic champion, the first having been relay team-mate Nova Peris-Kneebone, who herself had won with the hockey team four years earlier in Atlanta. It was now, once more, that Freeman took her victory lap with both Aboriginal and Australian flags – despite unofficial emblems banned by the IOC, and the Aboriginal unrecognised by the IOC. Yet her sense of entitlement was justifiably overwhelming. 'When I'd won, I was so conscious of being in a fish bowl, yet at the same time I wanted to be out of sight. My husband said I always ran away from people, that I am an armadillo. But, I'd just made people happy, that was great. Imagine *me*, actually inspiring people! I'd had that Olympic dream for 15 years of running a lap of honour with both flags, and I've only done it the first time I won a title.'

Receiving her medal, she sang the national anthem with the biggest accompanying choir ever assembled in Australia, then took her bouquet of flowers to her mother, Cecelia. The soul of Australia had momentarily been condensed into this one Aborigine: until this moment a *lesser* Australian. 'When we walked into new places, we were totally intimidated because we felt that, being black, we had no right to be there,' Freeman would reflect in her autobiography.

In honour of her triumph, she was elected by the IOC to represent Oceania in bearing the Olympic flag at the opening ceremony of the next Games, the winter event in Salt Lake

City, together with Archbishop Desmond Tutu (Africa), John Glenn (the Americas), Kazuyoshi Funaki (Asia), Lech Wałęsa (Europe), Jean-Michel Cousteau (Environment), Jean-Claude Killy (Sport) and Steven Spielberg (Culture). Freeman had not competed during 2001 but returned to the track as a member of the victorious 4 x 400m relay team at the Commonwealth Games of 2002, and retired the following year. We of free liberal nationalities roaming the world for many centuries can never fully comprehend the inhibitions imposed on the likes of Cathy Freeman. We owe her and her kin so much more than goodwill.

STEVE REDGRAVE
Sport Helped Educate Me

*'I'm just an ordinary guy who went
quite quick in a boat, really'*

There is hardly a more potent illustration of why sport matters than that from a family with ancestry dating back, if not to Roman charioteers, then the 11th-century Doomsday Book of 1086: way before a noted sailor by the name of Nelson, with his memorial column close by Westminster, but from the same East Anglian neck of the woods. Close by the Abbey of Bury St Edmunds was the Anglo-Saxon village of Hreod (red) Graef (pit), that becoming Redgrafe: from which descendants of the 60 inhabitants took the name Redgrave. Among subsequent multiple generations would emerge Britain's contemporary theatrical family, and elsewhere, a shy, unassuming, demure, educationally average schoolboy who would inexorably become an Olympic monument to unparalleled achievement. Steve Redgrave, five-times gold medal champion across 16 years, surpassed being simply superlative. As his prestige escalated quadrennially, his modesty remained unwavering, 'Sport has given me everything I have.'

Any schoolteacher, in any language, has in Redgrave's example a definitive lesson in life: that effort, discipline, integrity, collaboration and conviction can transform ambition into reality. This is despite threatening obstacles en route, such as diabetes and colitis, to which Redgrave's response was, 'They had to live with me rather than I with them.' Not unlike, you might be tempted to say, Horatio minus one eye and one arm. Is courage exclusive to warfare? Moreover, what has coincidentally distinguished Redgrave, alongside his fellow oarsmen, is that unlike contemporary champions in track, football, cricket or tennis, he has predominantly been out of pocket. He returned from his fourth Olympic pinnacle in Atlanta in the red, with National Lottery grants wholly exhausted in training to get to the starting line, and often a ten- or 12-hour day. And for four years, or in Redgrave's instance, *twenty*, having been left at the bus stop so to speak aged 18, by Prime Minister Margaret Thatcher's attempted embargo on the 1980 Games in Moscow.

Locked down like the rest of us through the winter of 2020 – though nowadays as national coach in China rather than at tranquil Marlow on the Thames – Redgrave is unequivocal about the value of sport, 'For children, and teenagers, sport, especially in competition, teaches us about ourselves and society: that we cannot all be winners, and how to deal with failure. It makes you a more rounded person. Discovering how to win at the same time makes losing more understandable, acceptable. Sport enables you to be comfortable in your own skin. Before becoming involved in sport, I kept my opinions in shadow, shy and insecure, wouldn't say boo to a goose. Rowing is an expensive sport, but lacking wealth for competitors, though success does enable you to earn a living elsewhere. Without sport, I would have kept myself to myself, but sport helped educate me. Yes, there was a position in the 80s, my ambition then to be an Olympic champion in sculling in 1988, and I nearly quit. Sculling had been a reflection of childhood – a bit of a loner, out on the water on my own.' In those critical years, between the age of 20 and 22, between sculler and becoming a rower, Redgrave was maturing.

Oscillating between single sculls and a coxed four, Redgrave had enjoyed the 'promotional' experience of a gold medal at the 1984 Los Angeles Games, partnered in the coxed four by Martin Cross, Andy Holmes, Richard Budgett and cox Adrian Ellison. Reverting to sculls the following year, and disillusioned with 12th place in the World Championships, his career faltered, then he was re-orientated with world championship gold in coxed pairs with Holmes and cox Patrick Sweeney at Nottingham in 1986. The dye was cast: this trio won the world title at Copenhagen in 1987 and headed for Seoul's Olympics and the rare attempt at a double title, seldom contemplated. I was a distressed viewer when they failed on the second leg, the coxed pairs: six races over 2,000 metres, including two semi-finals, in one week. Never in modern times had any pair won coxless and coxed events. As Redgrave and Holmes silently sipped champagne with their coxed pairs bronze medal, they looked as if they had just won a one-way ticket to Devil's Island, never mind their coxless gold.

With Sweeney, they had come within three seconds of double gold. Having crushed Romania in the coxless but now confronted by world champion Abbagnale brothers from Italy in the coxed, Redgrave and Holmes suddenly found themselves drained. They were last over the first quarter, then hauled themselves back to second place behind the Italians, only then to be overtaken at the line by GDR, respectively two seconds and one second adrift in medal order. I thought I had been witnessing something special in British Olympic rowing, blithely unaware of what was to lie ahead over the next 12 years.

An immediate change was at hand. Following a world championship coxless silver with Simon Berrisford in 1989, former GDR coach Jurgen Gröbler initiated a strategic tactical switch for 1990 – pairing Redgrave with Oxford University's massively powerful Matthew Pinsent, and controversially shifting Redgrave to bow with Pinsent as stroke. Gröbler's 'relegation' of Redgrave behind a superior powerhouse proved triumphant and after World Championship bronze in 1990, the pair claimed four consecutive world golds with the Barcelona Olympic title thrown in for added splendour. Witnessing this socially contrasted pair storm to success at Barcelona's Banyoles course was to witness a masterpiece of technical and temperamental co-ordination. The integration was mutual: the intellectual exchanges within the boat had been anything but exclusively the Oxford man's. 'He [Pinsent] has achieved almost everything at the first attempt – and has a great future,' claimed Redgrave, to which Pinsent countered, 'He is very aggressive, competitive, and a great racer. He makes great calls – I've learned a lot from him.' The catalyst, one sensed, had been the younger man's humour and tolerance of the older man's severity. There was more pleasure in the partnership, Pinsent reflected, than in twice winning the university Boat Race. Together they were anything but finished.

Yet what now followed was an intensity, off the water, of public and media scrutiny which became close to intolerable. Their World Championship dominance continued with three further titles, yet the paramount focus by the media was inevitably on Atlanta's Centenary Olympics of 1996: a perceived certainty within a British Olympic Association not as yet the medal-funding machine it was intent on becoming.

Heightening the intensity was that the British pair were now 'the team to beat', a global target, a boat on a hunt for history. Could the two men, one with a growing family, handle the unrelenting pressure? Recollection of past certainties on the track, say, could be unnerving: consider Australian Ron Clarke, American Jim Ryun and Britain's David Bedford, all having stumbled. The moment arrived for Redgrave and Pinsent, and they did not.

The margins in Atlanta were narrow, but emphatic enough: a length over Australia, two over France with bronze, and a place in 3,000 years of Olympism for Redgrave where few had trod: a fourth gold in four consecutive Games in one of the most physically demanding of all disciplines. A lone Brit had done it early in the 20th century – Paul Radmilovic, three times a member of Britain's water polo champions and a 4 x 200m swimming relay: a naturalised and innovative Croatian. And then of course there were three others: Alada Gerevich of Hungary, winner of seven golds, one silver and two bronzes in fencing from 1932 to '60; Paul Elvstrøm of Denmark, Finn-class yachtsman from 1948 to '60; and American Al Oerter, discus champion 1956 to '68. Oerter was there to add his congratulations, while Redgrave himself tried to come to terms with having achieved the supposed impossible, famously remarking that if he ever again got in a boat, somebody should shoot him. While his sporting idiosyncrasy was as technical as that of Gerevich, Elvstrøm or Oerter, the physical intensity was another world.

The motivation, so distant from economic incentive, was hard to define. Pinsent, himself now a two-time champion, was openly in awe of his partner of eight years and thousands of hours of preparation. 'He deserves it ... we don't do it for the fame, but for the way it makes us feel,' he reflected with almost teenage innocence; the youngster governing the throttle in front of the master holding the steering wheel and calling the shots. Those of us surrounding the quietly celebrating couple in the aftermath, Redgrave with an infant daughter asleep in his arms, could but wonder where life would take them from here: globally saluted, but nothing in the bank, simply the consuming sense 'it's over'.

But was it? Redgrave, nowadays financially secure, a revered doyen coaching in China, graced by knighthood yet emotionally as unaffectedly modest as ever, recalls the post-Atlanta turmoil, 'The pressure had been immense. The media's shift between Barcelona and Atlanta was almost intolerable. Everyone wanted a piece of the action, wherever Matthew and I went. After Atlanta, undecided, I didn't speak with him for a couple of months, trying to assess "where next?" I discussed the situation with Jurgen, realising there was still some incentive to continue.' Redgrave's loyal wife Ann, herself an Olympic oarswoman in 1984 and by now a doctor to the British team, read his underlying desire. Yet a further four years of exclusive application, stretching once again every sinew of mind and body, were to be punctuated with various different anxieties.

Firstly, diabetes. Characteristically, Redgrave confronted the problem head on, as though climbing the Eiger. Disease would not prevail. He simply adjusted his diet. Secondly, here was Pinsent questing for a heroic third title – now, at Gröbler's discernment, in a coxless four – yet Redgrave was the man still commanding most of the public attention. It was uncomfortable, and he admitted during training, 'It's tough, rowing with someone who gets all the publicity. I've never gone out of my way to have that. In any other sport, the media would be flocking to talk to someone already with two gold medals ... so Matthew's in a very difficult situation.' As a mark of the quartet's unity, this issue never broke the surface. Redgrave's three colleagues, including Tim Foster and James Cracknell, acknowledged his integrity: that all four of them were beholden to total commitment, imperatively Redgrave himself if he were still to be included on merit.

Pinsent had decided immediately after Atlanta that he should move up to a four. Crucial to this adjustment had been Gröbler's selection of the two additional oarsmen. Cracknell was a junior world champion in 1990 who missed the double sculls at Atlanta through illness, but was now a source of power alongside Pinsent. Foster had won a junior pairs title with Pinsent and was a four-oar bronze winner at Atlanta, as well as being an adroit technical pace-setter. All was synchronised until an inexplicable first racing defeat at the preceding world championships at Lucerne, in both semi-final and final, respectively by New Zealand, and then Italy, New Zealand and Australia, relegating them to fourth place. Everyone was dismayed, bar Gröbler, who announced, 'I still have complete confidence.' They had two months in which to put things right.

And they did so – sustaining Redgrave's exemplary ambition of achieving five 'Olympic rings' of gold. Establishing an early lead over Australia at Sydney, then resisting a fearsome challenge from Italy in mid-race, Foster's pace-timing would prove superbly judged. Closest to pursuers at stroke, Pinsent's exceptional power contributed to a dramatic final surge that drove their bow home by a nose: a margin of 38 hundredths of a second, and Redgrave's Olympic immortality, though forever a shared triumph. Outwardly, he remained unchanged: 'I'm just an ordinary guy who went quite quick in a boat, really.' Pinsent, notwithstanding his own triple triumph, was euphoric on Redgrave's behalf, 'I said beforehand that Steve had achieved the title of ultimate Olympian irrespective of the result. Today, he's placed himself as the greatest Olympian that Britain has ever produced, arguably by any country anywhere.' As the victors slumped, gasping for oxygen, Redgrave momentarily close to oblivion, Pinsent had clambered past Cracknell to embrace his private hero, then fell in the water. Their mutual lifetime had been welded.

It would be superfluous to itemise Redgrave's subsequent honours beyond the gold pin of acknowledgement, additionally presented in recognition besides his medal by IOC president Juan Antonio Samaranch. Honorary doctorates, memorial rowing lakes dedicated to him and Pinsent, statues at Marlow: what Steve Redgrave had given to society, beyond sport, and what sport had given to him, were beyond material measurement. Suffice to say that twice bearing Britain's flag at subsequent Olympic opening ceremonies – including into the stadium at London 2012 – was a testimony to the nation's debt to him for moral example. When being white and male today evokes extended woke liberal social criticism, Redgrave is a beacon to his race's sense of dignity and equity.

JONNY WILKINSON
Helicopter Among the Tractors

'I have been given too much respect'

Rugby Union is effectively two games in one – an opinion not exclusively mine. There are those carrying the ball, initiated by a boy doing so at Rugby School, hence the name, and there are those hefty individuals scrambling to win the ball for the carriers. The ball-winners can be quite brutal against the opposing carriers and enjoy an aggression-orientated fan-base. It is the carriers who often have a distinctive elegance and symmetry which engages the emotions of those beyond the coterie of rugby addicts. Jonny Wilkinson, helicopter among the tractors, was one of those: echo of Wales 'ghost' Barry John.

Though not physically equipped, I admire rugby's open play: handling the oval ball is more spontaneous than association football's esoteric kicking, which in the 19th century became more the global game. Open rugby, antelopes in contention with lions, is as exhilarating for both players and audience as any physical contest. In more than a century of rugby, few have come closer to subtlety than Wilkinson, there being simultaneously the mostly obscure complexity of his own haunting emotions: intent on being supreme, yet throughout his 17-year career, privately questioning his convictions, his commitment, this obsessive Buddhist-like self-examination being evident in his autobiography.

An irreconcilable element of rugby is the frequency of injury, inevitably often serious, almost by design of its clinically conducted challenge. Wilkinson's career was punctuated by recurrent injury, but for which he would have been twice the phenomenon he was. I was familiar with this risk by association. A close friend at my Cambridge college was Jim Hetherington, equally gifted at rugby and soccer, the two of us often training together. A multiple goalscorer for the Peterhouse soccer team, he simultaneously fearlessly played full-back for the university's rugby XV, and in 1958/59 was selected six times for England. Recklessly brave, hurling himself headlong at marauding opponents, he suffered concussion blackouts at Twickenham against Australia and Ireland, and was medically advised prematurely to retire. The catalogue of injuries experienced by Wilkinson read like an orthopaedic consultant's annual diary – a jewel of the game repetitively fractured by its intentional environment.

Yet in spite of this multitude of fitness reversals, Wilkinson's 17-year scroll of honour after leaving school at Lord Wandsworth College – against which I regularly competed in athletics – was gold-plated: 91 caps with England (in spite of missing three whole international seasons following the 2003 World Cup win); 1,179 points for England, including a world record 36 dropped goals; the highest points score in both the Five/Six Nations Championship and the World Cup; the first England player to score over 1,000 points; record scorer in the Calcutta Cup against Scotland, with 27 points, scoring from all four techniques (drop, penalty, try, conversion); the most points, 89, in a single Six Nations season; in the 2007 World

Cup becoming the leading all-time scorer with 277 points. Just imagine what he might have done without a plague of injuries, an impediment which confines a majority of players.

Yet behind Wilkinson's accomplishments, requiring the temperament of an archer with the accuracy of a darts master, lay someone with these anxieties, an inner soul-searching which questioned his ambition for perfection, the indiscipline or absence of team spirit in others. A *Guardian* review of his autobiography, which was exclusively titled *Jonny*, complained that Wilkinson's 'lengthy answers to questions ... revealed little'. Yet evidence was there exposing an ambivalence about being English: that he felt more a sense of 'belonging' when in 2009 he departed after 13 seasons with Newcastle Falcons to join Toulon; that by 2010 he doubted whether he still had the motivation to represent England, never mind being forever remembered for the last-minute dropped goal that had won the 2003 World Cup.

Born in May 1979, as a teenage novice international Wilkinson had often fled to the privacy of his hotel room. There had been times when he wondered whether English colleagues sufficiently asked themselves why they were selected and what was expected from them: that the objective was not simply 'party time'. Here were the reflections, on a game so long considered 'a gentleman's excuse for a disciplined rough house', by a player searching for ideals, of suffering the same mental anxieties as any office drudger, of dismay at invasive media, of the search for values amid total unrelenting commitment. Wilkinson was no average rugby rowdy.

Abandoning entry to Durham University aged 18 to become a professional with Newcastle, within a year Wilkinson was elevated to the England squad, experiencing a grim baptism in summer 1998 tour defeats by both New

Zealand and Australia, returning to Newcastle to succeed Rob Andrew as fly-half and place kicker.

Wilkinson made his World Cup debut in 1999 against Italy, scoring one try, converting six and hitting five penalties for 32 of England's 67-7 points victory. With England then losing 30-16 to the All Blacks, he was rested against Tonga and on the bench for the losing quarter-final against South Africa. The following year he played throughout the Five Nations, then toured South Africa, kicking all the points in the 27-22 Test victory in Bloemfontein. Against Italy in 2001, Wilkinson overtook Andrew's Five/Six Nations individual match record with 35 points, and victory by Falcons in the Powergen Cup over Harlequins saw him elevated as fly-half and kicker for the Lions tour of Australia, in which he equalled the Lions' best individual score with 18 points. That autumn, in peak form, he struck all England's points in a 21-15 surge against Australia, then seven penalties when defeating South Africa 29-9. In a blistering sequence for any kicker, in the autumn of 2002, Wilkinson's boot was instrumental in defeats of all three main southern hemisphere rivals: New Zealand, Australia (coming from 31-19 behind) and finally the Springboks by 53-3, a brutal contest in which Wilkinson had his shoulder dislocated in a late, red-carded assault by Jannes Labuschagne. Rugby's elite inevitably top the hit-list of the unethical.

The year 2003 was arguably the apotheosis of Wilkinson's career. In the opening Six Nations meeting with France, the reigning champions, England won 25-17, then defeated Wales, Italy and Scotland, with Wilkinson named captain against Italy, culminating with a Grand Slam victory against Ireland. On the subsequent southern hemisphere tour, Wilkinson was the lone scorer in a 15-13 defeat of New Zealand, and was then dominant in their first ever victory in Australia by 25-14. All this was followed by England's marksman contributing 18 points in a 45-14 rout of France, prior to commencement of the World Cup in which he was youngest member of the squad.

England launched their World Cup campaign in Perth at a canter, Wilkinson contributing 16 points in an 84-6 amble against Georgia. He then kicked 20 of 25 points against the Springboks, who were restricted to six of their own. A quarter-final with Wales saw Wilkinson ratchet 23 points in a 28-17 progression, capped by a third defeat of France in the year for a semi-final triumph – Wilkinson scoring all of England's points for a 24-7 path to the final against Australia. The outcome of that is special in cultural drama, the definitive hallmark of Wilkinson's imprint upon sport.

Back in my time at Cambridge in the 1950s, when I would often share lunchtime at the university's sports club with England lock forward David Marques and Ireland's beguiling scrum-half Andy Mulligan, I detected an unspoken but prevailing attitude: that the ultimate objective of rugby was scoring a try, the physical overthrow of the enemy's castle. A drop goal, from far beyond the line, was, should we say it, somehow sly, a sporting branch of MI5, though no one would ever politely say as much. Indeed, the points for a drop had been reduced from four to three. Forty years and more later, both Andrew and his England successor were the magicians of this art, Wilkinson the record accumulator. Now, in Sydney, with the score 17-17 and less than a minute of extra time remaining, England heeled out of a ruck: a moment in time for me as frozen as the winning pass by Stanley Matthews in the FA Cup Final.

The ball is flipped to Wilkinson, some 40 yards from the posts. The entire stadium is gripped, as though riding the crest of a big dipper. This seemingly lone figure in white pauses, glances, swings. Like some bouquet sweeping across a rainbow, the ball climbs, arches, and glides between the posts for an instant, irredeemable, majestic triumph. Wilkinson need never kick another ball.

In fact, it was soon learned that he had, yes, another injury, a cracked shoulder bone, duly missing the Six Nations of 2004. He was briefly named England captain in place of the resigned Lawrence Dallaglio but was obliged to withdraw with a blood disorder. He was out of the game for 18 months but returned on the Lions tour of 2005, though his position was challenged by 2008 with the emergence of 20-year-old Danny Cipriani; simultaneously, Wilkinson's club career, if not in jeopardy, was at least viewed with concern. Elite contribution to England remained and in the 2007 Six Nations England routed Scotland 42-20, Wilkinson scoring 27 points with five penalties, two conversions, one dropped goal and a try – thus breaking the Calcutta Cup record of 24 points by Andrew. Following this came 15 points against Italy, thereby making Wilkinson the highest Six Nations scorer with 421 points. Further injuries followed.

During the 2007 World Cup, Wilkinson missed early matches against the USA and South Africa, but scored all England's points in the 12-10 quarter-final win against Australia, becoming the World Cup's highest scorer with 231 points, though he was unable to turn the tide in a losing final against South Africa. Further injuries clouded the next two seasons with Newcastle and in 2009 he moved on to Toulon – an ambience of temperamental comfort for so long being subliminally elusive. His 182 appearances for the Falcons would be followed by 141 for Toulon, culminating with a rare European and league double in 2014, winning the Heineken Cup and the Bouclier de Brennus trophy. In the Heineken

Cup he kicked 13 points in the final against Saracens, then 15 in Toulon's 18-10 French final victory over Castres.

Aged 42, modesty remained ingrained in a man who had equally donated dignity and delight in a rugged recreation. 'I have been given too much respect, others deserve it more. Some will realise I've been a bit of a fraud – part of great teams where others should get the credit.' Maybe. Wilkinson owned some pages of history, never mind his lingering sense of self-examination and undue modesty.

USAIN BOLT
Rescuing His Sport

'You can break records ... but
champions are remembered'

There are two justifiable reasons, one unavoidable and the
other irresistible, for recognising Usain Bolt as among the
foremost sporting phenomenon of the 170 or so years that
leisure activities and ball games have become institutionally
administered. Was this super human, the wonder of the
world, utilising biochemical enhancement in obtaining world
records? Stephen Francis, coach of Bolt's Jamaican fellow
record-breaker Asafa Powell, offered an explanation of this
astonishingly improbable athlete, 'It's not understandable how
he does what he does, he's just using what he has. You can't
stop people doubting, but along comes someone who is truly
exceptional. You have Beethoven, Isaac Newton, you have
Einstein ... and you have Usain Bolt.' The outcome is beyond
previously acceptable imagination.

Here is an athlete, born in August 1986, in the little
village of Trelawney, Jamaica, who before he is almost old
enough to wear long trousers is truncating not just junior
but world records and leaving Olympic rivals trailing almost
anonymously: in detail, 11 world championships, winning

384

100m, 200m and joining the 4 x 100m relay teams from 2009 to 2015 (four consecutive championships) alongside triple-triple Olympic championships from 2008 to 2016 (the first relay gold was annulled in 2017 for a colleague's retrospectively deemed drug-positive for a banned respiratory inhalant). And, hooray, being innocent in a century or more of drug tests.

This one man, jovial Afro-Caribbean, almost single-handedly rescues a billion-dollar universal sport, all but on its knees in disputes, credibility torpedoed by incessant wilful cheats, including coaches, doctors and agents. Prior to Bolt's second Olympic Games, 2008 in Beijing – he had failed in the 200m heats at Athens in 2004 – there had been ten years of unrelenting exposure, infamously including another Afro-Caribbean in Canadian Ben Johnson, who had defamed not merely themselves but their arena, driven by professional greed and always being one step ahead of the judicial authority of the World Anti-Doping Agency, instituted in 1999. Bolt habitually and happily took incessant drug tests, meanwhile contentedly welcoming a prize money fountain which afforded him more luxury limousines than a Jamaican embassy's car park: two or three of which he seriously bent without lasting damage to the legs which gave him take-off for under ten seconds. International scepticism was furthered by the absence of any Caribbean independent testing authority, but Bolt's national federation and his personal coach, Glen Mills, repeatedly invited anyone to monitor their medical accordance.

What distinguished Bolt's development, as with Carl Lewis of America 20 years earlier, was the uniformity of physical profile during teenage years, free of sudden upper-body abnormality or an abrupt leap in performance, which was consistent while being remarkable. At 6ft 5in (1.96m) by the time he was 15, a key to his exceptional stride was the length of his shins beneath a sprinter's dense thighs – which create leg speed – the overall leg length giving him the immense stride which carried him clear over the middle 40 metres in the 100m. Bolt attributed his frame to the local diet of yams and bananas (as a successful junior sprinter, with 100 yards in ten seconds, as an adult at Cambridge of 5ft 8in I immediately found rivals leaving me trailing over the last 30 yards).

Bolt as a youngster was casually more interested in cricket and football, but by 12 years old he found he was fastest in the school. 'Until I was 17, I was just running for fun, no idea at all of becoming an Olympian, until Glen Mills said he thought I could do well, and I began to train seriously.' At 15, he won both 200m and 400m in the Central American and Caribbean Junior Championships, and in the World Youth Championships he recorded 21.73s for the 200m, prompting former prime minister P.J. Patterson to arrange schooling in Kingston so that he might train with the Jamaica Athletic Association. Progress accelerated. At the World Junior Championships, coincidentally staged in Kingston, at only 16 he won the 200m in 20.61s, the youngest ever; a year later, four gold medals came in the Caribbean Junior Championships and national junior records at 200m and 400m, which he repeated at the Pan American U20 Athletics Championships with a world junior 200m record of 20.13s. By 2004, he became the first junior to go under 20 seconds for 200m, with 19.93.

Offered several US college scholarships, Bolt preferred to remain in Jamaica. Mills intensified his professionalism, sensing Bolt's optimum might be 400m, and suggesting this. Bolt's inclination, however, was instead now for the 100m, amplified by a 10.03s performance in Crete in 2007. The Olympics beckoned, even more so with a World Championship silver at 200m in Osaka, Japan, and, spectacularly, a 100m in 9.76s at home in Kingston in May 2008, only two hundredths behind Powell's recent world record. Aged 22, Bolt was more than ready for Beijing, sharply revealed when, at the Reebok Grand Prix in New York, he shaved Powell's world record to 9.72, with legal following wind of 1.7 metres per second – only his fifth senior short sprint.

For any journalist, the Beijing Games were to be a double revelation, cultural as well as social. While the architecturally novel Bird's Nest stadium was, if you had no ticket, as secure as Pentonville or the Scrubs, the surrounds during performance deserted but for regiments of police, the crowded streets were thronged with students, many eager to practise their English, brazenly inviting an obvious 'foreigner' to join them for a coffee and to be interrogated, 'Do you know Usain Bolt?' He was famous across China even before he had completed his first heat. I was 'accosted' on every other stroll from the bus stop to my hotel. Bolt was not to disappoint. 'I'd view the Games as the pinnacle, Glen and I had aimed everything towards Beijing. Don Quarrie, our Olympic legend, had told me this was it: he hadn't actually coached me, but guided me particularly on corner-running, the 200 being my speciality more than the 100. On the grand prix circuit, my 200 hadn't been so good, but in Beijing it all came together.'

It certainly did. In the final 20 metres of the 100m, totally confident of victory, Bolt eased, glancing sideways, waving an arm – and improving his world record with 9.69, with zero wind, two tenths ahead of Richard Thompson in second place. Here was a figure transforming the image of his sport. 'I wasn't thinking of a world record, just feeling sheer happiness, looking to the right as I thumped my chest when crossing the line.' Bolt's joyous celebration on the track drew myopic condemnation from Belgium's IOC president Jacques Rogge, alleging it was 'disrespectful'. Truth was, it was what track and field needed: personality in conjunction with integrity. In my official history of the IOC I was glad to quote this supreme successor to Carl Lewis and Jesse Owens, 'I didn't mind that Jacques Rogge disapproved, I didn't feel it [my behaviour] was too serious – just ask my colleagues and rivals. The public enjoys it when competitors show their personality, some exuberance adds to the performance. Whatever I do, it's spontaneous, my nature, just me enjoying myself. People like to see more than simply the race, they want to see what you're like as a person, so I think my style helps a bit – I hope it gives some credibility back to track and field, following doping scandals. I was first tested at 17, recently must have had more tests than anyone. I'm all for it.'

More was to follow in Beijing with another world record, 19.30s in the 200m final in spite of a head-wind of 0.9 metres per second, lowering the supposedly immune time of past Olympic champion Michael Johnson of America, and becoming the first since Quarrie to hold both world sprint records simultaneously – a totemic Jamaican surpassing all those sons of the island previously recording milestones before him such as Herb McKenley, George Rhoden, Arthur Wint, Lennox Miller, Quarrie, Linford Christie, Donovan Bailey and the disgraced Ben Johnson. This young man, who had primarily trained on a grass track and at a gymnasium without air-conditioning, had twice stunned the watching world; in the 200m, with a lead wide enough to park a bus, and joining the eight previously to have achieved the Olympic sprint double: Hahn (US, 1904), Craig (US, 1912), Williams (Canada, 1928), Tolan (US, 1932), Owens (US, 1936), Morrow (US, 1956), Borzov (USSR, 1972), and Lewis (US, 1984). Bolt's third gold, in the sprint relay, would be taken away years later on a failed drug repeat test, a respiratory inhalant utilised by Nesta Carter. Bolt, however, was anything but finished. 'Now I'll go to Berlin for next year's World Championships with even more focus. I never have nerves before a race, and I'll be even more single-minded. Glen and I always have a plan, but I leave the detail to him. I don't necessarily go for grand prix prize money – Glen stresses that only championships really matter – you can break records, but you are remembered as a champion.' How true, a principle ignored by many others.

We gathered in Berlin's Olympic Stadium in 2009, the scene of Owens's triumph 73 years earlier, in awesome expectation which was swiftly fulfilled. In the face of challenger Tyson Gay, Bolt improved his 100m world record to 9.58s – still standing today – with Gay 13 hundredths astern, even if ahead of Bolt's Beijing record. In the 200m final Bolt was further astonishing as his Beijing record was improved by 0.11s at 19.19, thanks primarily to an improved start reaction, hitherto the only 'weak' link in a tall sprinter. As host city, how do you recognise such a monumental visitor? As a history-maker, Bolt himself received a souvenir relic of the dismantled Berlin Wall. The World Championships two years later at Daegu, South Korea, would witness his own, temporary, dismantling: a false start disqualification in the 100m, followed by non-record 200m victory, and an improved relay world record with Jamaican colleagues Blake, Carter and Frater in 36.84.

For a while in 2012, Bolt was being out-gunned by compatriot Yohan Blake, winner of both sprints in the Jamaica championships, but Bolt reversed the order at the London Olympics with a 9.63s Games record to Blake's 9.75, a few hours before the celebration of Jamaica's 50th anniversary of independence. This was followed by inflicting a double defeat on Blake in the 200m with 19.32 to Blake's 19.44, Bolt becoming the first Olympian successively to defend both sprint titles. The now famed quartet duly lowered the relay world record to 36.84s. Such was Bolt's status, he was in London as much part of the sporting furniture as Britain's own Afro-descendant, Mo Farah. His enduring dominance was almost routine: at Moscow's World Championships a year later, in the rain, he retained the 100m title in 9.72, the fastest time of the year and eight hundredths ahead of Justin Gatlin. The 200m was a relative runaway, the first champion with three consecutive 200m victories, then he duly collected the sprint relay.

Supremacy further continued at Beijing's World Championships in 2015. Though America's Justin Gatlin, reprieved and discredited by positive tests, was fastest on the circuit tour, Bolt protected his incredible reputation in both sprints – winning the 100m by one hundredth, 9.79s to Gatlin's 9.80s, and the 200m, with 19.55s, the fifth fastest of the year and his fourth consecutive victory. What now? Approaching his 30th birthday, he headed for his fourth Olympics at Rio amid the drug scandal enveloping Russia. Though no longer quite the unassailable Achilles of 2008 and '09, yet again he adroitly defended both sprints to universal comfort for the athletics world at the expense of reinstated cheats Gay and Gatlin. Collecting both sprints and once more the relay, Bolt possessed the incredible triple-triple (bar the one suspended relay). While two times suspended Gatlin was jeered in Rio, Bolt was revered as a humble hero who had risen above endemic scandal to immortalise Jamaica's and his reputation.

Fate ultimately overtook fame at London's World Championships of 2017 when collapsing with a pulled hamstring on the relay anchor leg, having taken bronze in the 100m. It is a cliché, but world sport cannot expect to see his like again. He could now retire back home in Jamaica to a life of family, financial security and memories. For me, it was a privilege to have once shared an hour's conversation in Monte Carlo with a legend as modest as any village schoolmaster. Bolt is Jamaica's uninhibited gift, his spontaneous nature as enviable as his talent in an era when cheats have poisoned our simplest of sports.

ROGER FEDERER
Physical Poetry

*'I don't lie awake wondering
what went wrong'*

It has been engaging for so long to have enjoyed a journalist's career stretching from Matthews to Messi, Zátopek to Bolt and, perhaps most strikingly, from Hoad to Federer. The story of Roger Federer – temperamentally disrespectful Swiss teenager transformed into the ultimate of composed, unrivalled and gracious tennis champions, simultaneously donating much of his mountainous endorsement wealth to a charitable education fund – has been a gospel of emotional generosity, on and off court. To be as technically supreme yet unassumingly modest is a rare accomplishment, the courtesy not instantly spontaneous with that nine-figure income.

It was early evident that Federer possessed enviable talent but temperamental excess as tantrums in defeat caused his parents alarm. His father, a pharmaceutical sales representative, and his South African mother, would treat his sulks and outbursts with silent condemnation. Young Roger would later acknowledge he had been 'out of control', that his parents were ashamed of him, and his prospects were severely threatened. 'Nobody believed I had the temperament to be a champion,' he remembers. The realisation was painful: champion was his ingrained ambition, prominent German Boris Becker his image for success. A combination of the influence, when aged 12, of Peter Carter, an Australian coach with the Swiss Tennis Federation, and Federer's own emerging sense of reality, adjusted his wayward, racket-smashing path. Further maturity was imbued by Swedish coach Peter Lundgren. Via his own conversion to maturity, having turned professional at 16, Federer sensed the importance of education.

The shock of Carter's death in a holiday car crash further rationalised Federer's perception aged 21, two years on from having won Junior Wimbledon. A year later, 2003, winning what was to be the first of 20 Grand Slam titles on Wimbledon's grass, he created his philanthropic Federer Foundation – a charity that over two decades would spend some €26m across six South African nations, enhancing the lives of more than half a million schoolchildren, thousands of teachers and hundreds of primary schools. Admiration for the foundation should exceed that for Federer's astonishing guile for striking a tennis ball, by which the foundation has been funded, and by the imagination of a man as studiously calm in competition as if awaiting the teatime waitress in the Savoy's sun lounge. Modesty never arrived better dressed, without affectation, admired and respected as warmly in the dressing room as in the grandstand, yet the ambition undiminished. In a mid-career interview, he said, 'Sometimes people ask me what else is left for me. What they don't realise is that this is what I've been waiting for … winning Wimbledon, beating Sampras and Agassi, being number one in the world. It's not a problem to stay motivated, and I don't let things get on top of me, I don't lie awake [after a defeat] wondering what went wrong.'

Not much went wrong between 2001 and 2010. In that first of those stunning years, Federer marked his frontline potential when outplaying renowned champion Pete Sampras in Wimbledon's fourth round, though subsequently he lost to Tim Henman in the quarter-final. 'I knew there were improvements I could make,' he admitted. There were: winning Wimbledon the next year, defeating the acclaimed Andy Roddick of the USA in the semi-final and overwhelming powerhouse server Mark Philippoussis in straight sets in the final with an elegance that charmed all those weary of serve-and-volley grass court specialists. Now the Federer bandwagon was moving up a gear. In 2004, he claimed three Grand Slams – his first hard court title, in Australia, defeating Marat Safin, then his second Wimbledon over Roddick, and at the US Open the champion of 2001, Lleyton Hewitt of Australia, was beaten in straight sets including two games won to love. This was the first 'triple' year since Mats Wilander of Sweden in 1988, Federer thereby becoming world number one for the first time. The style and ability to direct any shot to any part of the opponent's court from any position was mesmerising. Obliterating Andre Agassi in an early round in Australia in straight sets, at the net he told the dismayed American how much he had enjoyed the conflict. 'That makes one of us,' jested Agassi.

Prior to 2005, only three players had won more than two consecutive Wimbledons: Fred Perry of Britain in the 1930s, Bjorn Borg with five from 1976 to '80 and Sampras with four from 1997 to 2000. Now this was emulated by Federer, with another victory over the unfortunate Roddick – Federer having lost semi-finals in Australia and France respectively to Safin and Rafa Nadal – and then winning the US in Agassi's last Grand Slam final. Inevitably Federer was now being acclaimed as the greatest of all time; as possessing the focus of Borg, the agility of McEnroe and the power of Sampras, plus a fourth disarming ingredient: unpretentious charm. With a contemporary synthetic racket, Federer could conjure shots, especially on the backhand, that were beyond, say, Rod Laver, twice a quadruple Grand Slam winner in one year. As veteran Laver, usually present at Wimbledon, reflected, 'A lot of the shots Federer produces are just uncanny.'

In 2006, Federer again won three Grand Slams, losing only the French to Nadal, while having a match record for the year of 92-5, and being the first man since Laver in 1969 to reach all four Grand Slam finals, plus winning his third ATP Championship title at the end of the year. He repeated the four-final feat again in 2007, winning Australia without dropping a set, a feat last achieved at a Grand Slam by Bjorn Borg in 1980 in Paris. At Wimbledon, Federer equalled Borg's five in a row, defeating Nadal in five sets, a duel rivalling the Borg–McEnroe battle of 1980. Here was yet another instance of Federer's single-handed backhand, especially on grass, so often being deceitfully cunning in its acute dipping angles: reminiscent of the old, slower days with wooden rackets of, say, Romanian Ilie Năstase or Spain's Manuel Santana, each masterful for drift and spin.

The eminence of Federer must have been heartbreak for Roddick, so repeatedly victim of the Swiss, and once again in the Wimbledon final of 2009 – the longest in Wimbledon's men's singles history, Federer finally securing his 15th and then record-breaking Grand Slam after four-and-a-quarter hours by 16-14 in the fifth set. It could have gone the other way, Roddick achieving the only two breaks of service in the first and fourth sets, Federer taking the second and third on tie-breaks, but Roddick having squandered two break points for a 9-8 lead in the fifth. It was luckless Roddick's third Wimbledon final defeat at Federer's hand, following 2004 and '05. In the second-set tie-break – Roddick having won 26 out of 30 that year – he had led 6-2, but Federer was able to close the gulf.

From 2010, Federer's mastery was to a degree restricted by the advance of Serbia's Novak Djokovic and the sustained power of an ageing Nadal, yet Federer's longevity persisted with further Australian titles in 2010, '17 and '18, and his seventh and eighth Wimbledons in 2012 and 2017, placing him alongside Nadal's Grand Slam total of 20 overall. 'Eloquence is heard, poetry is overheard,' said philosopher John Stuart Mill. Eloquence supposes an audience, while poetry is unconscious of an audience. There were moments during the Australian final between Federer and Nadal in 2017, never mind an ecstatic audience, when play was indeed poetic in its refinement: intermittent physical and strategic perfection from which would be remembered the stroke as much as the striker. I do not think it was an exaggeration to say that, although I viewed it on television, this was one of the best three matches I had seen in six decades, the others being victory by Sampras over Becker in the ATP final of 1996 in Hanover, and Borg's fifth consecutive Wimbledon of 1980 against McEnroe. What made the duel between Federer and Nadal so memorable was the improbability of such skill, following a prolonged absence by both for surgery, at their respective ages: Federer 35 and Nadal 30. When Becker had wrestled agonisingly with Sampras 20 years earlier, he was thought elderly at 29.

There was indeed a Grecian yet undemonstrative serenity about Federer, and therein lies his secret: the extreme opposite of Andy Murray, whose demeanour when losing a vital point suggests he has broken a finger. Federer moved from point to point, won or lost, with rarely a gesture beyond an approving nod. A tie-break? A fifth set? You would suppose it was just a warm-up. Federer's remarkable triumph had been declared impossible by most informed observers on the circuit. He himself had considered it unlikely even to reach the semi-final, yet a six-month absence for a knee overhaul seemed to have freshened his mind against an opponent so often his conqueror. Habitually generous and gentlemanly off court, Nadal is essentially a physical bully: a destroyer with relentless power down either flank. Poised to serve, with first a repetitive routine of eyebrow-sweat removal and an ungainly adjustment of the seam of his shorts, he has the air of a paratrooper about to leap from his plane. No messing. Federer awaits as though for the afternoon newspaper.

The drama of tennis is exaggerated by its scoring system, and thus it was now in Melbourne, Federer claiming first and third sets, Nadal the second and fourth, and gaining a break for 2-0 in the fifth. The tide seemed irrevocably with Nadal, pacing between points as impatiently as if the whistle for the last train had just sounded. Not so Federer, from whose expression you can rarely tell the score. However, it had to be acknowledged that in an almost intolerable climax, he enjoyed a double stroke of luck: a net cord on his shot falling over dead in his favour, another by Nadal leaping into the tram lines. Federer's 18th Grand Slam title was his first in five years, Nadal's haul remaining level for the moment with Sampras on 14. It was visible in the aftermath that Nadal knew victory could have been his, but he remained characteristically sporting. Almost in disbelief, Federer admitted, 'I would have been happy to lose. If a draw is possible, I would like to have drawn.' They equally brought honour to the match.

What Federer has given to sport, and to life, has been not simply a thousand memories, but an element of physical poetry, the vision of something enjoyably beyond the scope of regular mortals, so we as bystanders are able to reflect on his happiness.

MARCUS RASHFORD
Inspirational Benevolence

*'Thankfully I had the talent to kick
a ball around'*

Marcus Rashford, such a prominent young footballer for Manchester United and England, benign youngest of five children of a single-parent first-generation Caribbean mother, has been decisively instrumental in forcing national economic policy adjustment for free school meals during the school suspension enforced by the coronavirus pandemic of 2020. It is coincidental that Rashford's income, exclusive of his commercial endorsements, is some 40 times that of Prime Minister Boris Johnson, whose hand was initially pressurised by Rashford in mid-2019 and then again during the pandemic. Here is contemporary democracy at work, within the social imbalance of capitalism. Rashford is nowadays said to be worth in excess of £65m, having emerged from a childhood devotedly guarded by a Christian mother, Melanie, of St Kitts origin, in the absence of a deserting Robert, now a 'celebrity' father and Marcus's assistant agent: a contemporary family structure, in which the young son's natural physical attributes, nurtured by Manchester United from the age of seven, have matured for him to become not merely material saviour of the family – and then some – but a national figure of inspirational benevolence. He has co-ordinated aid, alongside political intervention, for millions of impoverished children whose destitute plight Rashford recognises from years when occasionally there was no food on the family dinner table. As he aptly reflects 'never blame the children', while fulsome in praise of his mother's will to survive in former times of desperation. Intimate associates of Melanie testify to her characteristic fortitude.

In the cultural chasm between football's allegedly indolent millionaires and unemployment's innocent poverty-stricken, I can admit a minor, distant but well-intentioned influence some 60 years ago: aware that as a young representative of the *Daily Telegraph*, I was better paid in 1960 than Bobby Charlton, teenage sensation at Wembley. I campaigned, almost alone in Fleet Street, to create the economic financial 'freedom' in football which – courtesy of incestuous management greed in the game and the advent of television's 24-hour electronic commercial 'entertainment' – has led ultimately to today's chronic overinvestment in players by indiscriminate club investors. For nine months I tracked all negotiations between the Professional Footballers' Association chairman Jimmy Hill, the stilted Football League, and the Ministry of Labour until the £18 a week maximum wage was abolished and Fulham's chairman, comedian Tommy Trinder, upped the ante by rewarding England captain Johnny Haynes with £100 a week.

Bred in the century-old tradition of amateur sport – vainly upheld by the Olympic Games in the face of overwhelming evidence until 1988 – my generation institutionally had considered that professionalism in sport was for the 'uneducated'. I played for a club, Pegasus (combined of players from Oxford and Cambridge universities), which in its brief existence of 15 years generated 17 England amateur international players. At Cambridge, we played once annually on level terms with Tottenham Hotspur's, sometimes against such First Division opponents as England striker Johnny Brooks or playmaker Tommy Harmer. John Blythe, for Cambridge, was all but a double for the immaculate Denis Viollet, a survivor of Manchester United's Munich crash. Pegasus foundered when impecunious undergraduates became willing to accept 'pocket money' from phoney amateur clubs. As part of the British training squad for the 1956 Olympics in Melbourne, although ultimately unselected, I was invited by Spurs manager Bill Nicholson, our coach at Cambridge, to train at White Hart Lane, but by then I had opted at 21 for journalism: the assistant coaching staff at White Hart Lane inevitably regarded me as an ineligible amateur alien, while my school old boys' team, winners of the FA Cup in 1881, would have excommunicated me instantly had I ever contemplated the professional arena. In our old boys' cup matches, spectator cheering was unseemly but clapping was approved. When John Howlett, an electric centre-forward for Cambridge, who in subsequent business life played for leisure with non-league Nuneaton, scored a goal against Oxford described by the *Daily Mail* as 'one of the best ever seen at Wembley' in front of an 18,000 crowd, there was no ecstatic hugging: just a trot back to the halfway line with exchanges of 'nice one'.

Rashford has the benefit, in the 21st century, that coaching is far advanced from the mid-20th, bar a handful of clubs then, such as Spurs, West Ham, Manchester United and West Bromwich Albion, already sensing the concept of 'Total Football', in which all players must be creative when in possession, otherwise defend. Rashford has come through the junior ranks at Old Trafford, schooled first by academy development coaches, with Fletcher Moss Rangers, then United's Schoolboy Scholars scheme, prematurely promoted to train with the first team by David Moyes in 2016, and tactically monitored by former midfielder Nicky Butt, the under-19 manager. By degrees, Rashford became the 'complete' modern footballer. Back in the 1960s, players were still predominantly stereotyped: defenders, schemers, wingers, strikers. The game was still dominant in Britain for the long ball or dribbling. Such is now the financial value placed on a skilled *and* intelligent player such as Rashford that he can have built personally a home with five bedrooms for approaching £2m: when I first watched Fulham against Spurs as a 15-year-old, few if any players possessed a car, many travelling to a match by bus with the fans, their homes rented rooms.

What is exceptional about Rashford – beyond being the youngest England player to score on his international debut, against Australia in 2016, since Tommy Lawton in 1938 – has been his clairvoyance, aged 22, to comprehend, and act upon, widespread social inequality and desperation, his interventions far-reaching:

- October 2019: Established the In The Box campaign with Selfridges, providing the homeless with Christmas essentials, which he and his mother personally delivered
- March 2020: During the COVID lockdown, collaborated with charity FareShare, to provide meals in Greater Manchester to those deprived of free school meals, raising £20m to aid four million children
- June 2020: Pressurised every Member of Parliament for the extension of free school meals

during the summer holiday, reaching more than one and a quarter million children

- September 2020: Established the Child Food Poverty Task Force in collaboration with multiple grocery suppliers, manufacturers, charities and delivery companies
- October 2020: In the wake of receiving an MBE, initiated a petition campaigning to increase the value of Healthy Start vouchers, raising 300,000 signatures and supported by the Co-operative Group in Manchester, although the proposal was rejected by Parliament
- October 2020: Challenged Rishi Sunak, Chancellor of the Exchequer, on levels of Universal Credit income at £20
- November 2020: Following the Child Food Poverty Task Force campaign, the Government announced £400m in poverty funding over 12 months
- December 2020: Initiated with Macmillan Publishers the provision of educational books for children
- January 2021: Protested via Twitter regarding inadequate food packages through the Compass Group

Commenting on his charity work and MBE investiture, Rashford has been candidly modest, 'When you come from a background of struggle and pain, as I did, it often switches to become your drive and motivation. In sport, you have to have something behind you that is pushing you. Sometimes we didn't have even a loaf at home – embarrassing, but true. All the struggle and sacrifice our mother had made ensured we appreciated her ten times more, not to see the experience as a weakness. I can understand how food poverty is contributing to social unrest. Once, it was my own reality – thankfully, I had the talent to kick a ball around to pull us out of that situation. As for my MBE, as a young black man from Wythenshawe, never did I think I would be receiving that, let alone at the age of 22. It's a very special moment for me and my family, but particularly for my mum, who is the real deserving recipient of an honour.' In times of stress, with six to feed, Melanie Rashford would supplement her income as a Ladbrokes minimum-wage cashier with late-night cleaning jobs.

The environment of Old Trafford's fame has of course been motivating for a youngster with Rashford's talent. 'Yes, I've wanted to follow in the footsteps of Bobby Charlton and Wayne Rooney, so receiving that award was an amazing feeling, after the early years of striving for maturity, knowing that this was essential. What I also understood, on the school meals issue, was the importance of protecting childhood, recognising that so much more needed to be done for the many that were struggling. Taking a few steps in the right direction helped create a new chapter in their lives, even if there was a shortfall for more than a million of them. We've managed to reach many kids, but some are still struggling. It's difficult to jump ahead, but all schoolchildren are equal, we should never give up.'

Rashford's benevolent involvement in the schoolchildren's welfare has been no flash in the pan. Early in 2021, in continuing search for economic benefits, he attended a *Financial Times* Business of Football summit, acknowledging that he is at times a target for criticism. 'When the coronavirus arrived, it was the first time my mind shifted from football, my head was all over the place. I needed to concentrate, to try to achieve something. The cost to the taxpayer? Incalculable. The system is broke, it needs to change. Whatever Boris Johnson had to say before, his U-turn mattered most. There had been criticism of the Premier League's players by Julian Knight from the Committee on Culture, Media and Sport, and by Health Secretary Matt Hancock, saying we were in a moral vacuum, that we ought to contribute, but we didn't need public pressure, the financial contribution would have happened.

'Being a footballer with one of the biggest clubs in the world of course is going to bring attention, and I knew what I was stepping into with my involvement. However, there were people who had opinions before they ever met me or spoke with me. I've come to terms with that, part of my life. Apart from the effect it will have on me, the campaign's much bigger than that. I'm willing to take the little bits of aggravation from wherever it comes. We've taken a lot of steps in the right direction. I've raised awareness for this topic, so I'm pleased we've had some progress, but I'm still hungry to do more.

'Before this campaign, I hadn't been one to speak about my upbringing. I just got on with my job of playing football. The time came for me to speak out. We found ways to help, and the businesses who joined were much more powerful than I was. I was dead proud of everyone being so kind-hearted and willing to do so much. It's been an amazing journey. We wouldn't have had to say this if it had started 15 or 20 years ago, and I hope we will see benefits in ten or 15 years from now.'

Rashford's development owed much to his observation, inspirational, of Rooney, though he acknowledges a contrast in playing profile. 'We're different, Wayne showed such versatility – you could put him anywhere on the field and he'd make it happen. And besides all his goals, he was so professional, whether operating in midfield or attack, the goals still came. My main regret is not to have played at all under Alex Ferguson, though I was happy he was apparently "aware" of me. What he achieved was astonishing – the courage in the way he approached life.'

Application is there in Rashford's nature: he is almost bookish in his study of the bureaucracy behind retailers' food distribution to the community in his quest for egalitarianism. In the opinion of Henry Winter, the most experienced of contemporary correspondents on the world front, Rashford's temperament exemplifies what is needed in an 'occasional' team such as England's: 'calm, flexible and dedicated'. An England coach has to be sure of what he is getting. Gareth Southgate should detect in Rashford that element of continuity conspicuous in 1996 with Darren Anderton and Steve McManaman on the flanks of Alan Shearer and Teddy Sheringham. Reliability.

It has been a rewarding task to have watched England's team under the direction of the 16 managers and coaches since 1946. Alf Ramsey succeeded Walter Winterbottom in 1963, prior to which, misguidedly, an FA selection committee ran a saloon-bar lottery, any player observed having a useful performance last Saturday was given a go, Winterbottom's opinion supplementary. In my opinion only two managers, Alf Ramsey from 1962–73, and then Terry Venables from 1994–96, have recognised the fundamental principle at international as opposed to club level: determine those players not simply with technical class but consistent character. Whenever possible keep an unchanged team, success being dependent upon continuity, the factor behind any club success. Southgate should know this from his experience as a player for Venables. By the World Cup of 2022, in the wake of the Euros, Rashford might even be superior to Harry Kane of Spurs in a front trio with Rahim Sterling. He would benefit by a perception that he is fundamental to England's attempt to repeat the triumph of 1966, rather than the reserve role in which he functioned, aged 20, in Russia's finals of 2018, and again in 2021. However, evidence indicates that Southgate may be too experimental in selection, with the emergence of fresh young talent in the Euros, for England to blend into that crucial continuity that could enable Rashford truly to impose his talent in Qatar.

Forget his involvement in the nightmare penalty shoot-out against Italy, engulfed in failure with two other youngsters, Jadon Sancho and Bukayo Saka, in a 2-3 tally for Italy. The pressure – of month-long expectation, a 60,000 euphoric Wembley crowd escaping 14-month Covid lockdown, the cliff-edge horror of the TV-contrived Russian Roulette climax, antithesis of sport – overwhelmed the youngsters who bravely had volunteered. Rashford's error – confused run-up, hitting a post – was the more inexplicable for an erudite mind, fluent reader who a month earlier had extended his children's benevolence with a 50,000 book-aid through Macmillan Children and food charity Magic Breakfast.

The social media avalanche of racist abuse which then overwhelmed the trio is alarming evidence of a minority but vicious undercurrent infesting a predominantly tolerant nation. We must pray the trio rise above their double misfortune inflicted through sport.

Rashford courageously promised: 'I will never apologise for who I am and where I came from.'

POSTSCRIPT

*'All battles regarded as
military masterpieces have been
ones of manoeuvre'*
Winston Churchill

This recollection of sporting lives has, I hope, stirred emotions such as nostalgia, awe, personal ambition, ideas of liberation, perhaps discrete envy, a route to fulfilment. What has guided me, above all, an abstract sense from even early childhood – probably inherited from my oddly erratic actor father and grandfather – is a feeling for *style*. It is style that colours life, for the individual and for an audience. Depending on the context of the drama – all sports carrying this inherent element – style can be just as appealing as being valiant, dedicated, generous or astute.

It is why I warmed to the charm, say, of elegant Fred Couples, irresistible when claiming he is content to be the world's *fifth* best, while enjoying the occasion even more than you are. Danny Blanchflower, the celebrated theorist and captain of Tottenham Hotspur and Northern Ireland, maintained that sport was more fundamentally about glory than victory: occasionally the glory can lie with the runner-up, opponents optimistically sharing a mutual allegiance, rivalry and camaraderie being an essential equation. Witness Jesse Owens and Lutz Long, Pelé and Bobby Charlton, Emil Zátopek and Ron Clarke, Henry Cooper and Ali, Roger Federer and Rafa Nadal.

Style and technique are not synonymous. Technique can be studied and acquired; style is spontaneous, as much mental as physical, and even exponents such as Stanley Matthews or Usain Bolt are unable to define themselves, as when my father attempted to divulge the rapture he experienced in Shakespeare's *Hamlet* or *Julius Caesar* at my tender age when still unscrambling quadratic equations.

Style can also embrace improvisation, a key element of sport and something I perhaps inherited from my otherwise tranquil mother: as a 1920s teenager abandoning her staid middle-class background to join that touring immigrant balalaika orchestra fleeing the Bolshevik revolution; or in revenge on her preferred elder brother, eating his stamp collection. I suppose that streak of eccentricity helped me understand the impulsive Jack Johnson or iconoclastic Alex Higgins.

The one sporting genius here recalled who has not had identifiable, individualistic style is someone who repeated the same ferocious, identical split-second muscular agony a few million times over 20 years: Steve Redgrave. Style in rowing resides, I would say as an observer, in character. Redgrave's five Olympic titles, from 1984 to 2000, are immeasurably heroic and a reflection of Antarctic explorer Captain Titus Oates. For any ten opportunist politicians or local councillors, give me an athlete who has gained two or more four-yearly Olympic or world championship medals in any individual sport not determined by arbitrary judging.

By such trailblazers as dear Steve Redgrave and Winifred Brown, as Kip Keino and Cathy Freeman, Jesse Owens, Emil

Zatopek and Josiah Thugwane, are nations founded. Indeed sport matters: in many ways to many millions across the globe, as it has to me. As a youngster, sport was emotional and motivating, as a journalist illuminating about people and perceptions. Owing to old-time conventional amateur ethics, I 'retired' at 22 to find a 'proper' job: a rival winger for the England Amateur XI was Warren Bradley of amateurs Bishop Auckland ... who a year later was an emergency signing by Jimmy Murphy for Manchester United, post-Munich. Bradley making over 60 League appearances and twice selected for England professionals. Fancifully, I harboured daydreams of an Old Trafford shirt, having scored a runaway goal for Pegasus against Queens Park at Hampden.

We at Cambridge were so fortunate to have been coached by emerging Spurs manager Bill Nicholson; a reflection of why local educational facilities are always an essential path – in gymnastics, swimming, etc. – to exposing potential talent. My moderate javelin summit, for Cambridge and then Achilles Club, was 12 feet short of Olympic qualifying in 1956 without ever having had access to a single hour's coaching: a sport as technically esoteric as embroidery.

ACKNOWLEDGEMENTS

"Acknowledgements" by journalist-authors tend to be an apology for unintended but omitted gratitude for years of collaboration from colleagues in meeting evasive deadlines. Irrespective of ability, journalists often survive by single facility – accumulation of personal telephone numbers of 'contacts', which can run to hundreds. A prominent ageing and bibulous freelance attempted to sell me, aged 22, his 'contacts' library for £600, then the rate for a one-room apartment or a year's salary. Newly married and broke, I risked my own initiative.

So recognition is due of willing scribes, home and abroad, some no longer with us, who over 65 years and 25 books helped paddle my canoe when lacking facts: steering my attempt to portray the infective appeal to society of sports, from global to a game of conkers.

The Fleet Street 'club' was, and remains, a fluctuating balance between integrity and encroaching rat-race of declining circulation: the *Express* in the 70s four million daily, today *half* of that *per week*. In 1996, I worked 69 consecutive 12-hour days for *The Times* without a day off: be sure no-one noticed except my late wife Marita, partner for 61 years, enduringly managing the family while I rode the coat-tails of domestic and international events. Friends envied my diary, oblivious of domestic rupture. Without Marita's allegiance, my schedule would have been unsustainable, never mind the invaluable confidential phone numbers: fellow hacks, governing bodies in many sports, coaches, performers current and retired, agents, sponsors, lawyers. Thank heaven for stoic typists, latterly Susan Buck and Karen Game; Pitch Publishing's valiant crew led by Paul Camillin, Graham Hales and Duncan Olner. Special thanks also to Thomas Bach, IOC President, for donation from Lausanne Picture Archives of various legends, likewise to Wimbledon's All England Club for racquet icons.

Encyclopaedia of domestic collaborative friends:

Neil Allen; Derick Allsop; Vera Atkinson; Trevor Bailey; Chris Baillieu; Patrick Barclay; Philip Barker; Ian Barnes; John Barrett; Jonah Barrington; Jayne Bateman; Michael Beloff; Pat Besford; Henry Blofeld; Trevor Bond; Mihir Bose; Richard Bott; Simon Briggs; Malcolm Brodie; Oliver Brown; Eddie Butler; Alec Cameron, David Cannon; Tom Clarke; Duncan Clegg; Mike Collett; Pat Collins; Peter Corrigan; Chris Davies; Barry Davies; David Dein; Frank Dick; Mike Dickson; John Dillon; Chris Dodd; Hubert Doggart; Patrick Eagar; Richard Eaton; Martin Edwards; David Emery; Clive Everton; Jeff Farmer; Bob Ferrier; Liz Ferris; Ben Findon; Peter Fitton; Barry Flatman; Malcolm Folley; Roddy Forsyth; Brendan Foster; Norman Fox; Norman Giller; Doug Gillon; Brian Glanville; John Goodbody; Edward Grayson; Geoffrey Green; Stan Greenberg; David Hands; Tony Hardisty; Nick Harling; Bob Harris; Mike Hart; Colin Hart; Simon Hart; Ian Hawkey; Reg Hayter; Paul Hayward; Barry Hearn; Jimmy Hedley; Michael Henderson; John Hennessy; Jim Hetherington; Leon Hickman; Jimmy Hill; Christopher Hill; Chris Hilton; Derek Hodgson; Fred Holder; John Holt;

John Hopkins; Alan Hubbard; Sidney Hulls; Doug Insole; Brian James; Cliff Jones; Ken Jones; Frank Keating; Peter Keeling; John Keith; Paul Kelso; Glen Kirton; Maeve Kyle; David Lacey; Ken Lawrence; Jim Lawton; Alan Lee; Sarah Lewis; John Ley; Phil Liggett; Martin Lipton; David Lloyd; Andrew Longmore; Joe Lovejoy; Charles Lyell; Jacqueline Magnay; Lewine Mair; Colin Malam; Dan Maskell; Jenny McArthur; Paul McCarthy; Erskine McCulloch; John McKenzie, Ian McLeod; Tom McNab; Norris McWhirter; Michael Melford; Bill Meredith; Alan Mills; Keith Mills; Alex Montgomery; Ken Montgomery; Cliff Morgan, Jim Mossop; Neil Moxley; John Moynihan; Morley Myers; Patrick Nally; Andrew Napier; Barry Newcombe; Simon O'Hagan; Brian Oliver; Peter O'Sullevan; Bob Oxby; Dick Palmer; Charles Palmer; John Parsons; Jayne Pearce; Keith Perry; Tony Pickard; Barry Pickthall; Mitchell Platts; Derek Potter; Jeff Powell; Keir Radnage; Alix Ramsay; Fred Reading; Dennis Roach; John Rodda; Jack Rollin; Mike Rosewell; Alyson Rudd; Dickie Rutnagur; Bob Scott; Caroline Searle; Janine Self; Sri Sen; David Shaw; Denis Signy; Alan Smith (Football); Alan Smith (Ski); David Steel; Sandra Stevenson; Mickey Stewart, Bob Stinson; Ivo Tennant; Jon Tibbs; April Tod; Steve Tongue; Dan Topolski; Peter Tozer; Roger Uttley; Graham Walker; David Walsh; Adrian Warner; Mel Watman; Doug Weatherall; Mel Webb; David Welch; Clive White; Jim White; Nick Whitehead; Gerry Williams; Marcus Williams; Alan Williams; Tony Williams; Doug Wilson; Neil Wilson; Harry Wilson; Steve Wilson; Henry Winter; Colin Wood; John Woodcock; Charles Woodhouse; John Wragg; Vince Wright; R F Wright; Norman Wynn; Martyn Ziegler.

Overseas friends:

Alan Abrahamson; Mark Adams, Istvan Agic; Ali Bacher; Lajos Baroti; Charlie Battle; Alain Billoin; Miroslav Blazovic; John Boulter; Andreas Brugger; Francois Carrard; Philippe Chatrier; Ron Clarke; Toni Damacelli; Alain Danet; Massimo Della Pergola; Sonny DeSales; Natalie Durot; Dick Ebersol; Franco Fava; Gilbert Felli; Wilfrid Gerhardt; Bud Greenspan; Istvan Gyular; Matti Hannus; Sven-Arne Hansen; Phil Hersh; Karl-Heinz Huba; Kosuke Inagaki; Leif Josefsson; Markus Kecht; Fekrou Kidane; Nissim Kivity; Christian Klaue; Rudi Krol; John Landy; John Lucas; Alain Lunzenfichter; Wolf Lyberg; Haris Lymberopoulos; Bill Mallon; Emanuel Mavromattis; Wilf Meart; Gianni Merlo; Oleg Milshtein; Bora Milutinovic; Lex Muller; Kazimierz Oleszek; Egil Olsen; Ivica Osim; Joe Pamenski; Robert Pariente; Michael Payne; Gal Peleg; Branko Perovanovic; Stojan Protic; Fedor Radman; Alex Ratner; Leopoldo Rodes; Manolo Romero; Stratos Safioleas; Matti Salmenkyla; Hartmuth Scherzer; Jean-Claude Schupp; Evi Simeoni; Dragran Stojkovic; Artur Takac; Dan Tana; Jonny Tocco; Dezso Vad; Andras Varela; Eric Weil; Herb Wind; Andrew Young; Francoise Zweifel

BIBLIOGRAPHY

Albertville Olympic Games '92. David Miller. IMS Studio 6
Athletic World Records. Lionel Blackman. Book Guild.
Atlanta Centenary Games '96. David Miller. IMS Studio 6
Ayrton Senna, Hard Edge of Genius. Christopher Hilton.
    Patrick Stephens.
Billie Jean King. Frank Deford. Granada.
Born to Win. John Bertrand. Bantam.
British Olympians. Ian Buchanan. Guinness.
Champions of Europe. Brian Glanville. Guinness.
Coming Back. David Miller. Sidgwick & Jackson.
Complete Book of Olympics. David Wallechinsky/Jaime
    Loucky. Aurum.
Cup Magic. David Miller. Sidgwick & Jackson.
Days of Grace, Arthur Ashe. Arnold Rampersand. Heinemann.
Encyclopaedia of Track and Field. Mel Watman. Hale.
Encyclopaedia of World Sports. Marshall Cavendish.
England's Last Glory. David Miller. Pavilion.
Father of Football, Matt Busby. David Miller. Stanley Paul.
From Where I Sit. Dan Maskell. Collins.
The Greatest. Muhammad Ali. Book Club Associates.
History of Modern Track and Field. Roberto Quercertani.
    Vallardi.
100 Years of Olympic Games 1896–1996. IAAF. OSB

IAAF 100 Years. IGAM-Cuneo.

Jack Johnson and His Times. Denzil Batchelor. Sportsmans Book Club.

Lillehammer Olympic Games '94. David Miller. IMS Studio 6.

My Game. Lew Hoad. Hodder.

Modern Encyclopaedia of Tennis. Bud Collins. Visible Ink.

Nagano Olympic Games '98. David Miller. IMS Studio 6.

Official History of Olympics Games and IOC, 1894–2018. David Miller. Mainstream/IOC

The Olympic Games. Killanin/Rodda. Barrie & Jenkins.

Olympic Guardians. David Miller. Pro Sport Publishing.

Olympic Revolution. David Miller. Pavilion.

Olympics Past and Present. Qatar Olympic Museum. Prestel.

Our Sporting Times. David Miller. Pavilion.

Papa Jack. Randy Roberts. Robson Books.

Running Free, Sebastian Coe. David Miller. Sidgwick & Jackson.

Running My Life. Sebastian Coe. Pavilion.

Seoul Olympic Games '88. David Miller. IMS Studio 6.

Stanley Matthews. David Miller. Pavilion.

This Life I've Led. Babe Didrikson & Harry Paxton. Literary Licensing.

Usain Bolt 9.58. Shaun Custis. Harper Collins.

World Cup Anthology '06. Chris Freddi. Harper.

World Cup '70. David Miller. Heinemann.

World Cup '74. David Miller (English Edition). FIFA.